I Hate Campaign Hats

I Hate Campaign Hats

Police Stories of a Young State Trooper
Making His Way with
Faith, Love, and Silly Humor

Randall Stevens

Printed in the United States of America.

ISBN-13: 9798706540708

Cover design by Barry Moser
Cover photo by Jim Gipe (http://pivotmedia.com)
Editorial services by Tucker Seven

I dedicate this work to my late wife, Marion,
for her love, guidance, support,
and encouragement throughout our life together,
to our daughters, Pamela and Jillian, and
in memory of my parents and my brother Brad.

I also dedicate this book to my wife, Anne,
who persuaded me to finish what I had set aside
so many years ago, and who filled my life with
love and happiness when I needed it the most.

Contents

Introduction

The original intention of writing this book was to present a career tale beginning at the State Police Academy and ending in retirement, but I soon realized a narrative of that nature and length would be drudgery for me. I'm proud of the tests I passed to achieve rank, the positions I held, the stations I commanded, the bureaus I worked in, and the cases that I solved, but a memoir tracking daily life would surely be a bore to most.

Having taken two written examinations and enduring the same number of employment exercises, I can honestly say that, at the time, I found nothing funny with any of it. On reflection, however, seeing all the laughter that seemed to follow me early and throughout my career made me want to share my stories. Almost every cop I know has some funny stories to tell, along with impressive career accomplishments and noteworthy criminal cases, and those are wonderful things, but I was never stirred by position or arrests that made headlines. One would think there might be something wrong with me, and I wondered about that myself sometimes, but the heightened feelings we humans experience in everyday life are the ones that moved me—and amusement does that most of all. More importantly, I realized it was the anecdotes I remembered, cherished, and contemplated that stimulated my emotions. So, with encouragement from a friend who is an artist and writer, I began the good practice of keeping notes and making mediocre attempts at writing. Fortunately for literature in its broadest sense, life got in the way and forced me to hide my box of efforts on a moldy basement shelf until the Covid-19 pandemic lockdowns of 2020 and the widespread vilification of police in general for the actions of so few. I felt that by sharing these stories people might see themselves, or someone they know, in these pages, and begin to understand that police are, in fact, no more or less fallible, and no better or worse than the rest of us.

This is not a crime drama chronicling brilliant investigative work, prosecutors, court scenes, or heroes and villains. It begins with a young man joining the state police and adapting to the paramilitary yet often comical barracks life. The journey provides some nerve-wracking and humorous glimpses into the narcotics bureau, undercover work, patrol, the public, and some other human beings, who from time to time put on a police uniform.

The reader will hear the story of how he met his first wife and question whether it was coincidental, or something meant to be. Also, private, intimate truths, lessons learned, and lessons taught in a forty-year marriage, ending with a cancer, that needed telling.

Is the story of finding a second wife a matter of destiny, providence, chance, good fortune, coincidence, or, once again, meant to be?

These are simply the anecdotes most memorable to me. So, remaining as true to the facts as my senior memory allows, I offer this memoir as a creative nonfiction, or true stories well told, recalling events that are as meaningful today as they were some thirty to fifty years ago. Many of these anecdotes are zany, humorous and feel good, some are heartbreakingly sad, or a mixture of both, as life so often is; but they are real stories of people and life. And they are worth the telling.

The Hat

At the age of twenty-one I had never thought about a campaign hat. Why would I? I had no idea what it signified, or what it was used for, other than to put on one's head. I couldn't have described one if I had to, and at that point in my life, I could not have cared less. So, for those as ignorant as I was, simply put, a campaign hat is a Smokey Bear hat.

My first encounter with a campaign hat was, to be more accurate, with the man beneath a campaign hat, who proudly wore it as a uniformed member of the Massachusetts State Police Academy staff. The Academy was a machine modeled closely after Marine boot camp and it molded and churned out new Troopers. I wanted to be one of them.

Fate, destiny, and luck are things I had never spent much time thinking about. At that age, my mind was mostly attuned to the fastest cars and girls. Cars I knew about, but girls, fast or slow, I didn't have a clue. To continue, I have never considered myself lucky in games of chance, but then, as now, I feel that I have been blessed in terms of health and happiness. It seems to me that fate and destiny are less tangible than luck. Perhaps this is because people don't usually go around proclaiming their fate or destiny the way they do their luck. In any case, I don't know what specific term or terms applied to the circumstances surrounding my appointment to the Massachusetts State Police, but clearly, one or all of them played a part.

In the fall of 1966, I took the entrance exam. I thought about nothing else, and after having taken the first step, it was all my young and fairly empty mind wanted. Waiting to hear the result was torturous, but several weeks later I received notification that I had passed, and was instructed to report to the academy for a physical examination.

I had always been in good physical condition, and although skinny as a rail I was strong, wiry, and loved playing sandlot football with my friends. I even had the best batting average on my intermediate baseball league team. So I was unconcerned about being rejected for any medical reasons, but I *was* slightly worried about my weight. I was 5 feet 11 inches tall and weighed only 147 pounds, which was three pounds below the minimum weight requirement. It was common knowledge that the state police were sticklers about size. They liked their troopers BIG, with capital letters.

The physical was pretty routine: blood pressure, pulse, heartbeat, bend over, say "Ahh." I'd worried needlessly about the lack of three pounds, for after getting off the scale they recorded my weight on the medical form without so much as a murmur. It was at the test for color blindness that I hit a brick wall.

I waited confidently and patiently in line, listening to each man in front of me complete his test. When my turn came, I stepped smartly to the table and handed my application to the Trooper, who was seated with his campaign hat on. I stood staring down at the top of his hat, wondering why on earth he would wear a hat to administer a color test. No matter, he confirmed that I was Randall Stevens, took my paper, smiled, and placed it to one side. The booklet they used contained nearly thirty color perception plates used to detect red-green color deficiencies, and was famously known as the Ishihara Color Deficiency Test. It was the first in its class of successful color tests, and named after its designer, Shinobu Ishihara, a professor at the University of Tokyo, who first published his tests in 1916. Professor Ishihara died in 1963, and I'm sincerely sorry for his passing, but I must admit that I wished he had kept the damnable test for his own people in Tokyo.

The officer placed Professor Ishihara's test book flat on the table and turned it to the first page. Then he and his hat nodded, indicating that I should begin. Seeing only colored circles, I said nothing and waited for the next page.

"Well?" asked the officer.

"Well, what?" I replied.

"Read the number," he ordered.

Panic struck. What frigging number? I thought.

I looked again, but all I could see was colored circles. My mind raced—something was very wrong, and I had no idea what. The Trooper grew impatient and his expression clearly showed it. My brain screamed, say something, anything. This had to be some sort of a test within a test—a trick? Did they think I was listening to the men preceding me? Maybe they thought I wrote the numbers on my arm? I didn't know. Stumped, it was no use. Unable to think of a suitable response I fell back on the truth (which is supposed to set you free), and told him what I saw: nothing.

He twisted his head, hat included, in such a manner that I thought it must surely have hurt. He stared at me for what I thought was an eternity before flipping to the next page.

"Read the number."

I flushed and was losing my composure as the line behind me began to crowd my space. Apparently this was entertaining, at my expense. All the breathable air had either disappeared or been sucked up by the mob of applicants pushing closer to see the show. I heard an unrestrained chuckle from the rear as I leaned over the "devil's" test book to get a closer look. Two others leaned with me. Plainly, they wanted to help. I squinted hard, to no avail. I could have put my nose on the page, and it wouldn't have made any difference. I just couldn't see it. Swallowing hard, I took a guess.

"Twenty-three," I almost shouted.

The officer's head snapped up at me with a wide-eyed expression. "Twenty-three, you see the number twenty-three?"

"Yessir," I confirmed, as every pair of eyes within a dozen feet looked at me in disbelief.

I was humiliated and easily could have cried. I was surrendering and wanted to call it quits, just run away, but no. I wasn't gonna get off that easily. They were having too much fun.

"Try again," he said.

"Fourteen."

"Again!"

"Eleven."

Slowly, ever so slowly he turned the pages, and one by one I guessed. Wrong.

The entire episode lasted less than three minutes, but it felt interminable. When I had finished with Professor Ishihara's stupid color test, no one had to tell me that I was also done with the state police. One might have accused me of being overly sensitive at that point, but what had felt like salt poured on the wound was seeing the large letters they'd written on the bottom of my medical form: DISQUALIFIED—COLORBLIND.

The ride from the academy in Framingham, Massachusetts to my home in Auburn was very hard. In my short and sheltered existence, I'd never faced such disappointment. I kept telling myself that it wasn't the end of the world, that compared to the tragedies and disappointments endured by others I had no right to be so bitter. Yet I couldn't help it. The rejection was absolutely devastating, and I kept seeing the testing officer look up at me from under his silly hat.

The next days were spent calling every influential friend I had ever known, attempting to get another test. My list was short. Who the hell did I know at twenty-one, except other twenty-something-year-olds? But thankfully my father was on the phone, too. He was as sorry as I, but never let it show. He kept saying not to worry, and that it would all work out. I prayed for some of his optimism to rub off.

By the end of the next week the worst feelings were over, and I accepted the thought of life without a state police uniform hanging in my closet. It was then that we got a call. A state representative friend of my dad had managed to get me an appointment with the State Police Surgeon General to review my test. I was on cloud nine.

I was uneasy about the appointment. My father must have noticed or sensed it, because without a word he had taken the day off from work to go along. (I digress for a moment. Fifty years later, as I begin writing my stories, I'm finally realizing how blessed I was to have such a kind, caring, and thoroughly wonderful father. How easily we under-appreciate those who have given and done so much for those they love. Even though he's gone, I love him more than ever. We never stop learning or loving.)

The Surgeon General's office was located in the Prudential Center in Boston. I was happy that Dad went with me. I'd have gotten lost for sure. All the way down the Massachusetts Turnpike, Dad quizzed me on the color of cars we passed, while keeping the conversation light and full of hope. Before I knew it, we were driving beneath the Prudential building at Copley Square. I had always been amazed wondering how they had built a skyscraper straddling the interstate highway, and every time I'd driven underneath it I'd tried to count the support columns holding it up. There never seemed to be enough for my liking. Maybe it was my imagination, but I always thought that drivers seemed to speed up going underneath. I know I did. The thought of a column collapsing was enough for me to boost my exit speed by twenty miles an hour.

We cruised for several blocks before finding a parking space within a reasonable walking distance. The Center's lobby was large, but we found a wall directory, slipped into an elevator, and pressed the button for the sixth floor. Normally, I liked the sensation of a fast elevator ride, but my stomach was so queasy I nearly threw up.

The Surgeon General's office was nothing special; in fact it bordered on stark. Antiseptic white gave the room a coldness, and the matronly receptionist never raised her eyes above her work as she waved us toward seats. There, I would await my fate.

I was a nervous wreck. No matter how hard I tried, I couldn't sit still. I stood up, sat down, paced, then flipped through magazines. I crossed, uncrossed, and recrossed my legs. Deep breathing worked best, but I was drawing stares from other patients. The lady sitting next to me had given up her magazine altogether in favor of watching my gyrations. My father, who had settled across the room, was upset with me—his hard stare and raised eyebrow were dead giveaways. If the nurse hadn't come in just then calling my name, he would have probably tried tying me up.

Dr. Michael Estes had his back to us and was rummaging through his bottom cabinets as we entered the examination room. He appeared to be about sixty years old, wore dark-rimmed glasses, and had salt and pepper hair that hung mostly over his ears and curled up from his collar. He wasn't tall, just over five feet seven inches, but I got the impression he was a strong and forceful personality. Aside from needing a haircut, he was a handsome man, neatly and expensively dressed.

Peering over his glasses, the doctor politely introduced himself and got right down to business. He knew exactly why we were there. Directing his attention to me, he held up a color chart he had taken from his cabinet.

"Now, Randall, can I call you Randall?"

"Yessir, mostly I go by Randy, but Randall is fine."

"Okay, Randy, I want you to identify the colors for me."

It seemed more an order than a request, giving me the feeling that our visit was an imposition and that he was examining me but really didn't want to. Then again, I was beyond hypersensitive. The moment of truth had come, and my mind flashed back to the officer under his campaign hat giving me strange looks.

"Red, green, brown, yellow, orange, blue, black, and white," I said, pointing at each.

"Okay. Now I'd like you to point to the dark colors and identify them."

I studied the chart for a second, then quickly pointed at the four darkest colors and identified each one correctly. A broad smile accompanying the approval in his voice put me at ease.

"Good, good," said the doctor. "I think I know what your problem is. Let's go into my office."

Ushering my father and me through an inner door, he offered us seats as he moved behind his desk and settled into a great leather chair. The office was rich and warm, nothing at all like the reception room. Framed degrees hung on the wall behind his chair, and several prints balanced the room. I took particular notice of Norman Rockwell's *Saturday Evening Post* cover print of the "The Runaway." It was the first time I'd seen the print, and I noticed it was from the September 20, 1958 issue of the magazine. Ironically, I was born on a September 20, and Trooper Dick Clemens, who had posed for Rockwell's painting, was *not* wearing a campaign hat. Was that a good omen? I didn't know, but I dismissed all thoughts and focused my attention on Dr. Estes. I wanted to hear what he had to say.

Removing his glasses with both hands, Estes slowly wiped his eyes and began talking about colorblindness. I was surprised to learn that it affects many more men than women, something in the genes, he said. I wasn't paying attention to the details. I wanted the bottom line. He continued by saying that my particular difficulty related mostly to shades of basic colors, especially red and green. He called it a red-green colorblindness. Shades of these colors, he said, would be the hardest for me to discern, and identifying certain colors individually would be harder unless they were seen in comparison to one another. The shaded circles in the test booklet quickly proved a red-green color perception deficiency, but, he added, I was not totally colorblind, because I was able to see and identify the strong basic colors on the color chart.

"I see no reason, Randy, why you shouldn't be able to perform the duties of a state police officer."

My first thought? Screw you, Professor Ishihara!

"What? Do you mean it?" I asked in shock.

"Oh, yes, I'm quite sure. You have a color deficiency in a certain range of colors, but it shouldn't hamper you in law enforcement, as long as you're aware of the problem and deal with it smartly. You'll do fine. Now, let me give the academy a call, get you reinstated and arrange for the agility test."

Dad's face glowed. I'll never forget the sound of utter happiness in his voice, as he whispered, shaking the Surgeon General's hand, "Doctor, thank you, that's just wonderful."

The trip home was wonderful too, a different ride from the drive in, and thoughts of the Prudential building collapsing on top of us never entered my mind.

The days leading up to the agility test passed slowly but were filled with a renewed feeling of joy and anticipation. My confidence was back, and I wouldn't allow myself to imagine anything else going wrong. I had given a lot of thought to what Dr. Estes had said about my condition. I took his advice and at every opportunity tested myself identifying colors. Shades of red, brown, and green were the most difficult to tell apart, especially in low light, or if I was a distance away, but if I could get close enough to compare them to one another, more often than not I could pick them out. There were, however, times when I knew a color was either red, brown, or green, but I had no idea which. In my early years as a road trooper, radar details could be a bane. I'd call out a speeding green Ford, then watch the offender drive right past the pick-up crew without any one of them waving the car over. I was too far away to see their faces, or obviously hear them, but knew someone had to ask. "What green Ford?" Many a happy motorist made it, unwittingly, through my radar details.

I could see someone standing at the front of a small building as I drove into the Academy's parking lot. He was obviously waiting for me, because he started in my direction before I was out of the car. As I got closer, I noticed that he was wearing a baseball cap, sweatpants, and a sweatshirt, each with an academy staff emblem. Trooper John Tobin introduced himself as a drill instructor. He was my height, strong, thickset, and rock hard—someone I would never want to mess with. His voice was low and calm as he explained what would be required of me as we started off toward a group of buildings. We entered a large Quonset hut. It was very possibly a remnant hut from World War II. The Quonset hut was basically a prefab steel building that be could quickly assembled, disassembled, and moved as needed. They were perfect as wartime structures and mostly used by the Navy. This hut was one of several used for housing and training the Academy recruits.

Once inside, Trooper Tobin flipped two switches on an electric panel and turned on half of the overhead lights. At first, I thought we had entered a long, dark, wide tunnel, but lights revealed a well-equipped gymnasium with testing stations set up around the perimeter. Each station was clearly labeled: PULL UP, BROAD JUMP, ROPE CLIMB, and DUMMY LIFT. On the officer's order I began with the rope climb. Hand over hand without the use of my legs, I zipped to the top and back down with ease. While moving to the next station I spoke to the officer for the first time since entering the gym.

"Excuse me, sir. Where is everyone else? Am I the only one?"

"That's right, we finished testing everyone last week. You're the last one."

"Do you know when the class is scheduled to start, sir?" I was careful to add the *sir*.

"No, I don't. I don't think they've decided that yet. It'll probably depend on the size of the class they want. If they have enough recruits, it will start soon. If not, they'll call additional people from the eligibility list. If that happens, we'll have to wait for them to complete physicals and agility tests. That's why all these stations are still up."

Questions filled my head and I could have asked a dozen more, but I didn't want to push my luck. I was grateful for the information he had given me, so I decided to button up, the less said the better.

It took about forty-five minutes to finish the tests. Trooper Tobin gave me the option of either doing pull ups, palms outward, or the 150-pound dummy lift. Since the dummy weighed more than me, I opted for the pull ups, which were easy. I struggled through the mile run huffing and puffing but finished within the allotted time. We left the outside track and went back inside. Trooper Tobin finished his paperwork while I sat patiently catching my breath.

"Okay, that does it," said the officer, slipping his report into a manila envelope and ushering me toward the door. "You passed okay. I don't know when you'll be called for the oral interview, but I don't think it will be too long. Good luck."

Stepping from the building, we were met—actually more like challenged—by an older handsome sort of man in his late forties with grey hair. His features, like Tobin's, were hard and strong. His face was weathered with the look of someone who had spent most of his life outdoors. Huge hands dug deep into his pockets as he stood before us with an aura of authority, a campaign hat firmly attached to his head at that perfect downward angle. Scary!

"Good afternoon, Trooper Tobin."

"Good afternoon, Commandant," replied the Trooper, assuming a posture of attention.

"You there!"

"Me, sir?" I answered with a surprised look.

"Yes, you. What are *you* doing here?" he asked as Tobin walked away.

The Commandant's stare sent me rigid. My heart pounded harder than during the mile run. "I—I just took the agility test, sir."

"I can see that. I saw you crawling around my track. What are you doing here *today*?"

Before I could answer, he spun on his heel, clasped his hands at the small of his back, and started toward the parking lot at a brisk pace. I didn't need to be told that I should follow. Running to keep stride, I talked rapidly telling him of my problem with the color test, and how Dr. Estes had retested and then reinstated me. It was Dr. Estes, I explained, who had told me to report for the testing.

"I certainly hope I haven't been an inconvenience to you or your sta—"

"Sooo, you're colorblind," interrupted the Commandant with an amused glance, like he was enjoying himself.

"No, sir! I'm not colorblind." I dared not tell him that I was partially colorblind. I had no idea what the Surgeon General had actually put on my application, and I certainly didn't want this man digging into it. I could feel myself starting to come apart. I wasn't finding any words.

The man's face was stone, as cold blue eyes searched the parking lot, before settling upon a red Ford Mustang convertible about twenty feet away.

"What color is that car?" he demanded.

"It's red, looks like a candy apple red, sir."

"And the top?"

"It's white, sir."

He glared at the car until he spotted a sweater draped over the passenger's seat. Smiling, he pointed directly at it. "What color's that sweater?"

"It's green, sir, actually looks olive green."

"Awright, dismissed," barked the Commandant. I sensed disappointment as he turned and walked away without another word.

Flabbergasted, I watched until he rounded the corner of a building. When I was sure he had gone, I climbed into my red Ford Mustang, threw my olive-green sweater into the back, and drove home. Only the oral interview remained between the Massachusetts State Police and me.

Colonel Robert Murphy and Major John Mason, the two highest-ranking state police officers, conducted the oral interviews of potential new recruits. The Commissioner of Public Safety, a political appointee, was not a member of the Uniformed Branch of the state police, but oversaw its operations, and as such was superior to Murphy and Mason. It was unusual that the two highest-ranking Commissioned Officers within the department would concern themselves with employment interviews. It would be like the CEO of IBM interviewing a newly graduated college student for an entry level position. The authority that these officers held over the rank and file was staggering, and men like Murphy and Mason couldn't let it go—they coveted power. Terms like delegation, authority vs. responsibility, and management by objectives were foreign to them. Leadership style, especially in the paramilitary organization of the state police during those years, was autocratic. More opinionated critics would have called it dictatorial. Officers who committed minor infractions were routinely disciplined with a transfer far from home. It was a blatantly unfair practice, giving cause for some serious thought on the matter. Since that time, however, the department has undergone major reorganization, with one result being that transfers were not as arbitrary and recruit interviews were delegated to subordinate officers. Had the reorganization taken place in late 1966, it might have benefited me.

I sat, my butt puckered, in a straight-backed wooden chair with no cushion, facing Colonel Murphy and Major Mason, who were seated on a raised platform behind a large rectangular table, resplendent in full dress uniforms, complete with campaign hats. What was with these people and their campaign hats, did they wear them to bed? It made me very nervous.

Each of the senior officers scribbled feverishly in folder after folder, while quizzing me on an unending variety of subjects. I wasn't sure if it had been preplanned, but I suspected the seating was supposed to have a psychological effect on the interviewee. Sitting in a lone chair, strategically placed in the center of the room, responding to questions from rigid interviewers, it was more an interrogation than a casual interview. Answering their questions, I began to settle down and gave confident responses without hesitation.

"I see it says here, Mr. Stevens, that you're still at your present job."

"Yes, sir, that's correct, Major. I was promoted to production supervisor three months ago."

"You have a lot invested in the company," added Mason. "Are you sure the state police is what you want?"

"I'm positive. I worked hard to get this far." Little did he know, I thought.

"Our Academy is very strenuous. Many applicants like yourself never make it through. Have you discussed with your present employer the fact that you might be leaving? And also the possibility that you might return to your old job should you leave us?"

I didn't like what he was trying to tell me, or maybe it was just the way he said it, but there was no doubt he suspected that I wouldn't cut it. I thought carefully for a second before I answered. I wanted to sound sure of myself, but not cocky.

Nothing could have prepared me for what happened next. Before I said a word, Colonel Murphy's face scrunched with anger as he looked at the paper before him and uttered, "What, the *hell* is this?"

With his eyes about to burst from their sockets and his face puffed scarlet, he screamed at me, "*How did you get in here?*"

I blanked, and not knowing where he was going, I timidly pointed at the door behind me, through which I had entered the room. He glared at me silently.

"What do you mean, sir? I don't understand." I absolutely didn't. I actually became fearful.

"How much do you weigh?" he sputtered.

"One hundred and forty-seven pounds," I answered.

Exploding from his seat and knocking his chair nearly off the platform, Murphy said, "I mean, Mr. Stevens, you *can't* be here *unless* you weigh 150 pounds!" Turning to Mason, he said, "Major Mason, find out who the hell approved this man's application. Never mind, never mind, I'll find out myself."

He raced from the room, and somewhere far down the corridor, I heard doors slamming and a loud but muffled voice.

When Colonel Murphy left the room, Major Mason removed his campaign hat and placed it on the table in front of him with the badge pointed right at me. I stared back at the damn hat, convinced that it was somehow responsible. Mason's eyes avoided mine as he, very politely, told me the interview was over. But he was unable to hide a tinge of facial color betraying his embarrassment.

I can't describe exactly how I felt leaving the Academy. There was no anger, only sorrow. I even felt sorry for the poor slob who had approved my application.

Try Again

A couple of days after the oral interview, I went back to my old job in the production department at Riley Stoker Corporation in Worcester, Massachusetts. Riley Stoker manufactured large gas, coal, and oil-fired steam electric generating plants for utility companies. In later years, most plants retrofitted their smokestacks with coal scrubbers to remove the toxic particles, allowing the use of "cheap" coal without pollution.

I liked my job and it kept me busy. At least while at work I didn't dwell on what had happened at the Academy. Only my closest friends knew that I had applied to the state police, and in light of the outcome, it was a good decision—I didn't want to offer excuses or have to explain to every Tom, Dick, and Harry why I hadn't made it.

Nearly a year passed before I saw an ad for another State Police exam in our local paper. I hadn't fully recovered from the last effort, and not wanting to think about it, I tossed the ad aside and put the whole idea on a back burner.

The production department office at Riley Stoker was located on an exterior wall of the building. The office floor was below the level of the outside sidewalk, and the bottom of our windows were level with the sidewalk. Pedestrians strolling by stared down at us working, making me feel like a fish in an aquarium. I hated being on display, and I also hated being stuck indoors on bright sunshiny days, summer or winter. I worked happier and felt better when it was raining.

Donald Mans was the production manager and head of the department. His desk was located at one end of the room, and the assistant production manager, Tom Tully, sat at the desk next to him. Directly in front of the two managers there were two rows of three desks. I had one of the front desks and the production supervisor, Bill Lobil, occupied the other. Typists held the rest of the workstations, and at the very rear was pipe-smoking Harry Davis, who filled the role of our company's travel agent, but was supervised by Mr. Mans.

It's hard for me to describe Mr. Mans. And by the way, he *was* addressed as Mr. Mans by everyone except his assistant, Tom. I don't want to say that our boss was a bad person, because I don't believe deep down that he was, but he did have a mean streak that often showed when dealing with his subordinates. Too often, he would belittle his workers in front of everyone to the point of embarrassment. In my view, he embarrassed himself as much as the unfortunate target of his ire. Harry Davis always got it the worst. I often found myself leaving my desk for a trip to the men's room until he was done abusing Harry. I found it very disturbing.

Fortunately, I had managed to escape the boss man's displeasure, except for one morning when he discovered that I had allowed a vendor to deliver a shipment of insulation to one of our construction sites before it was needed. He called me on it and began questioning me loud and hard in front of the office. I wasn't quite sure of what I had done, so I asked permission to check with my counterpart in the construction department. He waved for me to go, so I went next door and asked my coworker and friend, Ken Rivers, what had happened.

Cutting to the chase, Ken told me that a railroad car full of insulation arrived on site a month ahead of schedule and there would be extra work to store it, but that it was not the end of the world. No doubt though, I had screwed up.

I returned to my desk upset at myself for messing up. Addressing my boss, I freely admitted that I had made a mistake, was sorry, and would be more careful in the future. I told him that Ken had said that they could take care of the insulation, and things would be fine. Apparently, my apology wasn't good enough, nor was I contrite enough for his liking, so he started in on me. How could you let that happen? Don't you pay attention to your work? Didn't you check with construction first? When did you last talk to the supplier? He was getting madder and I couldn't get a word in, let alone a response. The office was still, and no one spoke as they listened to him pick me apart. Finally, he stopped and said, "We're done here!"

I hesitated for a second then said, "Well, I'm not done!"

The office collectively gasped.

With bright crimsoned cheeks Mans sputtered, "We will talk about this later!"

"I want to talk about this *now*!" I countered.

Mans crashed his chair against the wall as he rose and stormed out of the office.

I seemed to be developing an uncanny habit of causing people to knock over chairs.

I leaned back in my seat and lit a cigarette. A deathly silence had filled the office until Bill Lobil's desk phone rang. Bill listened for a second before picking it up. "Yes, sir," was all he said. Then facing me, he spoke uneasily. "Randy, Mr. Mans wants to see you in personnel." What the hell, I thought, I've got a phone on my desk; he can't call me? Angrily, I stubbed out the butt in my ashtray, stood, and addressed my coworkers. "Well, if I'm not back, it's been nice workin' with ya."

I strolled down the corridor towards personnel—in no hurry at all. Entering the room, I thought it odd that the personnel director, Jim Ross, was nowhere to be seen. Mr. Mans was seated at a desk in the first cubicle on the right. I went in and sat down opposite my boss. He had calmed down a little, but then started in on me again right where he had left off. I hadn't calmed down, and since I figured I was gonna be fired anyway, I interrupted him in mid-sentence.

"What do you want from me?" I blurted out. "I admitted that I made a mistake. I said that I was sorry and would be more careful in the future. What more can I say?"

"Well, I think—," he began to say as I interrupted him again.

"I'm not going to let anyone belittle me. I didn't deserve that. No one does. If you want to take me aside and privately discipline me, fine, but you have no right to embarrass me in front of the entire office. Furthermore, I'm not making enough money. I'm doing the same job as Bill Lobil. He's a production supervisor and makes more than I do." I had figured, what the hell, might just as well put it all on the table. I had nothing more to lose.

I paused, giving my boss opening to speak, which he did with a sour expression. "You're being more critical of me than I am of you," he said.

I stared back at him not saying a word. I had spoken my truth, and I was empty.

We sat quietly for a moment. Surely my boss was processing the exchange. "Okay," he said. "We can go back to the office."

I went directly back. He didn't. I had no idea where he had gone, but he was the boss and could go anywhere he wanted.

The next hour at work was kind of a daze. I couldn't focus, and none of my coworkers was talking. I can't even remember a phone ringing. Mr. Mans finally returned and began moving papers around on his desk. I think that even he was a little befuddled. So I decided that since I hadn't been canned, I should at least pretend to work. I lit a cigarette, shook out the match and tossed it into the wastebasket behind me, then picked up some correspondence. Seconds later, flames were shooting out of my wastebasket. "Oh, *shit!*" I yelled, grabbing the basket and running into the hallway. Fortunately, right outside our office was a janitor's sink big enough to dump the basket and douse the flames. Sheepishly, I returned with basket in hand and placed it under my desk as every face looked at me in complete and utter astonishment. Collapsing into my chair with a little chuckle I exclaimed toward the ceiling. "Wow, this has been some kinda day!"

Tom Tully began laughing first, then Bill Lobil, the secretaries next, and finally I saw Mr. Mans smile and just shake his head. I had survived the day, but all things considered, I decided it was time to move the state police exam to the front burner. No pun intended.

Two weeks after that memorable workday, Mr. Mans called me into the personnel office. It was a different meeting altogether. He confided that he had told his wife about "our episode," and further admitted that his wife understood how I had felt. It was completely unexpected. Additionally, I was going to receive a pay increase, and would soon be promoted to the position of production supervisor. It was a great ending. Thank you, Mrs. Mans. Because of you I was treated respectfully in every conversation thereafter with my boss. But my decision to retake the state police exam had already been made.

Harry Davis, however, was still used and abused quite regularly. He just didn't have the courage to stand up for himself.

I passed the written exam and, aware that it would be some time before a physical, I began gorging myself at meals, adding bananas, sundaes, shakes, and grinders. Anything fattening was fair game, but more than doubling my caloric intake proved fruitless. Despite stuffing myself to the point of nausea I didn't gain one single ounce. I was stuck at 147 lousy pounds. I couldn't wrap my head around the department's rigidity. Along with the five feet nine inch minimum height rule, applicants were to have 20/20 vision and were automatically rejected if they wore glasses. Once hired, however, a trooper's vision could deteriorate to the point of needing coke bottles to see, and that was okay. So why couldn't I be allowed to gain three pounds after they hired me? After all, they didn't fire a 150-pound officer if he lost a pound. Or did they?

I look back in time now and laugh at myself for the things I did next, but I was desperate to make the weight minimum. So I guess I'll give that silly young kid a pass.

I found an old belt in my closet. It was leather, but the entire length was wrapped with a cotton weave fabric of some sort. I took it down into our basement and went to my dad's old tool chest. Rummaging through the wrenches, old clamps, saws, and other rusty tools, I found a long piece of bar solder rolled up and tucked in a corner. The bar was half an inch wide and maybe 26 inches long. Most importantly, solder is very heavy. I unfolded the bar (it's pliable), and smiled to myself, thinking that it was perfect. A half inch slit in the cloth on the back side of the belt near the buckle was all that was needed to slide the bar inside. Taking a hold of each end of the belt, I wrapped it around my waist. I'd be able to slip it through my pant belt loops and close the buckle, but once molded it would stay in the shape of my midsection. No worries, it would work. As a last-minute thought, I picked up a good-sized piece of flat lead from the work bench, folded it into my wallet and put it in my back pocket. There it was. I was going to make up three pounds by hook or by crook.

I was sound asleep and woke to the Kingston Trio's "Charlie on the MTA" blasting on my mother's stereo in the living room. It was early. Usually it was very late Saturday or Sunday morning after partying the night before that I was serenaded with

Mom's music. I'm sure it gave her great pleasure. Sometimes she even sang along as I buried my head under the pillow. Surprisingly, I had slept well, considering what lay ahead. Sunlight filled my bedroom and warmed my legs, so I spent a few extra minutes soaking in the sunshine before going downstairs.

The house smelled of bacon, which to this day I consider one of life's most beautiful scents. My dad was cooking and had made me a huge breakfast of bacon, eggs, home fries, toast, and a waffle. My mom danced through the kitchen into their bedroom to make the bed. She really was a kick. When I started to eat, Dad grabbed two bananas from the fruit bowl, and dropped them next to my plate. "Eat those, too," he said. "You eat every bit of it. There's gotta be a couple of pounds there."

"I can't, Dad. I'm stuffed already."

"Never mind, you eat it."

A big breakfast was always my favorite meal. There were times I felt that I could do breakfast for lunch and dinner too, but this meal was sitting very heavy in my stomach. Butterflies were setting in and I wondered what my father would think if he knew about my weighted belt.

"Did you sleep okay last night?" he asked.

"Yeah, I did. Didn't have any trouble at all."

"Did you weigh yourself this morning?"

I really wished he hadn't asked that question. He knew the answer, because it was the same answer I'd been giving him for weeks. I suppose he couldn't help himself: he cared, and wanted to hear the number change as much as I did.

"Still the same, Dad, 147."

The physical was a carbon copy of the one I'd taken the previous year. I went from station to station submitting my 147 pounds to a thorough probing. I avoided the color and weight stations for as long as possible. Then, taking a deep breath, I got in line for the color test. I tried to stay calm, but thoughts of last year's fiasco came to mind. I recalled every single detail as if it had happened yesterday. Especially the tester with his dumb campaign hat. My heart pounded wildly. It was a good thing they had already listened to my heart and taken my pulse rate, or they might have called an ambulance to take me away. As I moved up in line, I listened to the men before me recite the numbers from Professor Ishihara's booklet. The tester only went through seven or eight pages for each person, then started over on the first page with each new man. Great, I thought, I only have to memorize seven or eight numbers and repeat them. I was three away from my turn when one of the guys in line behind me tripped, stumbling into the guy in front of him.

"Hey," said the one who'd been bumped, with a good-natured smile, "let's not get rowdy."

With all the stress, that was enough for me to lose all concentration. It was gone. I couldn't remember the first number in the sequence, and I was next.

"Excuse me, officer," I said addressing the trooper administering the test.

"Yes?"

"Ah, I took this test last year, I have a little trouble with reds and greens. I can tell you the basic colors. Your test will show that I'm colorblind, but I'm really not."

The officer, without a campaign hat, surprised me with his sincerity. "I'm sorry," he said. "I have my instructions and I only have this book to use. I don't have the authority to make any exceptions."

"Oh, I understand. I don't expect you to make an exception, it's just that the Surgeon General approved me last year." Here we go again, I thought.

"Look, I'd like to help, but there's nothing I can do. You'll have to take the test like everyone else."

Shrugging, I submitted, and failed.

It's impossible to describe the depth of disappointment I felt. Despair may have been a better word. It was a complete and utter loss of all hope, until I looked up and saw Dr. Estes appear out of nowhere. It hadn't occurred to me that he might be there, but then again, why not? He was the Surgeon General who oversaw the physical examination process. He had the final word on all the applicants as to whether they were fit for duty.

Estes was dressed in a white lab coat and stood by the door nearest our station. "Excuse me, officer, there's the Surgeon General," I said, pointing. "Will you ask him about my test last year? I'm sure he'll remember me."

An uncertain look passed over the officer's face, but he turned toward the doctor and waved him over. I didn't care about the people behind me getting impatient. I was desperate.

"Hello, Dr. Estes," I said. "Do you remember me from last year? I was at your office last fall after failing this test."

"I'm not sure," he said, peering over the top of his glasses, which rested low on his nose. "We use this book with everyone. It's our standard test." He spoke to me without a hint of recognition. Testing, once again, stopped at the table behind me and I felt a wave of embarrassment take hold. God, I thought, please don't let this happen again.

"Just a minute," said the doctor, addressing the officer. "Don't we have a box of colored yarn around here someplace?"

"Yessir, we do. It's over there on the other table." I followed the doctor, glad to get away from the others. Once there, he picked up a small box containing pieces of yarn in every imaginable color. My heart sank. Perspiration dampened my brow while he picked through the box. I glanced at the testing table, they all watched. I wished we could have moved farther away, and that he would hurry up. I was getting ready to chuck the whole thing and call it quits.

Shifting his bulk from one foot to the other he kept searching. Apparently, there was no hurry at all. Every now and again he would lift out a piece of yarn, adjust his glasses, then plunge his hand back into the box in search for more. He took a long time, but finally finished by extending his hand for my inspection. There, placed neatly side by side across his palm lay the pieces of yarn he had selected. Each was one of the basic colors, "Go on," said Dr. Estes with a smile. "Tell me the colors." And I did. And I passed the test.

As instructed, I took off my clothes, but purposely kept my slacks and undershorts on—I needed the hidden pounds! This was the last hurdle. If I could make the weight, I would be home free. There were no applicants waiting at the scale, just me. I felt relief, because after the color test I didn't need any more spectators.

The hall was nearly empty, and officers had begun dismantling their respective stations. Even the Surgeon General had disappeared. It was noticeably cooler, too, and standing half naked had nothing to do with it, for someone had turned off the heat.

"You're next on the scale, buddy," said the officer. "Got your paper?"

"Yes sir," I answered, giving him the sheet and taking a deep breath.

"You'll have to take off those pants," he ordered. Nooo, I thought.

The wallet and belt had been uncomfortable all morning. If I could describe it, it felt like an oversized handcuff around my waist, and was impossible to ignore. I half expected someone to tap me on the shoulder and ask why I was walking so funny, but no one did, and by noontime I'd become accustomed to the extra weight and forgot all about it. The consequence of forgetting occurred the instant I undid my belt buckle to remove my pants—it was then that the science of gravity pulled my pants to the floor, which landed with a *thunk* I will never forget.

"What was that?" the officer asked, looking for the source.

"What was what?" I said as innocently as possible.

Finding nothing, the trooper returned to his papers.

Gingerly, I bent over, picked up my pants and placed them quietly on the chair seat beside me. I tried to think. My first thought was how many pounds I had lost with the belt now on the chair. Things sure weren't going my way.

The officer stood and moved to the scale. He swung the height bar to the rear and adjusted the scale weight to zero. I was clearly taller than the five feet nine inch minimum height, so he was only interested in pounds. While he busied himself resetting the scale, I reached into the back pocket of my pants, grabbed the weighted wallet, and hung it onto the elastic band of my shorts. On his order, I jumped onto the scale. The moment of truth had arrived. I stood rock still and watched the officer work the scale as the left side of my underwear headed south under the weight of the lead. With a quick, short, downward stab I caught my shorts and yanked them back into place before he noticed. "You'll have to stand still there," warned the officer.

"Yes sir," was all I could manage.

"Okay. Just a second—there! That's it, 151 pounds. That about right?"

"Yes sir, it is."

I had made it!

Phil

Earlier I mentioned my belief that fate, destiny, and luck played a part in launching my state police career. My friend Phil Trapasso falls into the fate column. After ending up in the academy together, I am convinced that the adventures we shared growing up paved the way to our careers in law enforcement.

I could write a book about Phil and me, but to tell the story that I believe began our journey, I'll skip all the rest, and begin with the story about a skunk.

Phil and I lived next to each other in triple decker apartment houses on Maywood Street in Worcester, Massachusetts and first became friends in the fourth or fifth grade. We spent the summer months outside playing from early morning getting into all sorts of trouble, and rarely made it home in time for supper. You name it, we tried it. One day, and I'm guessing we were around eleven years old, Phil spotted a small skunk in the bushes between our houses. We both knew what a skunk was, but neither of us had ever been up close or seen one in the yard. This was exciting, a wild animal for us to check out. As we circled the skunk it scurried out from under the bush into the open, and Phil was first to notice that the little guy had its rear leg caught in a trap. The jaws had a firm hold.

"What are we gonna do?" I asked.

"Don't know," said Phil. "We can't just leave it there. Maybe we can pry it open with a stick."

So we found a long stick and began poking at the trap, being careful not to injure the skunk any more than he already was. It didn't work.

"We gotta get him outta there. We can pull it open and he'll run away," said Phil, full of confidence.

"I'm not gonna do it," I said.

"Yeah, you can. Go up from behind and open it. He didn't do nothin' when the stick was in there." I glanced at Phil suspiciously, but figured I'd try after seeing the *I dare ya* stare he gave me. Looking back, critically, it seems that I was a really stupid eleven-year-old, because the thought never entered my head to ask why he didn't do it. Duh!

Getting down on my hands and knees ever so slowly, I snuck up behind the skunk. The little stinker didn't mind us poking around with a stick, but as soon as my hand got near, he squirted me full in the face. "Gaaah," I gagged, coughing and choking. My eyes instantly burned and filled with tears, and my senses were overwhelmed with the obnoxious smell. I reeked. Meanwhile, my friend, helper, and fellow skunk savior, Phil, had deftly jumped backward out of harm's way and wouldn't come anywhere near me. I bolted for home.

Fortunately, home was around the other side of the house and up a flight of stairs to the second floor. The back door was open, but the screen door closed. My nose pushed against the screen as I yelled inside. "Mom," I called, as I saw her step from the kitchen into the back-door hallway. That's when my smell hit her. Her face scrunched into a grotesque mask as she grabbed her nose. "Oh my *God*, Randy," she whined. Taking hold of my arm and yanking me inside, she literally dragged me into the bathroom. Still holding her nose she began filling the bathtub. "Take those clothes off, and get in," she sputtered nasally. She was *mad!* Dropping my clothes on the floor, not daring to say a word, I climbed into the hot water. She was back in an instant, picked up my clothes and threw them into the tub with me. Next, I watched her twist the top off a container of Lestoil detergent and pour half the bottle into my bath. I wasn't sure which was worse, the skunk or the Lestoil. Apparently, my mother didn't know that tomato juice was supposed to neutralize skunk smell, or didn't care, or maybe she knew exactly what she was doing. My skin was on fire from the detergent and raw for days afterwards, but it worked.

I swore an oath that one day I would get even with Phil.

We weren't long out of high school. I was working in one local grocery store and Phil worked in another. I don't know where the idea came from, but it was actually dumb, because the Vietnam war was going on, and we were both vulnerable. Nonetheless, I suggested to Phil that we should join the Marine Reserves. Though eighteen, I obviously hadn't gotten much smarter since the skunk encounter, because he looked at me like I was nuts, but I kept at him and he eventually gave in, so maybe he wasn't too bright either. We went to the Reserve Center and signed up.

Phil went through the process with flying colors. I, on the other hand, had a problem with the physical. Apparently I had too much albumin in my urine. "What is that?" I asked the recruitment officer. "Albumin is an excess of protein in the urine. Not really an issue for you as a civilian, but if you were in a combat area, and living on rations without sufficient protein, it could be a health issue." The officer told me that if I wanted to, he could send in for a waiver, adding that they were sometimes granted. So I said yes, and he sent the request. A couple of weeks later, I received notice that my waiver had been denied. I wasn't going into the service, but Phil was, and not long after they shipped him off to Marine Boot Camp in good ole San Diego, California.

Phil was upset. Not so much that he was in, and that I wasn't, but that while he was suffering in boot camp, I spent most of the summer in a cottage on Cape Cod with some of our other buddies. I couldn't understand why he was so pissed. After all, I did send him lots of postcards. So, although it was six years post skunk, and the Marine outcome was not what I had initially intended, I figured we were even.

When I had made up my mind to leave Riley Stoker and take another shot at the state police, I suggested to Phil that since he was done with boot camp, and mostly just hanging around going to reserve meetings, that he should do it with me. So I pushed him. "Come on, Phil, take the test."

"Yeah sure, just like with the Marines," he argued.

"No, it won't be like that, come on," said I, but he wasn't listening.

"I'm done with your crazy ideas. I'm not ending up in boot camp for cops, and you spending your time on vacation somewhere sending me postcards."

This is more of the fate part, because Phil was way tougher than I was—he had already been through a boot camp, and I could only imagine what that was like. If we went into the state police together, I knew with all my heart that I wouldn't quit if he didn't. I wouldn't let the idea go, and hounded him until he finally agreed to apply.

The madness began the day Phil and I entered the State Police Academy in Framingham, Massachusetts. I'd heard from friends that the Academy was just like Marine boot camp. Phil knew for sure, but he didn't talk about it very much. I took it all as a warning, but a warning of *what*, I had no idea. So gallantly, and totally unmindful of what lay ahead, I wasn't the least bit nervous as one of the 93 trainees who walked onto the Academy grounds at 8:45 a.m. on September 16, 1968.

We stood around in small groups on a large oval driveway circling a grass field called the parade ground. I soon learned it wasn't there for us to sit on and watch parades go by. I was surprised at how small the complex was. In spite of being there twice for physicals and agility tests, I'd never really paid attention to the facility. Anyway, located just off the driveway were three Quonset huts. The one on the far right was the gym. To the left was a small wooden structure labeled "Mess Hall," and I remember thinking it would be impossible for everyone to fit inside. On the building next to the mess hall hung a sign that read "Administration Office," which housed the Academy Office and sleeping quarters for the staff. I was later convinced that this building was where each day's torture and dirty tricks were planned. The entire complex sat on maybe six or seven acres; I didn't know it at the time, but we would come to know every inch of the property intimately.

I squeezed the handle of my suitcase to get a firmer hold. It was chock-full of the clothing we were required to bring, and it was starting to get heavy. I could have put it down, but for some reason I felt more "secure" holding onto it.

It was a beautiful warm September day. The sun was lower in the sky, not directly overhead as in midsummer, and there were few clouds. The trainees had wandered the grounds, filling most of the parade field and the rear portion of the driveway in front of the huts. Phil and I had separated. Roaming by myself, I didn't recognize anyone, but one guy remembered me and grabbed my arm as I walked by. "I see you made it through the color test," he declared.

I was slightly startled, but glad someone spoke to me, even if I wasn't thrilled about the subject.

"Yeah," I answered with a laugh. "I take it you were there?"

"Yeah, I was there. Saw the whole thing. I thought the doctor would sink you for sure."

"Well, he had me worried. That was the second time I went through that. I took the exam before this one, but didn't make it. It hasn't been easy," I finished.

"I know what ya mean. I had trouble with my vision. They said that I was borderline. I knew I needed glasses, but wanted to wait. If I got glasses before this and my driver's license got restricted, I never would have made it. You smoke?"

"Yeah, want one?"

"Please," he said taking one from the pack I held out. "This place is supposed to be wicked hard. Have you heard anything about what they do?"

The poor guy was a bundle of nerves. His hands were shaking so hard he could barely hold the match to the cigarette. Luckily, his nerves weren't contagious. "No, I haven't. I know they do a lot of running and physical training. I guess we'll find out soon enough."

"Looks like we'll find out *now*," he said pointing toward the administrative office.

It was precisely 9:00 a.m. when the door opened and a staff of six uniformed state police Troopers appeared, complete with campaign hats. These men all held the rank of Trooper and they were our drill instructors, DIs for short. The first thing I noticed was that they didn't walk but *strutted* down the stairs with an air of arrogance. As they swaggered onto the parade ground, I studied them with a mixture of awe, uncertainty, and most of all, fear. One Trooper in particular caught my attention. He was about six feet three inches tall and maybe 230 pounds. I looked him up and down. There wasn't one single ounce of fat on the man. His chest was full and narrowed into a slim waist. The long-sleeved uniform shirt couldn't hide the strong, well-developed arms underneath. He wore a round blue campaign hat. The brim rested just above his eyebrows, the back rested high on his head. Had he worn it level or slightly back, the effect would have been minimal, its expression feeble. But the hat's angle was severe and sent a strong message: the person below is all business. The Trooper's face was built for the campaign hat—clear, sharp, all-seeing eyes, a handsome Roman nose, chiseled jaw, tight lips, and a thick neck. He was the perfect subject for a recruitment poster.

Round ornaments gleamed from each collar of his tailored, light blue shirt, accenting the full Windsor knot of his necktie. A silver badge rested on his left breast pocket, matched on the right with a name tag. The silver chain hanging from his shoulder was hooked to the pocket button below the name tag. A black garrison belt circled his waist. Light blue piping ran down the outside of both pant legs, accenting the dark blue slacks. The combat boots he wore were polished like black mirrors. He was a master of the spit shine.

As he moved closer, I was able see the swagger stick he squeezed tightly between his left arm and his side. His eyes searched constantly as he moved through the front of the crowd. I felt his gaze pass over me, seeing everything, yet it was like I wasn't there. He walked on without stopping, but I saw his name tag. The name was Hunt.

I left my new acquaintance behind and weaved my way through the throng, eager to begin training and not wanting to miss any instructions. Be that as it may, it was something that I needn't have worried about, because the DIs weren't going to let me miss a thing. I had lost Phil.

The suitcase I had been lugging around had become really heavy. I moved it from hand to hand every few minutes. I assumed the first order of business would be getting us unpacked and settled into our new quarters. After all, sleeping and locker assignments, unpacking, sizing, issuing uniforms, and general orientation for ninety-three men would probably take the whole day, and they surely wouldn't want to waste any time getting us settled. What I anticipated was going to be an efficient and orderly process, though, was nothing of the sort.

The DIs had positioned themselves randomly among us. Hunt's eyes moved from DI to DI, assuring himself that each was properly placed. While he scanned the field, I put my suitcase on the ground and waited for a welcoming speech.

"GET THOSE SUITCASES OFF THE DECK!" screamed Hunt. "GET 'EM UP. GET 'EM UP. GET 'EM UP!"

Startled, I hoisted my bag on pure reflex, but a trainee several feet away was too slow, and was instantly set upon by Hunt. By the bewildered look on the recruit's face, I guessed he was wondering what a deck was.

"YOU, WHAT'S YOUR NAME?" bellowed Hunt.

"Michael Collins," was the reply.

"*SIR, SIR,* YOU WILL ADDRESS ME AS *SIR. SIR, MY NAME IS MICHAEL COLLINS, SIR,*" screeched Hunt. "Where do you think you are, Boy Scout Camp?"

A trembling voice two octaves higher spoke. "Sir, my name is Michael Collins, sir."

"I CAN'T *HEAR* YOU, MISTAH," threatened Hunt. He turned to one of his colleagues. "Trooper Dunn, this one can't talk."

Dunn started toward Hunt as Hunt put his nose a half inch from Collins and whispered menacingly.

"You better make me hear you, Mister. I want people driving by here out front on Route 9 with their windows rolled up to hear you. Is that understood? SOUND OFF!"

"SIR, MY NAME IS MICHAEL COLLINS, SIR," came the terrified response.

Spinning on his heel to address the whole assembly, Hunt spoke in a voice as sinister as his expression. "You *people* will not speak unless spoken to. You will do exactly as you are told, nothing more, nothing less. You will face and look straight ahead. And you had better not eyeball me or anyone else. This isn't kindergarten, children. It's day one at the State Police Academy."

Trooper Hunt paused to let the message sink in, but he wasn't done. I watched him look us over with knife-like eyes. Then, with as foul and disdaining a look as I have ever seen on a human being, he proceeded to tell us just what he thought of us. "You *people* are disgraceful. I have never, never in my life seen a more disgusting lot. Not one of you will make a Trooper. Do you hear me?"

A few barely audible "yes sirs" wasn't enough for the DI. He flew into a rage, with arms and swagger stick waving wildly in the air. "SIR, YES SIR, SIR, YES SIR," he roared. "YOU WILL ANSWER, SIR, YES SIR, and I want to hear it *now!*"

"SIR, YES SIR," we screamed.

"Again!"

"SIR, YES SIR."

"That will do," said Hunt. "Trooper Dunn, line this pile of dirt into a column of fours."

So much for the welcoming speech.

The remaining staff descended on us like a pack of wolves—starving wolves. They had waited patiently while the alpha male fed, and now it was their turn. Shouting, yelling, screaming, jumping up and down, they molded us into a column. Trainees were being orally attacked from all directions as we formed up. All I can remember is a flurry of motion as orders came at us from every corner. We turned this way, and that. We stumbled, we fell, we cursed, we were cursed at, and we moved with no direction or purpose, as if someone had dropped a grenade into our midst and all ninety-three men scrambled for cover. It was chaos. We were confused, disorganized, and it suited our tormentors just fine.

Fifteen minutes later we were lined up in a column of fours standing at attention. I was shaking all over, aware of no one but myself. They could have shot the guy next to me, and I wouldn't have flinched. My heart was exploding in my chest with fear, and I was gasping for breath. A wave of exhaustion swept over me. This is impossible, I thought, you can't be tired. You just got here.

They were relentless in their harassment. The Trainees on the outside ranks got it the worst. They were made to do push-ups or sit-ups for doing nothing more than blinking an eye or turning a head. Luckily, I'd been shuffled to the center of the column, which spared me the onslaught. I think it was worse, psychologically, to be left wondering when they would get to me than it was when they actually did. Phil was still lost, but knowing he was there, somewhere, was enough.

I found myself talking to Jesus, praying the abuse would end and sanity would return. We had much to learn in fourteen weeks. I didn't know how they'd teach us anything if they kept acting like wild men. Anyhow, either God was listening, or the staff read my mind, for they ceased yelling and backed away, letting us settle down. They gave us about four minutes before we began training in a close-order drill, and since we had yet to be issued our M-1 carbine rifles for drill, we substituted—with our suitcases.

We marched on the oval drive around the parade ground to the rhythmic cadence sung by our instructors. Some men knew what they were doing; they had clearly been in the military. I listened to the cadence, but it was garbled, sounding as if they all had a mouth full of rocks, so I quit listening and concentrated on keeping in step with the guy in front of me. I only hoped he knew what he was doing.

Things got terribly worse, with any infraction being reason enough for discipline. Aside from being physically struck, it seemed there were no holds barred about what they could do to us. They were restricted only by the limit of their imaginations. If a drill instructor didn't like the tie one wore with his suit, or there was a sideways glance, a misstep, or a perfect step, it didn't matter. It was reason enough for punishment. Then, taking it to another level, we graduated from individual to group punishment. This new set of rules offered them the ability to make the whole troop suffer for any one person's screw up. It was the perfect form of discipline, because, according to one DI, we were all a "blot on humanity," and deserved it.

By the fourth trip around the track nothing was funny anymore, and my suitcase felt like it was full of bricks. The instructors began yelling from all sides. Several men had tripped or fallen, and lay sprawled on the ground, as others ran over and around them. A number of suitcases burst from the pounding, spilling the contents under the feet of the trampling herd. Socks, underwear, toothpaste, and all sorts of stuff was strewn everywhere. It was awful for those who had fallen. DIs hovered over them screaming, *"Get up, get up you maggots. You can't sleep here."* It seemed like terror had taken hold.

Looking back now, there was really no reason for us to have freaked out the way we did. It wasn't life-threatening, yet we behaved like they were after us with machetes. The run had become a test of survival and a message: endure or quit.

I hurled myself, and suitcase, over a small trainee who was on his hands and knees trying to gather the contents of his suitcase. My trailing foot caught his back, almost sending me to the pavement. Huge strides stretched my groin muscles, but I stayed up and kept moving. Somewhere close behind, someone gagged and threw up. Curses filled the air as those bringing up the rear trudged through the mess. The sickly smell of vomit was everywhere, and my suit, wet with perspiration, stunk. I started falling back as stronger runners passed me by in their stinking suits. My stomach heaved at the overwhelming smell, and I dropped out of the pack gulping for fresh air.

That first day I wasn't a strong runner, and it was very hard for me. From the rear I had a clear view of the damage inflicted. At least ten men were down, wheezing and gasping for breath, while another half dozen scrambled to grab their belongings and refill their suitcases. The track ahead of the fast-paced runners was clean and clear, but in their wake was a clutter of bodies and litter that I feared I might join at any moment. Why hadn't I listened to those who advised me to run and get in shape before starting the Academy? The question nagged at me. I could hear the "I told you so" from each advice-giver. Boy, was I dumb.

Twenty-five feet behind the main group, and barely on my feet, I heard the merciful words, *"Troop halt,"* from one of the DIs. God was still with me, because only by his grace was I able to scurry back into formation without being seen. I was totally drained, but still smart enough, or scared enough, to hide in the middle of the formation again.

They held us at attention, unmoving, for about a half hour. It was hard to keep track of time. I was only aware of what hurt and how much. The damage had been cleaned from the track, and all, except for the seven trainees who had already quit, were back in formation. Eighty-six left.

A chill, unhampered by the warm September sun, crept through my wet clothes. Shivering in silence was broken only by sporadic coughing, and to forget the pain, I focused my entire being on the wisps of slowly curling steam that rose from the shoulders of the man in front of me. I don't know how much time passed, but my memory tells me it was substantial, and when the order to march was given, I did so cold and stiff. My hope was that now they would get us to our quarters, or rooms, or wherever, but it wasn't to be, for they marched us to the supply building still dragging our suitcases for company.

Supply was located near the highway at the front of the compound. Again, we stood in formation while trainees went inside one at a time to get their equipment. The ordeal took forever, and while waiting at attention, our DIs delighted catching anyone who dared to move or even twitch.

The first two Quonset huts were our living quarters, and the DIs marched us directly there after the supply depot. Leaving us alone to unpack, we changed into our new khaki uniforms, stiff combat boots, and baseball caps. The DIs issued strict instructions about where and how to store our things, and once stored away, they gave us sheets and blankets for our bunks. Next came the lesson showing us how to make our beds, and a generous five minutes to complete the task. Simple enough. Sheets billowed all around the room as they were snapped into the air and settled onto our beds. We worked quickly, without angst. By the tone of our instructors about the art of bunk-making, it appeared the harassment was over and we would at last get down to business.

Five minutes later, to the second, Hunt and the others entered the hall and called the room to attention. Silence followed. I could feel tension mounting while I stood stiffly at the foot of my bunk, afraid to look, but I could feel the presence of Trooper Hunt at the end of the hall. He capsized the first bunk he came to without even looking at it. It hit the floor with an ear-splitting crash that echoed off the walls. I jumped, closing my eyes against the noise, trying to shut out what I knew was about to come.

"GET OUT. GET OUT. HIT THAT STREET. PICK UP THOSE PILLOWS AND SHEETS. GET OUTSIDE AND RUN. MOVE, MOVE, MOVE. IF I SEE ONE BED COVERING DRAG ON THE GROUND, YOU'LL RUN ALL DAY."

We did three laps, which was the equivalent of one mile, before they herded us back inside to give us another chance. I had learned that pleasing them was hopeless, and when we failed the second inspection, we ran again—this time we carried our mattresses. Eighty-one of the initial ninety-three trainees remained, including Phil, and I was sure of that, because I finally saw him again—running at the front of the pack with a mattress on top of his head.

Coming Together

I have no intention of dwelling on stories about the Academy, for each day was an adventure unto itself. What I found most noteworthy is that enduring, or "suffering" the experience with my fellow recruits, created a bond and lasting relationships—which are just as meaningful and strong half a century later.

Our first meal was a sheer joy. Our trainers were unrelenting, like a plague, and they watched our every move. I stood in the lunch line holding a tray with my eyes fixed straight ahead while inching forward. I had spent the better part of the day either in a line or in formation, staring at the back of someone's head. I never realized heads had such a variety of shapes. It's strange where one's mind will take you. I even wondered what the back of my head looked like.

My pointless musings about heads ended when I became aware of a DI standing just to the rear of my left arm. He remained outside my peripheral vision, which was fine with me as long as he didn't get any closer. I hadn't eaten anything since an early breakfast, and to my surprise, the stress, abuse, screaming, and running hadn't spoiled my appetite. I was starved! All through the chow line my nose told me they were serving root beer and scrambled eggs, but I was afraid to look and see for sure. Maybe, I thought, once closer I could sneak a peek without getting caught, but the drill instructor never left my sleeve, and I wasn't going to take a chance.

When it was my turn I moved toward the server's table; the DI moved even with me. It was Hunt. Slowly, he lifted his swagger stick and tapped my chest to stop my progress. My heart thumped, wondering what he was going to do as he lowered the stick and slipped it back under his arm. Then, in the same slow deliberate motion; he reached across the food trays; snatched the serving spoon from the mess boy; plunged it deep into a tray; and slammed a mountainous spoonful of mashed potatoes onto my plate, splattering my shirt in the process.

"Eat those," he growled.

"Sir, yes sir," I answered.

That was the first of several times Trooper Hunt took an interest in my diet. On a couple of other occasions, he scooped food from the plate of a "Farook Squad" member and piled it onto mine. Our instructors had created the Farook Squad for the overweight and out-of-shape trainees, who were made to run more and eat less. I still hovered around a 150 pounds, and Hunt, I dare say, made it his mission to fatten me up.

Each week we went home on Saturday afternoon and reported back to the Academy Sunday night. I recall very early one Monday morning about eight weeks into training, when Hunt once again showed an interest. We were standing in formation on the parade ground waiting to run; I happened to be in the front rank as Trooper Hunt came from the Admin building. Stopping in front of the troop, he looked right at me and yelled loud enough for all to hear, "STEVENS, WHAT'D YOU DO THIS WEEKEND?"

"SIR, I ATE POTATOES AND DRANK BEER, SIR!"

"That is well," he responded, turning away with a grinning laugh that was mostly unseen.

The tables were crowded around the small dining area, where we squeezed ten to a table built for eight. We were given the message that there would be no talking or unnecessary movement during chow, reinforced by several trainees doing pushups between tables on the floor. I stared at my plate, scarcely blinking as I shoveled food into my mouth. I remember the sensation of substance and hunger, but except for the potatoes hurled onto my plate, I have no recollection of what I ate, although I'm pretty sure it wasn't root beer and scrambled eggs.

After lunch we lined up for haircuts and waited once again. This time we filed quickly into formation, assumed the position of attention, and didn't move a muscle.

Short hair was the style for Academy trainees. The first man out of the chair reported to an instructor for inspection. His hair was nearly invisible on his scalp, and, as one might guess, it was deemed too long. A hippie, is what the DI called him, and he threatened the barber with non-payment if *we* didn't get our money's worth. "You see," the officer assured us with a sinister smile, "I'm here to look out for your interests."

By midafternoon, it was hard to maintain a positive attitude. I was mentally and physically exhausted and beginning to have second thoughts about what I was doing there. A trainee next to me had thrown his hands into the air and walked to the Administration building. Ten minutes later he packed up his belongings and drove out of the parking lot a free man. Too bad, I thought, he should have quit before the haircut.

Seeing how easily one could quit made it all the harder to stay. I didn't want to leave, but, quite frankly, I didn't know what to do. I looked for Phil, but couldn't find him, so I checked out others to see if they were faring any better than I was. They didn't appear to be. Even the ex-military guys looked haggard, and I'd lost track of how many had packed it in.

Menial tasks were created to keep us busy. Trainees were ordered to guard empty plots of ground containing invisible prisoners. Initially, they thought it was good duty because they were left alone, but it wasn't long before another DI discovered that three of the invisible prisoners had escaped. They ran a lap for each escapee. A dozen more men cleared the parade ground of pebbles, while another half dozen searched for rabbit holes to fill. Two trainees, believing they had found a rabbit hole, showed it to the officer, who promptly berated them for not knowing the difference between a rabbit and a gopher hole. And for wasting his time, they ran laps.

I had begun to believe that the instructors were harsh bastards and that their treatment was heartless as well as humiliating, but our behavior under the pressure was certainly responsive. When someone barked, we jumped, and when someone spoke, we listened. It became undeniable that Trooper Hunt and the DIs had a method to their madness; they knew exactly what they were doing. Suspected loners were studied and targeted for possible future elimination. Shirkers were observed, while those showing excessive anger were pushed harder to see their reaction. The fragile just up and quit, without having to be fired. We came together as a group and developed camaraderie. It was the recruits against the DIs, but more significantly, it became the group against those recruits who were outwardly disliked. Those who didn't fit in weren't embraced, and probably wouldn't make it, because out in the real world our lives could depend on one another. There was no room for anyone who couldn't be trusted or counted upon.

The next day we began all aspects of class instruction and it was intensive. They taught criminal law, the elements of a crime, motor vehicle law, search and seizure, search warrant affidavits, and much more. There was plenty to learn. A little-known fact, at least where I was stationed in western Massachusetts, was that troopers prosecuted their own cases at the District Court level. We had to know the law, court procedure, and have at least a cursory knowledge of how to prosecute a case.

The next three weeks were not any easier, or less strenuous, than the first. We ran three-to-six miles every morning before breakfast; I wasn't in shape and truly suffered for it. On Wednesday of the second week I strained my knee and couldn't run. I joined the collection of sick, lame, and lazy trainees each morning for the rest of the week doing calisthenics on the side-lines.

Monday morning, I taped my knee and tried to run again. I failed. I knew that if I didn't start running soon, I'd be out the door. The next morning, I gave it my best shot and completed the run, and from that point on everything was uphill. I was able to finish the most grueling runs, keeping up with Phil and some of the best runners. At the end of six weeks of training, it didn't matter what the drill instructors did to us. They couldn't hurt us anymore.

Graduation

As graduation neared my excitement grew, the intensity of our training and classroom instruction continued at a feverish pace, and the drill instructors had backed off and begun to reveal their true selves. They were human after all, even caring and showing a sense of humor. Trooper Hunt was the real surprise—in a word, he was funny, as in comical. He remained strict, stern, and all business in the classes he taught, but often lost his composure over classroom silliness, or more likely at a dim-witted question from a trainee. He'd turn his back on the class, trying to hide his laughter, but we all saw.

Graduating classes from the Massachusetts State Police Academy always provided good press for the media, so it wasn't surprising when a reporter and photographer from The Worcester Telegram and Gazette showed up to do a story on a local recruit. Phil was from Worcester, so why not. He was as surprised as everyone, yet embarrassed when they followed him around asking questions and taking pictures. At the target range they snapped closeups of Phil squeezing off rounds into a silhouette target. I knew Phil well, and he hated the attention.

Another afternoon, the newspaper duo wandered in while we were practicing hand-to-hand combat on mats laid out on the parade ground. The photographer busied himself taking pictures from every angle, while the female reporter flirted with a drill instructor. I hadn't been aware of it at the time, but I actually had my picture taken. Phil was on the mat when one of the instructors sent me to join him. We began wrestling, with neither of us gaining the advantage until Phil grabbed my arm and flipped me over his hip onto the mat. We stepped from the mat and two other trainees took our places.

The next weekend we went home as usual, and I had completely forgotten about the reporters. I was sitting at the kitchen table drinking coffee with my mother and our next-door neighbors Jean and Al, when my dad came home. He helped himself to a coffee and sat down. "Oh, my God," Dad exclaimed. "You haven't seen the paper." He wore a smile from ear to ear as he fumbled to pry his wallet from his back pocket. He was so excited, I swear his hands were shaking as he removed some folded newspaper pages and spread them on the table. "Look, it's a story about Phil. There he is shooting, here's another picture doing hand-to-hand combat, what a great story." My dad had a habit of getting up early on the weekends whenever I was home. He loved putting the top down on my Mustang, weather permitting, and cruising all over town. Today was no different, except that he had picked up the Sunday paper and had gone to all his morning stops showing off the article and pictures of Phil.

I read the story after Al had put it back on the table. I loved the article, and started snickering when I saw the picture of Phil throwing me to the mat during hand-to-hand combat. "Hey, Dad," I called. "Did you see this one?" I held up the photo. "Yeah, I did, it's great," he said.

"Take another look, who's the guy Phil's tossing to the ground?" Dad stared and his eyes grew wide. "Soooo, ya don't even recognize your own son," I teased. It was the first time in my life that I saw my dad blush. "That's a great article, but a lousy picture," I said. "If I hadn't known, I never would have guessed it was me." I wasn't going to tease him anymore either. My Dad loved Phil like another son, and that was fine with me.

Then came the day when we all gathered in the gym to be fitted for our new uniforms. We were trading in our khakis for the French and Electric Blue colors of the state police. It was hard to believe we were this close, but there was still enough time to screw up.

Pete Mazeikus, Phil, and I were together in a corner trying on uniform parts. The three of us had become friends. Pete was a good guy, unbelievably funny, and a straight shooter who told things just the way he saw them, whether anyone liked it or not. Both Phil and Pete were quick wits and smart asses who were masters of sarcastic one-liners. I respected and envied Pete for his candor and outspokenness, but I was more apt to keep my opinions close and my mouth shut. Looking back fifty years later, I'd like to think that I didn't want to hurt anyone's feelings, but it's more probable that I wanted to be liked, and lacked confidence in a war of words. In a battle of jabs, I couldn't keep up with either Pete or Phil.

We had taken our khakis off during the fittings and were hanging out in our underwear. Sitting on a table to my right was a campaign hat—a *real* state police campaign hat. Pete and Phil were in a deep conversation about something or other, so I wandered to the table. Picking up the hat, I held it like a delicate crown. On the wall behind the table was a mirror used by the guys who were into weight training, I guess to watch their muscles grow. Anyhow, standing in front of the mirror I warily placed the campaign hat on my head, then lowered my hands to stare at myself in the mirror. Not liking what I saw, I readjusted the hat by pulling it down above my eyebrows, and slipped the strap around the back of my head. In deep thought, I studied my skinny self and the oval face looking back at me. I remember thinking that I sure didn't look anything like Trooper Hunt did in his hat. That's when I became, embarrassingly, aware of Phil and Peter standing behind me. They had been watching my every move.

"You look just like a fuckin' nail in that hat," came the comment.

To this day, I don't know which one of them said it, and they both still claim ownership. But I learned two things. One is that Barney Fife and Smokey Bear looked better in the hat than I did. And two—I *hate* campaign hats.

Our class, the 52nd Recruit Training Troop, graduated from the Academy on December 16, 1968. I placed sixteenth of the sixty who had managed to survive. None of us knew where we would be stationed. The staff had said nothing, and truth be told I don't think they knew—it was above their pay grade. We could have been assigned anywhere within the Commonwealth and the rumors flowed like water. I didn't waste energy wondering where I'd end up. Most of the class felt the same, but some couldn't leave it alone, with endless speculation that their political connections would see to it they got a good station. I remained skeptical and paid them no attention.

The suspense ended graduation night when the Commissioner of Public Safety announced our assignments, and I'll admit it was satisfying to see so many predictions utterly wrong. Phil was sent to the Lee barracks, and I to the barracks in Russell. We had both lived in Massachusetts all our lives, yet had never heard of either town, never mind knew how to get there. I didn't care—I'd just been appointed to the rank of a Trooper in the Massachusetts State Police.

I settled in at Russell without any problems other than a few jitters and was assigned to a Trooper Coach. New troopers rode with a senior officer for three months before being turned loose on the public. Riding double was a continuation of our training. We had taken all we could from the Academy, but now it was for real and there was still much to learn. Others will disagree, but I have always maintained that it takes at least four or five years before officers gain enough confidence to know what they were doing. Time and experience are the key.

Russell consistently had a good mixture of cases to work on. Most of the area towns had a part-time police chief and maybe one patrolman. The State Police answered and investigated nearly every call except homicides and the more serious crimes. In those instances, we contacted the appropriate District Attorney's office, where a detective lieutenant and troopers working for the DA would handle the case, but were often assisted by road troopers, who gained invaluable experience.

There were many aspects to my probation period, but I think the most trying issue was learning how to fit into barracks life. This was a time when the state police force lived in the barracks. A civilian cook prepared our meals assisted by mess boys from the local state mental hospitals, and a janitor worked Monday through Friday taking care of the building inside and out. We shared our rooms with an officer working an opposite line schedule, so we were never "home" at the same time. Three days on and one day off, totaling eighty-four hours a week, made up our weekly duty schedules. The shifts were irregular and, depending upon what we were involved in, they could be brutally long. A workday didn't end because it was supposed to end at four o'clock, it ended when one had finished what needed to be done—no matter the hour.

New troopers were called "boots." The term's origin came from the Vietnam War era. It was an acronym for "beginning of one's tour." For new state police officers, it could have been "beginning of one's career" or "booc," but I guess someone figured it would be uncool to call us "boocs."

Fitting into barracks life was hard. In the opinion of all those assigned to a barracks, new boots were at the bottom of the roster. We knew nothing, we were nothing, and we wouldn't belong until we proved ourselves as acceptable. The station commander was a staff sergeant, and the second-in-command was a sergeant or a corporal. They were in total charge, unchallenged, and they had their own places at the dining table. Troopers also had their spots at the table, by seniority, and if there weren't enough seats for the boots, we would sit anywhere we could. Sometimes it was in the kitchen with the cook. Whenever we did manage to get a spot at the table we were pretty much ignored. I remember one time, it was only our second or third day, when one of the new boots inserted himself into a conversation at the dinner table. The second-in-command interrupted him in mid-sentence. "You have nothing to say that anyone here is interested in hearing. Keep your mouth shut and listen. You might learn something."

The young boot had been sharply put in his place. It was a lesson well learned.

My Trooper Coach, Dave Bernard, was great, and besides having four years on the job, he was smart and savvy. Dave was Italian with brown eyes, fair skin, and rapidly thinning black hair that he combed evenly over the top of his head. He was an inch or two taller and thirty pounds heavier than me. What I liked most about my coach was his silliness, sense of humor, and the compassion he showed toward people in his work. He had also recognized that I was self-conscious about my size, yet he never teased me or even mentioned it. Dave was well liked and more importantly respected by the other troopers and our bosses, which helped my "standing" in the barracks. If Dave liked me, it was easier for the others to follow suit. Senior troopers were glad to help with my education as well—they would talk about their ongoing investigations and encouraged me to ask questions. Whenever I did ask, they were eager to help by sharing things they were working on, their strategy, and the outcome they hoped to achieve. I was learning. I knew my place, though, and kept my opinions to myself. If I were asked a question, I'd give the best answer I could without sounding "salty." Being salty usually means to be angry or bitter as a result of being embarrassed. Not so, as far as the state police were concerned. If you were labeled salty, you were considered a know-it-all, conceited, arrogant, and self-important. It was one of the worst labels one could earn, especially a new boot. *Cowardly*, though was at the top of the list of bad labels.

Idiot

I had been extremely lucky to have Dave Barnard as a coach, and would later learn, on more than one occasion, just *how* fortunate. I've already said that he was a terrific teacher and fun to be with, but as in any job there were times when patrol was boring, especially if we were caught up on our investigations and there were no calls. It was on those days that Dave and I would wander the hill towns. We would discover farms and old houses in the middle of nowhere to stop at; we never considered just cruising by. Dave would drive us up to the house, barn, or right out into a field, where the farmers and hired help could usually be found hard at work. We would introduce ourselves and just talk, about anything. How are things going? Any problems around here? What are ya growing this year? These people had few visitors and loved our stops. They went out of their way to make us feel right at home and welcome anytime. They would offer us a cold drink, a cup of coffee, and sometimes a homemade pastry before we went on our way. Dave had said it was like a beat cop walking the city streets, only we were in cruisers. Acquaintances that I made and cultivated in the Russell area, as well as those at future stations, provided sources and knowledge of where to look and who to look at when working cases. People willing to talk are always the best sources of information.

One day near the end of our shift, Dave drove us down what looked like a cow path. He often did that, and I never worried because I thought he knew where he was taking us. This day, though, I asked, "Where are we going?" He smiled and said that he had no idea as we rounded a bend and came upon an ancient cemetery surrounded by a grove of trees that almost completely shaded the graves. I was pretty sure the fence encircling the graveyard was made of brittle cast iron, for it was broken in many places. The top rail of the entry gate was separated from the metal support post and was only attached by the lower rail. The gate was open halfway, with the bottom rail buried two inches into the moss-covered soil. Its days of swinging open to welcome visitors were long over, yet the scene was beautiful; it felt ancient to me. Partial sunshine landed here and there high-lighting the brilliant green of the moss. Clusters of tiny, light blue flowers poked through a few grass-covered spots un-claimed by the moss.

A sense of respectfulness washed over me as I walked among the headstones with a gentle step. I don't know where the feeling came from. It was peaceful, beautiful, and welcom-ing. This wasn't a Stephen King horror story cemetery. The headstones were very old, and many of the inscriptions were hard to read. Two hundred and more years of New England's winter and summer storms had worn away some of the engrav-ings, now filled with lichen. I found the graves of whole fami-lies, wondered what they looked like, and where they had lived. I shared a heartbreak reading the headstone of Sarah, who died with newborn child, and Jacob, who died at eight years of fever. Dave and I spent a half hour just meandering around before heading back to the barracks. I promised myself that I would return one day when I rode alone.

The days riding double with Dave were coming to an end. I was filled with excitement at the thought of going out on my own, and it couldn't come soon enough. Yet deep inside a nervousness tugged at my confidence. Was I really ready? Given the benefit of hindsight, looking back at my young self, the honest answer to that question was *hell no*, for in addition to being a naïve pupil, I knew nothing of the real world. We don't know what we don't know, is a saying Dave used often during the course of my training, and one that I had, eventually, learned to fall back upon in countless situations, often stopping me cold to rethink what I was doing.

On our next tour together, Dave and I were working our middle day. The middle day shift was split. It was called a "dipsy." The first portion was from 6 p.m. until 2 a.m. Then we'd return to the barracks, go to bed and finish the patrol from 10 o'clock the following morning until 2 in the afternoon. Enough of schedules.

This story begins around 1 a.m., when we received a radio call telling us to check a reported train derailment near the center of Chester. Chester only had a police chief. I couldn't say for certain, but I guessed the call was made to the Chief, who then called the barracks. Hell, it was a freezing cold, early March night, and if I'd been him, I'd have called the barracks too—— and gone right back to bed.

Tooling west on Route 20 was about a fifteen-mile ride. Dave kicked the accelerator, throwing the cruiser forward, and I grinned hearing the four-barrel carburetor sucking air into the Ford's 428 cubic inch engine with a hollow moan. Dave eased off on the gas as we swept down a long grade into Chester's center. We slipped into the sleeping town and parked behind some mill houses next to the railroad tracks. Unable to see anything of a derailment from Route 20 approaching town, we had talked, and figured this would be the best spot to begin searching.

Stepping from the cruiser, my breath was stolen by a blast of arctic air. It was freezing cold, the wind was constant, biting, and the windchill was well below zero. The clear, black sky held a million tiny points of sparkling diamond-like stars. This was radiational cooling at its best. There were only a few lights coming from houses alongside the tracks. Nobody was up, and they didn't even know we were there. I suspected the call had been a hoax. Dave was sure of it, but it made no difference, we had to check anyway.

I called the barracks to let them know we were going to be out of the car, then flipped on the outside speaker so we could hear the radio. Reluctantly, I left the car's warmth and joined Dave trackside.

This would be a good place to express my thoughts concerning our uniform winter coat, the reefer. In one word, inadequate!

I can't say for sure because I don't know, but I think it was a mixture of wool and something less warm. It was unlined, had front buttons, and it was stiff and hard to move in. The coat was tapered from the shoulders and chest down through the waist, then it flared, ending around the groin area. The gun belt, holster, ammunition, and handcuff case circled the waist. The cross strap hooked to the right rear of the belt, then passed over the left shoulder, attaching to the front of the belt. It was sharp looking. That's all the good I have to say about the reefer coat. Thankfully, in future times, the department changed the winter uniform to Mighty Macs, which were warm, comfortable, and didn't restrict movement.

Visibility wasn't good in either direction because of the westerly wind and the amount of snow it picked up. The train tracks, running along the river's edge, disappeared into the darkness and blowing snow less than a hundred yards down the line. Dave sent me searching east and he went west. It was tough going, bent against the wind, with blowing snow hitting me from every direction. I hunched my shoulders, scrunching my neck and head as far inside the reefer as possible. Imagine a turtle. Aiming my flashlight into the darkness I looked for any sign of a derailment. Fifteen minutes out I hadn't found a thing, so I headed back west to hook up with Dave. The snow stung my face and poked at my eyes as the wind roared up the valley. The slapping and cracking of bare branches on the huge oaks and maples, whirling high above me, became a din, drowning out all sound.

Unknown to me, Dave had called it quits a while ago and was almost back at the cruiser. He had turned his back to the wind and was walking backwards when the eastbound freight train came into view around a long easy curve. Back-to-back diesel locomotives dragged thirty cars of rolling stock at fifty miles per hour.

Dave had been walking twenty feet north of the tracks, parallel to the line, smartly putting a safe distance between himself and the tracks, but no one had ever told me it was bad practice to stroll down the middle of railroad tracks. Furthermore, no one had ever told me it was especially bad practice to do it in the middle of the night during a windstorm in subzero temperatures with blowing snow. Common sense should have told me, but as a city kid, born and bred, what the hell did I know about rolling freight trains. My expertise was limited to jumping on and off the stop and go trollies that took us downtown to the movies.

Dave watched me hopping from railroad tie to railroad tie, looking as if I didn't have a care in the world. It was then that he realized there was a very real possibility that I was about to be splattered amongst the trees. The engine's coupler stuck out from the locomotive like a battering ram. Dave screamed as the train raced on. He jumped into the air, wildly waving his arms and flashlight trying to get my attention. He turned on the train screeching, waving, stamping, and swearing. It was beside him now, and not long before I was going to become part of the scenery.

I, on the other hand, was oblivious. Warmed from walking and skipping westward, I moved faster, counting the ties as I hopped along. Something faintly probed my mind. Again, it nudged me, but didn't compute. The train drew closer, its roar hidden behind the wind. Out of the night, I thought I heard something. Then I heard him. Hands cupped around his mouth amplified his warning.

"LOOOOK OOOOUUUUT," Dave screamed, and I looked up.

The track in front of me was awash in light. An eerie yellowish glow from the freight train's large headlamp swallowed me as I jumped off the tracks. The freight tore by, slamming me with a wall of wind, spray, dirt, and snow. Thunder and vibration overwhelmed me, terrifying me. I envisioned a box car ripping loose and smearing me into the ground. I felt helpless against the thing, out of control. Spray soaked me, almost knocking me over. I imagined being inside a tornado.

On the ride back to the barracks, Dave told me every few miles that I was an idiot. All I could say was, "I know, I know." I was also thinking just how close I had come to permanently visiting the beautiful cemetery we had found a few days earlier.

My next-to-last thought before bed that night was realizing that the state police had already decided that we boots were ready to go it alone, armed only with a little bit of knowledge, overconfidence, the blind courage of youth, and a whole lot of luck. My last thought before sleep was that Dave had just saved my life, and I wasn't even off break-in.

Second Grade

I had finally completed probationary break-in, only to find myself truly alone and unchaperoned. It was kind of a naked feeling. I had never noticed people staring at me when I was with Dave. Was I admired, feared, respected, or was I being looked upon with disdain? The thoughts picked at me again and again, and the first few months without Dave's guidance reinforced just how little I knew and how tender my psyche was. Straightforward everyday police tasks were anything but routine for someone who had never done them before, and the inklings of doubt that I'd initially felt, and ignored, had returned. Feeling so unsure was scary, and I prayed that no one could see it.

I drove out of Westfield center headed west on Route 20 toward the barracks. The sergeant had ordered me back to the station for 12:45 p.m., where I was to escort the second-grade class from the Russell Elementary School on a tour of the barracks. The ride took about ten minutes, so barring any unnecessary stops I would be on time.

Each time I traveled that stretch of highway reminded me of the first day I had reported for duty at Russell. The newly graduated troopers, assigned to Troop B, were told to present themselves to the Troop Commander, at Northampton, before going to their assigned substations. The meeting consisted of nothing more than a short welcoming speech before they let us go.

Northampton, along with Lee and Russell, was another municipality in Massachusetts that I had never heard of. Obviously, I'd never been there, so I found myself faced with leaving a city I'd never heard of, to then find another place I'd never been to, or heard of, before graduation night. You would think that I might have brought a map, but I had never relied on them much—a fact to which my future wife would have readily attested, because my bullheaded refusal to consult a map, or heaven forbid ask someone for directions, drove her mad. (I'm convinced it's part of the male DNA.) So, true to form, a short distance outside Northampton, I took a wrong turn and got totally lost. Rather than take a stab at dead reckoning, I opted to backtrack and get right again. Why I gave in to backtracking, instead of believing that I'd eventually find my way, is beyond me, but then, I had yet to learn the lesson that one shouldn't walk along an active set of train tracks against blinding wind and freezing snow in the middle of the night.

I remember slipping through Westfield in my overloaded Pontiac Firebird stuffed full of my gear. I took the curves and turns slowly, because the car rolled like a tuna boat. Even without a heavy load, the Pontiac had a weak suspension and was prone to bottom out. I hated the car. One of the biggest mistakes of my short life was selling the red Mustang, which, fifty-odd years later, would have been worth a small fortune. Anyway, when I was packing the Firebird for that first trip to the barracks, I had to sit on the trunk to force it closed, jammed the rest inside the passenger compartment, and hung a pole from the door post hooks across the back seats to hang my uniforms. It gave me the extra space I needed, but the interior was claustrophobic. It felt like I was driving a closet.

The road followed the Westfield River. Its southern shore acted as a mantle, separating the river from the strong hills of Blandford and Russell that fell sharply to its banks. On the left, against the river's flow, hard and softwood forests dominated the landscape with steep outcroppings of ledge scored bare from blasting years ago. There was a lot of beauty in the valley, but one had to look past the old mills and mill housing that sat by the river's edge. I believed the area barely clung to economic survival, against what seemed to be more difficult times.

The sign in Westfield center indicated that Russell was eight miles away. Each mile seemed like three, and my excitement grew when I caught sight of the building. The barracks sat right alongside the road and didn't look anything like I imagined. The two-story brick structure rested on a large neatly manicured lot. It had been built in the 1950s, which made it the newest of all the other B Troop stations. The first floor held a foyer, main office, report room, cellblock, and garage. Connecting the first level spaces was a large rectangular guard room furnished with several overstuffed chairs, tables, lamps, and of course a TV.

My thoughts about my arrival that first day at Russell faded into the past as I flipped the left directional on, turned into the now-familiar driveway, and slowed to a stop. I could see the sergeant through the office window moving papers at his desk. I opened the front door and entered the foyer as the door alarm faded behind me. The sarge glanced up at the alarm, gave a wave, and while answering the phone he hit the button beside his desk to unlock the inner door. I snapped the door open and turned left into the main office, then sat on a desktop while the sergeant finished his call.

Sergeant Edward Summer was a large man, over six feet tall and well north of two hundred pounds. His black hair was streaked with grey and thinning on top. His face was full, with a large nose, wide mouth, and deep green eyes. Most often he wore an expression that made it hard to read his mood. I liked the sergeant, but at times I was a little fearful; maybe it was more wariness than fear; probably having to do with my inability to figure him out. But he'd been good to me; a willing teacher and always helpful. I had often seen his lighter side joking with the senior men, but whenever dealing with the new guys he was more businesslike.

Showing a class of second graders around the station wasn't my idea of how to spend the afternoon, especially when I found out that the sarge's daughter was in the class. Shouldn't I be saving our Mother Commonwealth from crime? I would have preferred almost anything to this. I was told of the assignment the day before. I had no say, and senior officers didn't want to do it, so the matter had been firmly decided. I was the junior trooper on duty the day of the visit, so it was all mine. One didn't complain, or even think about broaching the matter for discussion. Sergeants and corporals, in the stations they commanded, were the ultimate authority. They were not questioned or looked at cross-eyed. As I mentioned before, management was autocratic, and military style. Orders, instructions, and suggestions were almost blindly followed, and rarely, if ever, questioned. And, on one of those occasions, if one even dared, it was done with *extreme* tact. A second-grade class tour assignment was not one of those occasions.

Sergeant Summer hung up the phone and spun around in his chair. "Hi, Sarge, how you doin'?" I asked, sliding from the desktop.

"Good, good, it's been a quiet morning. I got lots done. Did you drop off that warrant at court like I asked?"

"Yessir, I gave it to Beth in the clerk's office."

"Thanks, they were looking for it yesterday. I gave it to Adams to drop off, but he forgot. Wait till I see him."

I ignored the remark.

"Look, Randy." He spoke in a formal tone. "I want you to give these kids a good show around. I know the teacher."

"Don't worry, Sarge. Everett and I gave a bunch of Cub Scouts a tour a couple of weeks ago. I'll just do what Everett did."

I was afraid that my confidence sounded hollow. The sarge never gave these visits any sort of notice, but he did have an interest in this one. I'd heard him say they were a pain in his butt, and he didn't like civilians wandering around *his* barracks.

"By the way," he offered. "I bounced that breaking and entering report you did on the Leary break-in on Montgomery Road. Get together with one of the senior guys to help you write it over. And I want you to check the pawn shops in West Springfield, too. Good chance you'll find a couple of their belongings there."

"I already did that, Sarge. There wasn't anything."

"Well, if you don't put it in the report, no one knows you checked. I don't want these things done half-assed."

"Yes sir," was all I said.

Summer had been on the job for twenty years and was from the old school. His idea of right and wrong came from his life's experience, on and off the job. It came from within the man and influenced everything he did. He, and others of his era, often administered their own kind of justice, usually right on the spot. No court appearance necessary; no social worker intervention; no big brother probation officer following an offender's progress; a swift kick in the ass when caught was all that was required; and, more often than not, it worked better than any arrest or court appearance.

For dinosaurs like Sergeant Summer, it was only during the later years of their careers that they had to deal with Miranda rights and stricter search and seizure laws. Supreme Court decisions changed police authority, scope, and procedures in a relatively short period of time. The chances are great that law enforcement will never experience movement as drastic or swift again. The new rules were hard for many of the old guard to work by, or even grasp. Many opted for retirement, but Sergeant Summer was one of those who embraced the change and moved with it. However, on this particular day, the sarge was not his usual self. He was out of sorts, and I suspected it had something to do with the class visit.

Leaving the office, I went upstairs into the kitchen, where our cook, Mary, was just taking a sheet of cookies from the oven. Mary Masella was a small woman in her mid-sixties. She had long black hair with only a few streaks of grey. It was all pinned up on the top of her head. Today, she held it all in place with a green and white kerchief. She always wore white aprons over simple print dresses, and I never saw her without nylon stockings and low-heeled black shoes. Her face was pale, and I could never tell if she wore makeup other than the ever-present bright red lipstick.

"We havin' cookies for lunch, Mary?" I asked, grabbing a couple and leaning against the counter.

"No, we're not havin' cookies for lunch," she mimicked. "They're for the kids. Eddie wanted me to bake them so they'd have a snack after you took them around. Did you know Eddie's daughter is in the class?"

"Yeah, I found out yesterday. I really don't want to do this, Mary. How come I got stuck with it? There's other guys on today."

"Don't ask me. I guess he just wanted you to do it. Maybe he figured you were the one closest to their age," she added, poking me in the side. I stuck my tongue out and swiped two more cookies. They were warm and delicious.

Mary asked me to get a fresh carton of milk and put it in the dispenser. They were too heavy for her to lift.

"Wait till you meet the teacher, Miss Pitt," Mary said, sliding another sheet of cookies into the oven and closing the door. "She's a real beauty," offered Mary, rolling her eyes.

"Oh yeah, how old?" I asked with a renewed interest in the second-grade class. Mary snorted a laugh waving her spatula back and forth. "Noooo, no, no, no, not that kind of beauty, a doozie, a real doozie. This woman knows everyone's business from Chester to Westfield. She's queen o' the gossips. I don't like her at all. My sister thinks she's okay, but then again, my sister tends to tittle-tattle herself. She lives alone with her elderly mother here in Russell. Not too far from the sarge, either, and she's never been married. I don't know why—she *is* attractive. Not your type though, honey. She's a typical old maid, just not that old. Can't imagine anyone having her for a wife. Ha! Her husband would never get her off the phone."

Mary put a large black pot on the stove's right rear burner and turned on the gas before continuing. "What upsets me most about that woman is knowing that she delights in the little tidbits of "material" she gets from those innocent children. A good friend of mine works in the school lunchroom. She told me how Pitt operates. She'd worm some little story of home life from one of the kids, and the next thing you knew, it was a tasty morsel of gossip at teachers' lunch."

Mary had worked herself into quite a huff. The more she talked the madder she got. She ended her rant by tossing her spoon into the stainless-steel sink with a huge clang.

"Easy Mary, easy," said John Delaney as he strolled sleepily into the kitchen and poured himself a coffee.

"Oh John, I'm sorry. Did I wake you?" Her expression was of true concern. Mary mothered each and every one of her troopers, and she was always careful to be quiet in the kitchen so as not to wake them up. To everyone's surprise, she even shushed the Troop Commander one day when he visited for lunch and got too loud.

"Naw, it's okay, I couldn't sleep anyway," replied John, taking a gulp from his steaming mug. The nine-year trooper had finished desk duty, which was called the night watch, at eight that morning. He wouldn't be able to go home until relief came in at three.

"I'm gonna try and sleep again after I finish this. What time are the little brats comin'?" he asked with a yawn and a wink to me, knowing he'd get a rise from Mary.

"Any time now," I replied.

"Okay, jus' make sure you muzzle 'em when they're upstairs, and keep the little shits outta my room."

"Don't you talk about the children like that, John Delaney," scolded Mary. Then, seeing his smile, she knew she'd been baited. "Oh, go on, get out. I got work to do."

John dropped his empty cup in the sink and headed back to bed after kissing Mary on the top of the head. It was an awkward sight to watch the six-foot-four-inch giant bend down to Mary, who was just a little over five feet tall.

"Are you gonna be here for lunch tomorrow, Randy?" Mary asked after John left.

"Yeah, I think so. I SDO tomorrow morning after night watch, but Trooper Walters took a holiday day off, so we're gonna be short. Sarge won't let me go home till the afternoon." (SDO, or "start day off," referred to a trooper's last working day before his DOR, or "day off regular." An officer's first day into work was simply called his first day back.)

"Good, because I'm makin' pot roast. You just go to bed in the morning, I'll have somebody wake you for lunch. And you'd better get out of those cookies too, they're not for you. Between you and the sarge, you'll have 'em all eaten before the kids get any."

Mary lived in the Town of Huntington, which was halfway between the barracks and Chester. It was typical of the other small, valley towns that depended on the paper mills for their livelihoods. Mary told me once that she had never wanted to work at the mills. After her brother, Tony, was hired as the barracks custodian, Mary applied for the job of cook and got it, saying that she never regretted the decision. The troopers at Russell never regretted her decision either, because she was a terrific cook, and loved her "boys."

Palming one last cookie, I left and headed down the corridor to our sleeping quarters. I couldn't shake the feeling of impending doom that had gnawed at me since the morning. My stomach was all butterflies knowing that Sergeant Summer would watch me like a hawk, and I fully expected him to follow me around hanging on every word. Mary hadn't helped matters by telling me about Miss Pitt.

When I got to my room, I removed my belt and service revolver, locking it away before cleaning up. Satisfied, I decided to have a peek at the other rooms, just in case. The sarge would scalp me if any of the kids saw something they shouldn't see.

Over the years of barracks living I've seen an astonishing array of items stashed away in bedrooms. From the animal kingdom alone, I've seen bear cubs, a horse, deer, a raccoon, snakes, a pig, ducks, and a couple of geese, each with a story of its own. It's safe to say that I wouldn't be surprised at anything I might find in a trooper's room. Happily, today, there was nothing unusual.

The children slammed the doors of the school van as they off-loaded and lined up on the sidewalk. Loud and excited voices gave me a chill. They were all here and ready to go, but I wasn't ready for them. I knew, just as sure as they were standing on the sidewalk, that something was going to go terribly sideways. And, if it did, salvation for me would be a transfer.

When I reached the bottom of the guard room stairs, Sergeant Summer had already gone outside and was bringing them through the front hallway door, where I was waiting.

"Miss Pitt, this is Trooper Stevens. He's one of our new troopers and he's been looking forward to showing the children around. I know you'll enjoy it." There was a hint of nervousness in the introduction, as well as an unmistakable message for me: Show them a good time, or else.

"It's nice to meet you, Miss Pitt," I added cheerfully, remembering every single word from Mary.

She forced a prune-like smile and extended her hand into mine. Then, apparently uncomfortable, she quickly withdrew it.

"Yes, how do you do," she said icily, and turned back to Sergeant Summer.

What little confidence I had drained away with each passing second. Maybe it was my imagination, but it sure seemed to have turned colder in the guard room. Mary had hit it right on the nose: a typical old maid. This lady wasn't going to be won over with charm. She was as personable as a fart, and I was totally outmatched.

For what seemed like a long time, I listened to Miss Pitt conduct a lecture-like conversation with Sergeant Summer. It was like she was talking to one of her students. He was noticeably uncomfortable, nervously looking at the floor, then his fingernails, and then, only out of necessity, he would look at Miss Pitt. She was paying no attention to his fretful shifts, for she rambled on in no apparent hurry to proceed.

Her body was trim, but not skinny. Her hair was pulled tightly back into a bun, with not a hair out of place. Behind unattractive wire-rimmed glasses were brown eyes devoid of makeup. Her facial features were sharp, except for full lips. As Miss Pitt presented herself, she was not appealing, but I could see the attractiveness that Mary had described. A hairstyle, makeup, new glasses, and clothes would transform this female into a fine-looking woman.

Tiring of the wait, and my growing restlessness, I decided to get things rolling, so, to the sergeant's relief, I cut into the middle of their one-sided conversation.

"Well, Miss Pitt, if we're all ready, I'll introduce myself to the children and we can get started." To hell with it, I thought. I'd do the best I could.

"Good afternoon, boys and girls, I'm Trooper Stevens."

There's just no describing the relief I felt when the sarge left us and went into his office. He had had enough of Miss Pitt, and ran away. As long as he stayed there, and didn't breathe down my neck, I felt I could cope with the kids and their teacher.

Turning to the business at hand, I ignored the teacher and concentrated on the students, asking them questions on anything that popped into my head. The response was more than I could have hoped for. They immediately began talking. Their fear, if they had any at all, melted away, and they soon began doing the asking. I made a game of it. When they asked a question I would redirect it to another child, thus involving the whole class. It worked great and their interest was piqued.

Miss Pitt loosened up, too. I could tell she liked the way the children were engaging, and she smiled profusely. Watching her in her element, surrounded by her students, I wondered if I hadn't been too critical of her. Maybe she couldn't help the way she was. Only God knows what trials she may have suffered on life's journey, and how she may have been affected. I had no right to judge her. It was clear that she truly loved the children and they seemed very fond of her.

"Hey, Miss Pitt, look at this." "Hey, Miss Pitt, look at that." "Wow, Miss Pitt, can we get one of these for school?"

I hated to admit it, but I was beginning to enjoy myself. I let the kids have hands on everything, much to the consternation of their teacher, but after my reassurances she gave in, and let them have their way.

They banged on the teletype machine while I explained its use. We pretended that Miss Pitt was a dangerous criminal and submitted her name through the NCIC computer. After the query, I wished that I hadn't done it, because it occurred to me that some prominent people had been sorely embarrassed by arrest for forgetting to pay a traffic fine. Paranoia grabbed hold as I imagined her name logged somewhere deep in the depths of the computer. Waiting for the response was endless. Over and over, I told myself that she probably didn't even have a driver's license. I gazed outside to clear my mind while twenty students stared over my shoulders at the teletype machine. It only took a few seconds staring at the school van parked at the curb before I realized Miss Pitt had been the driver. The epiphany nearly sent me over the edge, as that annoying little voice inside my head began talking to me. "Oh, you've done it now, Dummy. What are you gonna do if there's a warrant for her? You gonna arrest her in front of the children and lock her in a cell? What are you gonna say to the sarge with his daughter clinging to his leg screaming hysterically?" It was bad enough that I was listening to the stupid dribble of my subconscious, never mind answering. "But Sarge, how was I supposed to know there was a warrant for her arrest?"

Leaping to my feet, I waved my arms, as if herding sheep, to move everyone away from the machine and out the office door.

"Well, kids, I guess the computer must be slow today. We'll check later to see if an answer comes back. Now, who wants to see the cellblock?"

Every person who ever toured the barracks wanted to see the jail cells. "Who wants to go in?" I asked with a smile at Miss Pitt.

"Put Mike in, he's always gettin' in trouble," said a small voice in the corner.

"No," said Miss Pitt. "We don't need one of these for Mike."

"I'll go in, Miss Pitt, I'm not afraid, really." Mike squeezed between two boys and bravely stepped through the cell door.

"I wish all our prisoners went in that easily," I whispered to their teacher.

"I'm afraid he went in *too* easy," added Miss Pitt.

Once Mike was safely locked away in cell number 1, the rest of the class crowded into cell 2, and battered me with questions.

The biggest hit of the day was the cruiser parked in the back driveway. They thrilled at the siren and yelling over the public address system. Nearby neighbors always knew when a bunch of kids were touring the barracks. All in all, the day was going fine. The students were happy, Miss Pitt beamed, and the sarge was nowhere to be seen.

I ushered the gang back into the building through the garage, up the back stairs, quietly past our rooms, and into the dining area for milk and cookies. Tony and Mary had everything ready. The milk was poured, and a gigantic plate of cookies sat at the center of each table. By the time Miss Pitt and I entered the room, each kid already had a fistful of cookies. The teacher had become openly friendly toward me and began talking to Mary and me as Sergeant Summer came out of hiding.

"Oh, Sergeant Summer, this has been wonderful. We've had so much fun at seeing the barracks. They've learned so much today. I can't recall them ever being so interested in anything. Trooper Stevens was wonderful. The children loved him." On and on she raved, to the point where I was getting a little red-faced. Mary handed me a glass of milk, and we sat down at a front table while the sarge continued to get his ear bent.

Miss Pitt continued her high praise of me right to the end of the conversation, then walked to the rear of the dining room and tapped a tabletop to get her class's attention.

"Well, children, now is the time if you have any other questions to ask Trooper Stevens. We're leaving in a short while. We don't want to overstay our visit."

In a split second three hands flew into the air. This is what I dreaded most. I had been okay with the students, and had impressed their teacher, but I was concerned with Sergeant Summer present.

The boss had slid to a corner table with a full plate of cookies, safely out of the way of any stray questions. I wanted to tell him how nervous he was making me. I wanted to say that I'd done all right to this point, and I'd do the same if he'd just go away, but there was nothing to be done about it. He and his plate of cookies were staying right where they were. So, with a sense of foreboding, I pointed at one of the raised hands.

"Trooper Stevens, did you ever shoot anyone?" asked a redheaded boy with freckles.

I knew this was the type of question to expect and it was going to be hard to bring the answer down to a second-grade level. I thought for a second, then launched into a narrative on guns, their purpose, our training, and made it clear that the police didn't want to shoot anyone.

The sarge had his mouth full of cookies and was chewing about as fast as I was talking. I thought I noticed a nod of agreement, but dismissed it, realizing he had just swallowed.

Once the ice was broken, I began to feel better, and pointed to another boy at the middle table. "Did you ever arrest anyone?"

No problem, I thought to myself, if their questions don't get any tougher than this, I've got it made.

I don't know what got into me, but my confidence swelled. The sarge seemed pleased with the answer to the first question, so I decided to give the children an example they might be able to relate to. I was going to tell them about the Russell Inn.

The Inn was Russell's watering hole, but also frequented by many from the surrounding towns as well, and it was located right across the street from the barracks. It was a good place, with good food, but seldom a weekend went by that we weren't summoned to the Inn for one problem or another. Usually, it was a local resident who had had too much to drink, and occasionally there were bloody noses from a bar fight.

"You all know the Russell Inn across the street," I began, as the sergeant looked up and inhaled two more of Mary's best.

"Many times after drinking too many beers, people will argue and sometimes fight with each other. When that happens at the Russell Inn, the state police are called to go over."

There was no mistaking the upturned eyebrow. My boss stared hard and gulped three more cookies. What had I done? I was too close to home, his home. The sarge literally knew everyone in town and was known to frequent the Inn.

Too late now, I thought. I continued cautiously . . . another two cookies.

"So, we will send an officer to the Inn and sometimes we have to arrest the people causing the trouble."

I started to say more when the little girl beside Miss Pitt jumped to her feet and threw her hand toward the ceiling. Waving frantically, she looked with eyes that begged me to call on her.

The sarge's eyes were busy now, flickering nervously, between the little girl and me. His jaw pumped up and down, rolling in a sideways motion, and his lips were clamped shut. A pained look covered his face while he tried to swallow his cookies.

For a second, I was going to ignore the child, but I didn't, and I pointed. "Yes, what is it?" I asked.

"Oh, I know about *that*, Trooper Stevens," she offered while beaming proudly at her father. "My daddy goes to the Russell Inn all the time, and it's just like you say. When he comes home, Mommy fights with him every time."

A sound somewhere between a gasp and a choke came from the corner as half-chewed cookies exploded from the sarge's mouth onto his plate. A pot crashed into the kitchen sink behind me. Mary had dropped it while trying to control herself, but she lost the battle as laughter poured through the door.

I couldn't believe it. My mouth formed a sickly smile while I stood speechless. My face had turned scarlet and was only a shade lighter than Miss Pitt's. The sarge wiped cookie mush off the table with his napkin. I had tried so hard to impress him, yet all I had done was give Miss Pitt the story of a lifetime.

He didn't talk to me much over the next couple of days. I couldn't blame him. I wouldn't have talked to me either. I considered submitting a letter for transfer to another barracks. It seemed a wise thing to do.

On my next middle day, I had just finished an early breakfast when the sarge joined me at the table. We were alone. I didn't know what to say to him beyond good morning, so I studied the bottom of my empty cup. A full thirty seconds passed before he broke the ice. "Ya know, Rand . . . I wanted to strangle that little shit."

With that announcement, he shook his head from side to side and laughed. It was going to be okay.

Mrs. Fish

The volume of calls during my early months was light, mostly routine and minor in nature, but each was an exciting new adventure. Reminiscing brings the realization that I hadn't been overwhelmed with any assignment beyond my abilities, which was a good thing considering my experience, or lack thereof.

The previous sentence gives me pause to wonder why my assignments were easy, but upon reflection, I've had such thoughts throughout my lifetime. As I've aged and considered life itself— the trials of one's life; trying to find its purpose; then reading about, and working to discover one's awareness and inner soul— I have become convinced of a higher power within and beyond us all. When I think back on critical decisions, events, and incidents during my life, I have little doubt that I would not be as happy, peaceful, or possibly even alive today, had the selections gone a different way. I'm not suggesting I've been deserving of such providence, but considering my beliefs, and the saying, with biblical origins, that "God doesn't always give us what we want, but what we need," this higher power has certainly played a part in my life that I can't ignore. In the world in which we live, it's a never-ending struggle always to be "worthy."

There were many days when I would never get a call. Riding into the hill towns and practicing things Dave had taught me, I made good use of the uneventful hours, but a lack of patience and youthful exuberance frequently won out. I can remember taking stationary posts to watch traffic, and look for a violation—anything to be active. I'd even talk to the God of police, begging to be sent on a call. Years later, I'd park in a similar stationary position and beg them *not* to call me.

Adjusting to my newfound authority in the area of community relations, including with motorists, I'd say, for the most part, that I was fairly even with the public at large. But there were those few times when a rambunctious, swaggering, young trooper appeared out of nowhere, and he wasn't pretty. I cringe at the thought of those encounters. There truly were not many of them, but, my Lord, I'd catch someone driving ten or fifteen miles per hour above the speed limit, and I'd speak to them as if they'd just robbed a bank. It usually ended in an argument, and if you happened to swear at them, whoa. They would fire off a letter complaining to our Commissioner, or, depending on the motorist's level of anger, to the Governor, thus beginning an investigative process down the chain of command. In the end, the offending officer would write a letter answering the complaint to explain his actions. Punishment, if warranted, was swift and stern. It was a lose-lose situation.

It took only two letters and a couple of disciplinary sessions for me to realize what a complete jerk I had been. Replaying the incidents, I was appalled to imagine anyone treating a member of my family in the same manner. I was ashamed of myself, but a quick study. There were no more letters of complaint and I learned to set a pleasant tone with every motorist, or suspect, or person that I interviewed. When I encountered belligerence, arguments, or outwardly coarse people, I simply became more pleasant. The nicer I was, the angrier they became. No letter of complaint, and a win-win for me.

On another note, there were a few officers who could never get over "it," meaning their huge egos. They developed reputations that followed them wherever they worked, and many were out of favor with their fellow troopers. After retirement, many of these same officers had difficulty finding their own, civilian, identity beyond their badge and gun.

It had been a fairly quiet Thursday morning when I got a radio transmission ordering me to the home of a Mrs. Fish on Blandford Stage Road in Russell. A distant family member was concerned when they couldn't get hold of her. Knowing the home's location, and glad to abandon my traffic post, I headed right out. After getting lost on my first day on the job going from Northampton to Westfield, I made it a point to know every road and cow trail in the area. I even carried a map in my duffle bag— only, of course, for if I *really* needed it!

The single-family ranch was near the road with no other homes nearby; nothing across the street, and the next closest was three quarters of a mile away. From the road, the Fish residence appeared locked up tight with a single car parked in the driveway. It was early July and hot. We'd been in a heat wave for the past week, but no windows were open and there were no air conditioning units in any windows. It definitely looked as if no one was home.

I informed the barracks of my arrival and parked behind the tan Buick in the driveway. I walked up to the car and looked inside, then walked around the house, checking the doors and windows. Everything was secure and locked, so I made a second trip around, this time looking inside. The window shades were halfway down but the lace curtains allowed me to see clearly into each room. Everything was orderly. Peering through the back-door windows, I saw the empty kitchen sink and a spotless kitchen table.

After circling the home, I went back out front to check the car. I wanted to find the registration, or run a listing, to find out who it belonged to. It was unlocked, and the bench seat was slid forward as far as it would go, so I had to slide it back before I could fit in. Sitting behind the steering wheel I leaned over, opened the glove box, and pulled the registration from its clear plastic folder, which showed the car registered to Mrs. Fish. Where was Mrs. Fish? I wondered.

It was then that I noticed a single key in the ignition turned to the on position. The AC control dials below the radio were also in the on positions, but the dashboard instrument cluster lights were off. I turned the ignition to start the car, but nothing happened. The battery was dead.

Returning to the cruiser, I got on the radio and reported what I had found. I felt I needed to get into the house, but there was no way of doing so without a key, unless I broke something. The desk officer made a call back to Mrs. Fish's relative telling her of the situation. The woman was in another state, and since she knew of no one else with a key, she gave us permission to go through the back door.

It was easy to break the small windowpane closest to the latch and handle of the door. Reaching inside, I unlocked the door and went into the kitchen, the air was stale, stagnant, and very stuffy. In my opinion, lacking any expertise whatsoever, the place had been closed for some time. I studied the kitchen and slowly went into the living room. It was the same there, but I thought I heard something in the bedroom behind me. Maybe I was just jittery, but over the years and despite numerous explorations, searches, and inspections of vacant buildings or homes, not knowing what one might find was always "spooky," to say the least.

A month before, Trooper Pat O'Neill and I were in Huntington searching for a guy who had stabbed another player during a card game. We were told that he ran into an abandoned apartment building at the end of the street. O'Neill took the second floor, and I took the first. The fact that it was nighttime, and the building had no power, made things a little iffy. We had been trained to search buildings for armed suspects. So I knew what to do—I hoped. Holding a flashlight in my left hand and a handgun in the other, I started off room to room. God, it was dark—the house being at the end of the street, it received no outside light whatsoever. I only had a couple of rooms left to go and couldn't wait to finish. Entering the final bedroom, I was sweeping my light along the far wall when I sensed something on my left. I moved the light and pointed my firearm toward a German shepherd as it bounded off a bed and landed at my feet with a whine. I don't know why I didn't scream; I don't think I had the ability. There were only a few times in my career when I was as suddenly frightened or startled. One of them involved a bear, but that's another story. Thankfully, I didn't shoot the poor dog. He was really a nice shepherd, friendly, and I guess lonely, because he followed me outside, never leaving my side. We found the guy with the knife a week later.

For sure, the spookiness I felt going through Mrs. Fish's home was residual from that Huntington search for the angry poker player, but that didn't let me off the hook. I still needed to check the bedroom. Empty, good!

The house was small, so it didn't take long to check each room and end up back in the kitchen. Next, I went down the short kitchen hallway leading to the garage, but entering the hall I noticed a sickly, sweet odor that I hadn't noticed before. I opened the door from the kitchen to the garage and was engulfed, overwhelmed, and choked by the most awful smell of my life (worse than the skunk). My eyes watered, but not so much that I couldn't see Mrs. Fish lying on the garage floor. Her body was swollen and her face, hands, and arms, were a purplish black color. She was all dressed up with her pocketbook by her side.

It wasn't too difficult to put all the pieces together. A week earlier, Mrs. Fish was going to the grocery store. She locked up her house, then backed out of the garage into the driveway, and put the AC on to cool the car before her trip to the grocer. Returning to the house through the garage, she closed the automatic door and died on her way back inside. The car ran until it was out of gas and the battery died. The only unknown was why she closed the garage door when she went back into the house, but there are many logical and illogical reasons she may have done so.

We were able to contact Mrs. Fish's primary care doctor, who told us that she suffered from a serious heart condition. Given the undisturbed condition of the home and the absence of any indication of foul play, everyone involved, including the district attorney, was satisfied with the finding, which meant there was no crime scene and we could go about removing Mrs. Fish.

Cramer's Funeral Home arrived and backed their vehicle up to the garage door. It had been kept closed to keep curious eyes out, and it was interesting to note how many people were out for an afternoon walk on a humid eighty-five-degree day.

Once the garage door lifted the putrid smell went everywhere. The humid air was heavy and there was no breeze. I noticed the walkers had picked up their pace.

"Boy, that's a ripe one," said the "Funeral Man" as he strolled up to the body. I swear the smell didn't faze him. Bending over, he spread a body bag beside Mrs. Fish.

"Would you give me a hand here, Trooper?" he asked.

I hesitated, not wanting to get any closer, but gave in and moved beside him. I gagged on vomit just waiting to spill out of my throat.

"Okay, a quick move here. I'll take the heavy end. Grab her ankles, and, on three, we lift her into the bag." It sounded simple enough. So, on three we both lifted.

Mrs. Fish was wearing a dress and nylons that ended just above her knees. When we lifted, the rotted, wet, putrid, flesh, slop that was once her thighs, unsupported by nylons, went all over the floor. I had held my breath for the lift and was able to swing her into the bag, but instantly turned and ran to the door gasping for fresh air. The Funeral Man didn't miss a beat, produced a plastic spray bottle, and began spraying its contents onto the body. It was a powerful peppermint smell that instantly killed the stink.

"Where has that been?" I asked. "What the hell?"

Funeral Man smiled at me and said nothing.

It was another hour and a half before I finished at the Fish residence. I had found a neighbor willing to board up the broken pane on the rear door, leaving me confident the house was secure until the family could fix it properly. My job was done.

On the ride to the station I thought about Mrs. Fish, her condition, the smell, and the overall experience of my first dead body. I was sorry for the lady even though I didn't know her. I almost got sick at the sights and smell, but I didn't. I did some soul-searching, wondering if I should have had more compassion. Was I an unfeeling person unaffected by the death and unfortunate circumstances of others? I didn't know the answers then, but after years of seeing too many bodies and horrid criminal acts, I found what bothered me the most was anything involving children. I took the children home with me. The rest, I was able to leave at work.

The dinner meal had already begun by the time I got back to the barracks. Despite the day's events, to my surprise, I was starved. I had washed my hands downstairs then walked up to the dining room and pulled up a chair.

Almost in unison, the dinner crowd pointed at the door and howled, "GET OUT!"

I must have smelled like fish, or something.

Sunday Morning

I had waited anxiously for the class of new troopers to graduate from the Academy and fill our ranks. My classmate, Bill Wallace, and I had had our fill holding the title of "Boot Troopers." Sergeant Summer had begun to like me. I'm certain it was due to my "expert" handling of his daughter's class visit, or maybe because he didn't want me spreading the story around. In either case, it didn't stop the feelings of lowliness and subservience from being at the bottom of the roster. Twice in the last three trips, I'd been hauled from bed to go out on the road. Once was for a bad accident in Worthington and another to search for a lost hunter, which also makes this a good time to restate just how much I despised our reefer coat and winter uniform.

The area was hit with an early December snowstorm in the middle of deer hunting season. The call for which I'd been unceremoniously rolled out of bed was in the Town of Blandford, which is located at the eastern edge of the Berkshires and straddles the Massachusetts Turnpike. Blandford was the Turnpike's highest elevation at 1,451 feet above sea level, so needless to say, Blandford was getting whacked with over a foot of snow and gale winds. The twenty-year-old hunter had been missing for several hours and searchers hadn't been able to find him.

I drove to the rescue, where twenty volunteers were wandering around the hills, God knows where, with no search pattern or grid, and nobody in charge. It was near one o'clock in the morning and freezing cold. I was just one more body, and there was little I could do to organize the ongoing chaos. Actually, I was as concerned for the people wandering through the woods helter-skelter as I was for the missing hunter. Would more get lost?

I would like to claim that I had an idea of what to do next, but I didn't, and I was feeling about as lost as our hunter when a guy drove up on his snowmobile. The fortuitous arrival gave me hope that I could, at least, *appear* to be doing something. I explained to the gentleman that I needed his help looking for the hunter, but first needed to locate the searchers, and have them return to the staging area so that a proper search could be organized. That was the plan and he agreed, so I took off on the back of his snow machine holding on for dear life. It was my first ride ever on a snowmobile.

I couldn't get over how fast that thing went. Of course, my driver, or pilot—I wasn't sure what to call him—wore an insulated helmet, goggles, thick gloves, insulated boots, and a one-piece, thickly lined—you guessed it—snowmobile suit. I, on the other hand, wore a brimmed police cap, thin earmuffs, no goggles, the aforementioned unlined reefer coat, our traditional riding breeches, and our riding boots, unlined with smooth, thin leather soles, guaranteed to turn one's toes black with frostbite in an hour.

I will end this interlude by reporting that we located the searchers and got them back safely. The hunter walked out onto Route 23, all by himself, two and a half miles from the staging area, without a deer. I, on the other hand, was a block of ice, promising myself that I would never, ever, be that cold again. From that day forward, I was never without non-issue ski gloves, a non-issue stocking hat, non-issue lined winter boots, and I always made sure they were big enough to fit over my riding boots. I had sweaters for under the reefer, wore long underwear, and if it got too warm in the cruiser, I'd roll the window down. So it was for instances such as the search, and many others untold, that I couldn't wait to have troopers beneath me on the roster, so I could sleep through the nights, warm, cozy, and undisturbed.

Daniel Brandon was from the Worcester area. He was six feet three inches tall and weighed a good 220 pounds. He had a square-shaped face, with large blue eyes and brown hair. The pre-graduation haircut had left nothing but a short stubble, which Dan rubbed incessantly. It was a nervous habit picked up by many boots after graduation. I remember doing the same until my hair grew back. I liked Dan a lot. He was friendly and outgoing, which made it hard for me to treat him with the coldness normally afforded a new officer. For a while I tried to act like one of the drill instructors he had recently left behind, but I couldn't do it. I didn't look like one, and I knew that I wasn't scary looking to anybody. In terms of career and seniority, I was closer to Dan than to most of the other men in the barracks, so it was easier to be a friend.

I didn't have enough time on the job, and for sure not enough experience, to be his trooper coach. I wasn't disappointed, because I had enough trouble looking after myself, never mind someone else. Most of the top troopers liked the assignment. They took it seriously, teaching boots the ropes and giving them the benefit of their experience. Lifelong relationships were often developed between coaches and boots, and they took pride in a boot who was deemed outstanding, or "a good cop." Coaches would often brag about the best young officers, taking credit for breaking them in, but they were also quick to give credit to other coaches who turned out the good ones. Like in everything, there were always one or two coaches who spoiled the bunch. He was usually a salty know-it-all, with little time on the job, who took pleasure in having a boot in servitude for three months. Those relationships seldom turned out well.

The duty of forming Dan's career was given to Trooper Roger Korkowski. Korz was a character, a nut, funny, smart, and personable. He was the heart of the barracks and loved by all. There wasn't anything he couldn't or wouldn't do, especially for a laugh. I had no business judging who should or shouldn't break in Dan, because I hadn't been around long enough to know what skills one needed for the job. I had, however, been around long enough to know that Korz would have been my last choice. It had nothing to do with his abilities as a police officer, for he was highly qualified—it's just that you never knew what he'd get into, and I feared that Dan was in for an education. No matter what I thought, it was Dan and Korz together, for better or worse.

I had just finished a busy patrol in the rain. I'd covered two accidents and a burglary that had kept me up past two o'clock in the morning sending activity messages into headquarters. I was spent. All I wanted was something to eat and my bunk. Our cook, Mary, had always kept the refrigerator full. She purposely cooked extra-large meals so there would be plenty of leftovers for her boys after the late shifts. I was hoping to find some pot roast and potatoes to munch on. (Even to this day, I often think of Trooper Hunt whenever I put a potato on my plate. It's remarkable how a seemingly insignificant event, involving potatoes, can remain imprinted on one's mind for a lifetime.)

The hallway connecting all our rooms was dark except for the glow of light coming from the lavatory. After deciding to change before going to the kitchen, I crept silently down the hall toward my room. The troops slept at all different hours of the day or night, and waking someone could be hazardous.

Halfway along, I passed Dan's room when a large hand reached out, grabbed my arm, and yanked me inside.

"Whaaat," I sputtered.

"Shhhh, quiet," Dan pleaded, letting go of me.

"What's with you?" I asked, voicing displeasure. "I'm not in the mood, Dan. I'm tired and I gotta get up at seven."

"Oh God, Randy, you're not gonna believe this. I don't believe this. I'm gonna get fired for sure. I know it, and I'm still on probation." He hadn't heard a word I'd said. The poor kid appeared to be coming apart; sick-looking was a better description.

"Hey, it can't be that bad," I offered, trying to calm him down.

Dan sat motionless on the end of his bunk, staring at the floor. His shoulders were slumped, and his head hung so low it nearly rested on his chest. I couldn't recall seeing anyone so despondent. And, he looked scared.

"All right, all right, calm down and tell me what happened." I tried to lighten the mood by telling him I'd leave if he said that he and Korz had hidden a body somewhere.

He didn't see the humor.

"No, no, it's nothin' like that, but it might as well be. I'm gonna get fired just the same once the sarge finds out. I shoulda known something was up this morning when Korz asked Walter to switch cruisers and let us take the station wagon. Korz hates the station wagon, the last time the sarge gave Korz the wagon he made me drive it the whole patrol."

Dan kept right on talking, as much to himself as to me, and as if I'd been with them, but, obviously, I hadn't.

"So, we get out on the road and I ask him, where are we going? And he just sits behind the wheel smiling. I was gettin' real nervous so I asked him again. C'mon, Korz, where are we goin'? 'It's a surprise,' he tells me."

I was trying to be a patient listener, but I was so hungry and tired, it was hard to hide my irritation. I just wanted a pot roast sandwich. "Okay Dan. Tell me the surprise, please, just get to where you're going."

"A pig."

"A pig?" I asked with my eyes widening.

"Yeah well, actually, a piglet. We went to see that pig farmer in Southwick. You must know, it's the man Korz knows who owns the big pig farm."

"Ah, no, Dan, I don't know about Korz or his pig farmer."

"We went to the farm and Korz got a pig. He said it was for his kids. That's why he wanted the station wagon, to haul the pig around."

"Listen, you're not gonna get fired because Korz put a pig in the cruiser. If that's the worst thing you ever d—"

"No, Rand," Dan interrupted. "I didn't care about the pig in the cruiser, and I wasn't worried when he told me he was gonna have to smuggle it into his room and hide it until he went home. I figured once it was out of the car and in his bed, or wherever he was gonna put it, it was his problem, but I am gonna get fired for what happened at his sister's house."

Dan lapsed into silence, and my thoughts were trying to figure where Korz was gonna stash a piglet once he got it into his room. Don't they squeal? Don't they poop? Does it smell bad? I thought so. I envisioned the sergeant finishing a shower before bed and getting hit with the smell of pig poop. I could imagine him sniffing and checking every room. Korz would have more than a little pig poop to worry about if Sergeant Summer discovered a pig spending the night.

Korz remembered it was Sunday and his sister was sure to be home, continued Dan. He thought it would be better to leave the pig with his sister rather than risk hiding it in the barracks. The only problem was convincing his sister that she'd be happy to pig sit.

Dan said that he was baffled, that the whole thing was like a game to Korz. A form of play, actually, like how does he get this pig home from work without getting caught; his plan changed every minute. Korz was playing fast and loose and loving the challenge.

Dan sat up straight, and for the first time since he began telling his tale looked me in the eye, like, Okay, I guess I have to tell the rest.

They pulled into his sister's driveway, just as the ten o'clock Mass at Saint Mary's Catholic Church was ending with a hundred or so parishioners climbing down the front steps. A few churchgoers who had slipped out early stood near the end of the driveway waving and smiling at the cruiser crossing the sidewalk in front of them.

Dan paused once again and gazed at the floor, shaking his head from side to side. I got the impression he was trying to convince himself that if he didn't tell me the story, it didn't really happen. With a long sigh, he looked to me again and continued.

Korz had turned the ignition off and opened the door to get out, just as the piglet decided it was his time to escape. The animal leaped over the front seat, landing on Dan's clipboard, then smashed into the radio mount below the dashboard. Instinctively, Dan grabbed for the beast and got hold of its rear leg. The startled pig screamed and twisted, scaring Dan and pulling free.

Oblivious, Korz had already stepped from the cruiser, smiling politely at the growing crowd. The piglet's scream snapped his attention to the commotion inside the cruiser. With blinding speed, he blocked the animal's escape with his arms and legs while cursing Dan for letting go.

"FOR GOD'S SAKE, SIT ON HIM," hollered Korz, trying to grab the lightning-fast pig.

"DON'T YELL AT ME! IT'S YOUR GODDAMNED PIG, YOU SIT ON HIM. Look out, Korz, he's on the floor."

Korz knelt on the front half of the rocker panel trying to shove the snorting pig back inside and away from the door. "Grab him, grab him, I can't reach, he's gonna get loose, Dan, get him. Oh, God, don't let him get out," begged Korz.

Korz stood to shut the door as the pig spun on Dan squealing in terror and snapping at his fingers. Dan was quicker and let go ahead of the animal's teeth. Korz took the door in both hands, slamming it against the pig's rush, but he wasn't fast enough, and only succeeded in pinching the frightened pig against the doorjamb.

The murmured greetings and friendly conversations throughout the churchyard ceased as the pig's cries filled the air. The disturbance had everyone's attention. Smiling meekly at the crowd, Korz held the door firmly against the animal, hoping it would squeeze back inside. The piglet, on the other hand, had had enough of the two officers and their station wagon. It wiggled and squirmed savagely, dropped to the ground, then bolted into the crowd with two uniformed troopers in hot pursuit.

A young mother screamed and lifted her daughter safely into her arms as the pig dashed between them. Caution to the wind, the troopers chased full speed after the piglet. Left, right, in and out, raced the little porker through a forest of legs.

"Well, I never," came from one indignant lady as Dan bumped her into her startled husband.

"It's over there, Korz," pointed Dan, fighting his way through the host, all in their Sunday best.

"Near the steps, oh, 'scuse me, sir. No, no, near the guy in the striped suit."

A five-year-old boy watched in horror, his wide eyes switching between his mother and the chase. "Are they going to shoot it, Mommy?"

Korz headed toward the guy in the striped suit. The poor man had just come out of church, unaware of what was going on, to discover two very large state troopers charging him. Bug-eyed, he took two steps backward as the pig burst through the crowd and crashed into his shin bone. The gentleman clutched his shin in pain, almost falling over. The woman next to him screeched while an elderly gent with wavy, grey hair mumbled something about wasting his tax dollars.

"Where'd he go?" Korz asked. "Come on, come on, where did he go?" Unwilling to take his hands from the damaged shin, the man gestured with his head in the direction the pig had fled.

"Over here, Korz, he's in the bushes."

Korz joined Dan in front of the bushes on the far side of the church steps.

"Can you see him?" he asked.

"I don't know for sure. I think it's in the corner against the building."

"Okay, you slide around the back side and try and force him out. If you spot him, yell."

Dan slipped slowly to the back of the bushes. Both officers were acutely aware of the surrounding parishioners. Some were amused and giggling, but others, not so much.

"Imagine—on a Sunday morning. Do something, John, this is outrageous. They should be reported."

Dan was red-faced, sliding behind the nearest bush. The pig spotted him and crawled under a center bush. Korz had watched him go and inched toward the new hiding place. It had trapped itself with only one direction to run. The crowd was still. The troopers closed in.

The little piglet stood tense and alert. Its head straight and close to the ground, its ears unmoving, yet aware of every sound. Dan's next step was close enough and the pig ran from cover toward Korz, but seeing him once again, dodged his grab and squeezed between a bush and onto the steps. The little ham was running hard but slipping on the stone steps. With what he knew was his last chance, Korz made a dive at the piglet and grasped an outstretched rear leg.

Korz had once again become aware of the crowd. Dan was still, scarlet, and totally embarrassed. He stood frozen in his tracks unsure of what, if anything, to do or say. But not Korz. He was undaunted. Rising slowly to his fullest height, lightly brushing at his uniform, Korz swelled with dignity as he hiked up the piglet, then turned and made his pronouncement.

"The animal is diseased. We'll take care of it," then sauntered away, like he had planned it all.

I consoled Dan as best I could. I didn't admit that I was a little more worried than I let on, but I did tell him that if there was a complaint, or complaints about what happened, it would most likely be on Korz. At that point I told him not to worry, wished him good night, skipped the sandwich, and went to bed.

Dan spent many uneasy days waiting for the ax to fall. Every time the phone rang, he cringed. He even lost a few pounds. To this day I find it hard to believe that the sarge never found out. He knew too many people in Westfield. I truly believe that the tale of the troopers and the pig had eventually reached his ears. If I'm right, he never let on.

No Answer

I had always thought that most young people seeking a career in law enforcement do so with a genuine desire to serve. Additionally, being public-spirited, selfless, altruistic, or having any number of other higher traits makes for an ideal candidate. Having said that, and evaluating my own motives in retrospect at a more mature time in life, it would be dishonest to claim that I had all the perfect qualities. Oh, I had some beneath the surface, for sure, but was I actually aware of them? Did I assess them thinking that I would be a great applicant for the state police? I think not. So, as that twenty-one-year-old, I will declare that a position of authority and the notion of doing good were factors, but they were far overshadowed by the lure of excitement and action.

The police work at Russell provided a wide assortment of crime as well as routine calls that were often colorful, strange, different, and even bizarre, providing a full curriculum for our school of law enforcement. Nonetheless, the station was slow-paced except for our patrol of the southernmost section of Route 91. Each trooper was sent to patrol Route 91 south every third trip for all three shifts, 4:00 p.m. to midnight, 8:00 a.m. to 4:00 p.m., then finishing with a midnight to 8:00 a.m. stint. The 91 south patrol was where the action was, fast and furious.

In 1969, Route 91 through Springfield, Massachusetts was still under construction, with the northern two-thirds patrolled by men from other barracks. Russell's designated interstate patrol was approximately five miles, but in two segments because of the incomplete build. Traveling south, after covering the northern sector, one exited Route 91 onto Route 5 through busy West Springfield, and then across the Connecticut River's south end bridge into Longmeadow for the last three miles.

For the sake of perspective, Springfield is the state's third-largest city, and West Springfield is sizable as well. When you include the many suburban areas surrounding Springfield and the major north/south and east/west interstate roadways of 91 and 90, there was never a shortage of police work.

All the departments we worked with down south were fantastic, but I had always felt a special relationship with Springfield. We looked after each other. The policy for officers in the local police department cruisers was to ride double because it was dangerous to be alone. Troopers rode alone because it was our department policy. The local officers knew that, and quite often went out of their way to check that we were safe at whatever we got involved in. They also monitored scanners for any radio transmissions from troopers looking for help, which gave us added peace of mind.

I made career-long friendships with officers from many of the Springfield area towns. One of my favorites was a Springfield PD motorcycle cop named Frankie Santello. I was always running into Frankie on patrol. We'd meet at a local restaurant, diner, or coffee shop to catch up—and eat donuts. Frankie wouldn't touch anything fewer than 400 calories. I liked the honey-dipped.

I was never happier to see Frankie than I was late one night on a south patrol. I'd been sitting high on the south end bridge ramp watching cars pass below me headed into Connecticut, when one caught my eye. The tall roadway pole lights had given me a partial glimpse into a car which appeared to be full of passengers. Slipping off the ramp I opted to follow for a bit, staying about ten car lengths behind, so as not to be obvious.

It was a 1966 Chevy Nova. The headlights of my cruiser didn't quite reach to the car's back window, but I could see what looked like three large males in the back. I wasn't sure but there appeared to be three in the front as well. Six large men stuffed into a mid-size Chevy Nova seemed out of the norm. Certainly not unheard of, but . . . ? The car was doing the sixty-five miles per hour speed limit, not one mile faster, not one mile slower.

Closing by another car length I could see, hurried, herky-jerky movements by the passengers, which only added to the suspicion. I got on the radio, gave my location as southbound on 91, then ran a listing, and stolen check on the plate. It wasn't showing as stolen, and came back listed to a resident from Holyoke, Massachusetts. But something just didn't seem right! This was going to be a good check.

I pulled within three lengths of the Nova, hit my high beams, blue light, and aimed the remote spotlight into the rear window. No siren was necessary—they were well aware that I was behind them. The inside movement became more frantic as an arm reached over to the front seat, and the upper torso of the male in the right rear ducked toward the floor. Slowly, the driver pulled into the breakdown lane and stopped, leaving about three feet between the car and the guardrail.

Most often when officers pull a vehicle over, they will exit the cruiser and walk up to the driver's door to engage the operator. My Trooper coach, Dave, had taught me there were sometimes exceptions for how best to approach a stop. This was one of those times.

Once we were stopped, I could see that the occupants were black. Not that it mattered, for that wasn't why I'd followed them or stopped them. My gut screamed that they seemed all too suspicious. I had purposely parked the cruiser far enough back that the high beams shined full, along with the spotlight, into the car's rear window. I opened my door, slowly stepped out and closed the door short of the latch so it would not make a sound. Then I unholstered my handgun and held it at my side. I never took my eyes from the occupants of the Nova, who were glaring over their left shoulders to watch my advance. I walked around the back of my cruiser so as not to break the beam of my headlights, and walked up to the car on the passenger side along the guardrail. They had no idea where I was until I shined my flashlight into the car, tapped the window, and yanked the passenger door open in one motion. Then I squatted and leaned against the open door. Six sets of wide-open eyes stared at the barrel of my gun. "Don't even think about moving," said I.

Now, when I look back on what had taken place up to that moment, I can say that I had done pretty well. Yet, being naïvely careless, I hadn't thought beyond that point. Like, what are you gonna do now, Sherlock?

To digress: I wonder where all the "crucial" advice from that persistently stupid, subconscious voice living inside my head, which bombards me with chatter, was at that moment? Years later, I can see that it simply wasn't there. I believe that a being's spirit is actual self-awareness and is found deep within one's self. It takes practice to silence one's chatterbox nonsense, and experience real informational awareness and calm thinking.

There were many answers to the question, "What now, Sherlock?" But fundamentally, and most essential, I should have called for backup before ever getting out of my cruiser.

My mind churned. I had the drop on them, but it was going to be impossible to control this situation, and then I heard the Springfield PD Harley motorcycle pull in front of the Nova with lights flashing. Frankie jumped off his bike with a .357 Magnum pointed at the driver. He'd been listening to his scanner, knew where I was, and thought I might like some company. Thank you, Frank!

We took down two ounces of heroin, some coke, a half-pound of pot, and three handguns. The driver and two of the guys in the back had the guns. No doubt, had I walked up to the driver's side of the car, there was a very good chance that I wouldn't be around now to tell these stories. Dave hadn't been my coach for some time now, but I'm pretty sure it was the second time he saved my life.

There were many heart-pounding adventures to be had on the southern patrol, but in reality they were no more dangerous or heroic than the work of police anywhere.

Not all the action that we ran into down south was life-threatening. There was an incident one evening that was quite exciting and had a lasting effect.

I was on an evening patrol driving along Route 5 making my way from the north to the Longmeadow section of 91. Route 5 through West Springfield is also called Riverdale Road and is cluttered with restaurants, malls, motels, movie theaters, and whatever else one might imagine. The Friday night traffic was awful, and I was moving slowly in the travel lane when a guy driving a Camaro came from a side street spinning his tires and fishtailing into the passing lane. It wasn't really a terrible thing, for he immediately slowed after showing off in his hot car, but his little stunt, for all to witness, happening right in front of me, left no option. Pulling from my lane in behind the Camaro, I caught him looking at me through his rearview mirror and pointed to the side of the road. I put the cruiser's overhead light on, got out and walked up to the driver's window. We were in front of a multiplex cinema with seven movies showing, and Riverdale Road was lit up like a carnival midway. I didn't even need a flashlight.

Michael Smith was twenty-four years old, clean cut, with red hair, and dressed to party that Friday evening. He gave me his license and registration, said that he was really sorry, and I could see that he was scared. Motorists on Riverdale Road, and from urban areas in general, didn't often encounter the state police because those jurisdictions were the purview of the local police departments. Right or wrong, fifty-odd years ago we struck fear into the public, for we were rarely seen, and an unknown factor. People usually fear what they don't know.

The entire scene was noisy, and it was nearly impossible to carry on a conversation. Michael was only a year older than I was but responded to me as someone whose authority he wasn't going to mess with. Sensing that he was no threat, I had him return to the cruiser, where I learned that he was a construction worker and had recently bought the car. As we continued talking, the traffic congestion had gotten worse, with cars in both lanes nearly at a standstill. I liked the kid and had decided to give him a written warning so we could both get out of there.

I had just opened my ticket book when I heard a small thump. Traffic in the near lane beside Michael and me had stopped, and a silver 1968 Dodge Charger with a black vinyl roof bumped into the car in front of it. Looking from where I was seated, there was no damage to either car. It was an accident to be ignored, in no need of an investigation, and that was my intention until the young lady driving the Charger got out of her car to check the damage. She stood there motionless, a hand to her mouth, with an "oh my" expression, staring at the bumpers. I was thinking, "Oh my," as well, but I wasn't looking at car bumpers. There, just a couple of feet from my window, was a stunning tanned brunette. She had brown, pixie-styled short hair, a short-sleeve, three-button, lightweight, knit yellow top that fit perfectly. Very short white shorts, long deeply tanned legs, with low-heeled sandals completed the picture. I immediately decided that the accident did, in fact, need a thorough investigation. Saying goodbye to Michael, I sent him on his way without a ticket.

The operator of the car that was bumped by the young lady stood beside her conducting his own inspection of the "damage." The guy was about thirty-five years old, five feet eight inches tall, forty pounds overweight, with a round pocked face that needed shaving, and greasy black hair that needed a barber. One got the sense he could do with a shower as well. Stepping from the cruiser, I joined the two, telling them to move their cars into the breakdown lane, where Michael had been parked, and had them sit in the back seat of my cruiser. In those days, our cruisers were not equipped with cages protecting us from backseat passengers. Cages came several years later.

The object of my interest sat right behind me, and "Mr. Cleancut" sat next to her. I adjusted my rearview mirror, keeping a close watch on the girl. I talked to the guy, politely, but out of the side of my mouth, no need to keep an eye on him.

Neither car had any damage, so there was technically no accident report required. The guy started to annoy me when he engaged the girl in accusatory dialogue. It was her fault, yes, there was a scratch. Why hadn't she paid attention, etc., etc.

The brown-haired beauty answered courteously. She'd been distracted by the flashing lights of the cruiser and was sorry for hitting his car, but couldn't see a scratch anywhere. He started in again, until I shut him up. I think he imagined that I would take his side. Boy, was he wrong. "Look," I said to him. "I checked the bumpers of both cars and I don't see any damage to either one. This isn't worthy of an accident report. I think it would be best if you exchange information and submit it to your insurance companies. Let them figure it out if you feel that strongly."

I gave each of them, in turn, my clipboard with a lined sheet of paper to write down their information. When they had finished, I took their papers to review, and wrote the young lady's name and phone number on *my* pad. Her first name was Marion. I liked it. Handing back the paperwork, I noticed she wasn't wearing a wedding or engagement ring. She took and read the information from "Mr. Friendly" and then, in what must have been an afterthought, she asked him to look and see if she had included her phone number. He snottily replied yes.

After his snide response, I caught "Miss Dodge Charger" looking at me in the mirror, so I held up my pad so she could see where I had written her phone number. Smiling back in the mirror I said, "I've got it too."

I worked the midnight-to-8 a.m. shift to finish my tour of 91 south patrols, then headed back to the barracks to report in. Before starting my day off, I grabbed all my civilian clothes that needed my mother's washing machine. I'd come to like staying at the barracks on days off, and made the trip home every three weeks or so. My mother was glad to see me, and although I was capable of doing laundry myself, she always insisted on doing it. Barracks life was certainly different, and for me it was uniquely fun. Troopers tended to socialize together because our constantly changing days off made it difficult to hook up with old friends who worked Monday through Friday schedules.

On this trip home I did manage to go out with my hometown buddies, but all I could think about was the girl at the end of the phone number that I carried in my pocket. I had called her number early in the evening, but there was no answer. Trying once again before I left home to go back to work on Monday afternoon produced the same result. Guessing that she was probably at work, I decided to call in the evening when she got home. Nobody picked up.

It's amazing how different our world of communication is today as opposed to then. Answering machines first began selling in the United States around 1960 but didn't become widely used until 1984 when AT&T was restructured and made them more affordable. In the meantime, my imagination ran wild with thoughts of why she wasn't answering. Over the next week, I tried calling in the morning. I tried calling in the evening. The more I called the more disheartened I got. Looking as good as she did, I thought she had to be on a date. Possibly away on a trip? I was betting she had a boyfriend. Could she have two boyfriends? Is her phone broken? Maybe, I thought, she just doesn't want to talk to you, so I decided to call it quits with "Miss No Answer" on the eighth day.

Taste of Northampton

Our station had been unusually quiet and uneventful, and although there had been several bad accidents, none was on my shifts. Other troopers had been rolled from their bunks in the wee hours for various emergencies, but I'd been spared the calls and able to get some much-needed sleep. Busy work, nasty things, and the unusual frantic calls always came together, in cycles. If you doubt it, ask any cop, ER physician, nurse, firefighter, or EMT about the surreal, strange, and unexpected needs for emergency services, and you'll get the same response. "Oh yeah! Especially, if there's a full moon." Now, there was no full moon, and I wasn't in a crazy work cycle, but I'd been consumed by my own cycle of disappointment after being unable to reach the Riverdale Road beauty.

I had a good day off at home with my mom and dad, but on the ride back to work, anticipating a return to Route 91 south, I *could not* get that young lady out of my mind. It's a wonder I didn't crash into something or someone, for my head was not behind the wheel. Unable to throw her number away, I hoped the patrol would keep me busy enough to forget about her. I guess that by holding on, I was just being ever hopeful.

As was my habit, I arrived at work early and chose and washed one of the better cruisers for myself. But that didn't necessarily mean that the car I washed would be mine for patrol. More often than not, a senior trooper would pick the cruiser key right from your gun belt, saying, "Check the roster, kid." Junior men got the leftovers.

Sergeant Summer called me into his office just before I began my patrol, in an older unwashed cruiser, telling me that I would only have to do the evening and day patrol down south. Northampton was short a man and needed someone for the midnight-to-8 a.m. patrol on my last day. It was just what I needed, two shifts on 91, to forget Miss Dodge Charger, and my first taste of Northampton's station area.

The evening shift was busy. There was a personal injury accident, sending two off to the ER, another fender bender, one disabled vehicle, and a half dozen quality moving violations. The shift passed quickly, and I was back at the station before I knew it.

I got up early the next morning to shower, have breakfast, and drive the twenty-five miles through Westfield, Southwick, and Agawam to be on duty at 8 a.m. It was a beautiful day. The traffic was light and warm for early morning, so with my window down I inhaled the fresh air and took in the scenery.

Cruisers didn't have power windows or AC or AM-FM radios. They were bare boned except for the police package engine and heavy-duty suspensions. The Ford cruisers didn't lack power or handling, they were stiff and fast! Now, if my cruiser had been equipped with power windows, I'd have put the driver's window up and lowered the passenger's side, because the flapping and fluttering of my campaign hat was driving me nuts. Another thing that infuriated me was the Department's uniform code. Patrol supervisors held the rank of sergeant or staff sergeant, and one of their jobs was to ensure that a trooper didn't take a portable radio on patrol, or smoke in the cruiser, or God forbid, sit or drive without his hat on—military decorum at its best. Cruisers did have seat belts, but before the laws mandating their use we didn't often wear them, nor did the department require it. One last thing that especially twisted my ear was that when the Department of Public Safety went all-in creating K9 units, they purchased air-conditioned cruisers for the dogs, while droplets of sweat seeped under our hat bands to dangle from the tip of one's nose.

I got to the beginning of the six-lane divided highway section of Route 57 right on time. I took it up to the speed limit as a transmission came in ordering me to check a disabled car at the Massachusetts/Connecticut line. I acknowledged and headed off. About a mile and a half from my exit, onto and over the south end bridge, I came up behind a silver Dodge Charger in the middle lane. Slowing, I began to creep closer. It had a black vinyl roof and was a 1968. Could it be, I wondered?

Sure enough, it was the mysterious beauty of Riverdale Road who never answered her phone. She hadn't noticed the cruiser behind her, and only saw me when I pulled alongside. She was startled for an instant, then I saw recognition, a wave, and a big smile. She caught me completely off guard, for I half-expected a cold stare. My mind had worried that she'd been upset because I took her phone number, or that I'd stuffed her in the backseat with the unpleasant greaseball, or because I was gawking at her, which I was.

All in all, running into her again had me discombobulated because it was entirely unexpected. Dumbstruck is a better word, because I had frozen wearing what I felt must have been a stupefied expression. I gave her the biggest smile and wave I had, pulled in front of her and drove onto my exit to the bridge. In the rearview mirror I watched her take the rotary under the bridge. It was when I watched her disappear from sight that I woke up, and my only thought was *dumb, dumb, dumb, and dumb*, adding *half-wit* and *idiot* for good measure.

I called her three times that evening, and still there was no answer. I just didn't get it. She preoccupied nearly every waking thought and I didn't know what to do. I struggled to find sleep, feeling only anger and frustration at my utter stupidity. It was sadness that finally brought sleep.

I left Russell for the guest patrol in Northampton about 11 p.m. and arrived just before midnight. Sergeant Cally was the midnight desk officer. He took me around and introduced me to the troopers working that night, as well as the dispatcher, Ray Shea. I'd never met him but recognized his voice as one of the five dispatchers I'd become accustomed to hearing over Northampton's radio.

I was given a map of sectors 1, 3, and 5 showing the towns and major roads that I would be patrolling. Sergeant Cally gave me a quick overview and told me not to worry about getting lost. Just stay on the main roads, he advised, and dispatch would direct me to anywhere that I might be needed. Easy enough, I thought.

Cruisers in other sectors had received numerous calls. There were a couple of domestics, a three-car collision near the University of Massachusetts in Amherst, and a burglary in the hill town of Leverett. My sectors had been quiet, and I wasn't sent to assist any of the others. Being unfamiliar with the area made quiet and slow a good thing, except for the lingering sadness and thoughts replaying the Charger driving away under the bridge. I forced myself to focus on work.

It was hard to see much on a midnight shift anywhere, but I saw enough to believe that I could come to like working at Northampton. It was a college area with thousands of students from UMass, Smith, Mount Holyoke, Amherst, and Hampshire colleges making many Friday and Saturday nights insanely hectic. UMass had its own sizable police force with state policing authority, so they handled their own campus and sometimes beyond, but only when needed. Campus police for the private colleges were restricted to their properties.

Somewhere around 2:30 a.m. I found myself in the center of a picturesque Northampton, well-lit by streetlights along a Main Street of small retail stores, coffee shops, boutiques, and a few good restaurants. Back then, fifty-odd years ago, Northampton was inviting, charming, and one of my favorite places to wander around.

I turned onto Pleasant Street heading south. Pleasant Street is also Route 5, which follows the railroad tracks and the Connecticut River for seven or eight miles into the City of Holyoke. Once beyond the city lights, near the dike, the road was dark.

The Connecticut River is the City of Northampton's eastern border. The dike is part of the Northampton Local Protection Project built by the U.S. Army Corps of Engineers. Construction began in 1939 and was completed in 1941 at a cost of 1.1 million dollars. It was designed and built to protect the city from flooding by the Mill River and the Connecticut River and its upstream reservoirs. Stop-log modular structures were originally constructed where the dike crosses Route 5, which allowed engineers to control the water during floods. Southbound traffic crossing the dike drove up a severe incline, and northbound cars faced a drop off, kind of like a huge speed bump.

Continuing south, I could smell the river and the sweet fragrance of the crops planted, and nearing harvest, on either side. My wish was to drive around all night without a call, for it was calm, beautiful, warm, and clear. I approached the large electric generating plant located on the western edge of the river surrounded by mounds of coal, with a dozen rail cars waiting to add to the piles.

Interestingly enough, the plant was built by my previous employer, the Riley Stoker Corporation.

After glancing at the plant, my eyes were hit with high beams as a car screamed past me headed back toward Northampton. This wasn't a typical speeder a few miles over the limit—he or she was going over a hundred. I made a U-turn and started after the car. I didn't put my blue lights on, knowing that operators often become more reckless during a chase. I was at a hundred and twenty before beginning to catch up, and thankful there were no other cars on the road. Actually, this wasn't a chase because the driver wasn't running away; he slowed approaching the city and didn't even know that I was after him. Once again, the vehicle slowed while I was still a distance behind and moving just under a hundred and gaining. The driver slowed his car one more time and I lost sight of his taillights. Taking my foot off the accelerator, I was lost in the pursuit and aware of nothing, other than wondering why the taillights had disappeared. At that moment it dawned on me. *OH, MY GOD, THE DIKE!*

I flew off the dike at eighty-five miles per hour. I was certain that all four wheels left the pavement as both my feet tried pushing the brake pedal through the floorboards, but it didn't matter. When the cruiser bottomed I went airborne and slammed my head into the roof, splitting my campaign hat and smashing down with such force it encircled my head. Both my ears were bent outward 90 degrees, and I couldn't see with the hatband wrapped around my eyes. With both feet on the brake, and both hands prying the hat from my eyes, I skidded to a stop in the middle of Route 5.

The speeder was long gone and the cruiser was undamaged, so I pulled into a closed gas station and parked. Shaken and recovering, I planned on hiding for the rest of the night, praying that a patrol supervisor wouldn't come looking for me to do an inspection. How would I explain my squashed and torn hat split almost in two?

As someone who has always regarded his cup of life as being half full, as opposed to half empty, I was able to come away from the experience with a promise and a declaration to myself.

The promise was to never, ever, drive another vehicle without wearing a seatbelt.

And the declaration? I declared, then and forever, that I really, really hated campaign hats!

My Wives

Well, off I go on another 91 patrol to serve the Commonwealth, yet, truth be told, I was obsessed with my quest to find a "stupid" Dodge Charger. Okay, I give up, maybe I'm the stupid one. Every few days I would give that tired number a ring to the point of believing it pointless, yet I was unable to throw it away. A month and a half had passed since the last encounter. Why, Lord, couldn't I get over it?

I had finished covering a minor accident at the Connecticut line and said my goodbyes to the Connecticut Trooper who had also been sent to the call. If the mishap had occurred seventy feet farther south, I would have been the one visiting and Connecticut would have done the paperwork. But, no matter, I'd met a trooper from our neighboring state, and in all likelihood I'd be seeing him again.

It was time for a badly needed coffee, so I headed to Howard Johnson's on East Columbus Ave. Route 91 was largely built as an overpass through Springfield, which ran parallel between East and West Columbus with underpasses connecting the two streets. The Sunday morning was overcast, but another warm day with fresh air despite the cloudiness. I took the South End Bridge/Columbus Avenue exit, driving straight onto East Columbus toward my destination ahead on the right. I was almost to the entrance of HJs when a car exited the underpass onto East Columbus right in front of me.

There she was, silver Dodge Charger and all. I didn't know if it was going to be strike three you're out, or third time's a charm, but I wasn't about to miss the chance to find out. Lights, siren, and flashing headlights startled the mysterious Miss and her female passenger as she pulled to the side of the road.

Walking toward the car I could tell that she hadn't recognized me. She was deep into the pocketbook beside her, searching for her license and registration, while the passenger watched me approach. As a matter of habit, I stood slightly to the rear of the door as she rolled down the window with her papers in hand.

"I don't need your license and registration again," I said with a smile, "I know who you are. I've been calling you. Is your phone broken?"

"Well, no," she answered hesitantly, and puzzled. "You've been calling me?"

"Yeah, I wanted to see if everything turned out okay between you and the guy you bumped into. He was kinda a jerk," I added.

The look of puzzlement turned pleasantly surprised. "He was a jerk all right," she said, then asked curiously, "When have you called me?"

"Oh, actually, quite a few times. That's why I figured your phone had to be out of order."

"At night? Did you call me at night?"

"Yeah, mostly at night, usually in the evening, then I'd try you on the weekends." I wasn't going tell her how many times.

"I'm sorry," she offered sincerely. "I'm not home very much. I have three jobs. I work full-time days, then part-time evenings, and another for random hours on weekends."

"Wow. I thought I worked a lot. No wonder I couldn't get you."

My mysterious Miss, Marion, introduced me to her girlfriend, Coral, saying they'd been out for a ride together going nowhere in particular. Coral had long blonde hair tied in a ponytail. She had a pretty face, a nice smile, and wore a sweatshirt with jeans.

Marion told me how the guy in the other car kept harassing her over the "damage" to his bumper. Through his insurance company he'd been able to get her work phone number and called repeatedly. Maybe the guy was smarter than me after all. I could have done the same thing and saved myself a lot of anguish. Marion continued, telling me that he finally went away when she threatened to call the trooper who was there that night, and who had said there wasn't any damage.

We talked for about fifteen minutes right there beside the road. She seemed genuinely interested, so I asked if it would be okay for me to call her to say hello sometime. When I asked her when the best time was to call, she gave me her work number and said, "Call me anytime."

That day was the beginning of a two-year relationship, resulting in a thirty-eight-year marriage producing two wonderful girls, six years apart.

A book about my marriage to Marion, and our forty years together would be a massive story, as would the tale of any marriage that length. For me to recount all the trials, tribulations, the ups and downs, the joys and heartbreaks, would be impossible, and many are just too personal. There are humorous and heartwarming stories during my police career involving Marion that can be told later. But for now, it's important to reveal a little of Marion's personal history to understand our lives hand in hand, and how we were brought together. I've come to believe that spiritual intervention was responsible for our union, as well as why, and how, I was brought together with another later in my life.

Marion was three years old when her mother died. They lived in Connecticut. Her father remarried, creating a new family for Marion, her older sister, and their new stepmother. He and his new wife eventually had a daughter together, but then Marion's father tragically died of injuries from an automobile accident. Marion was eight. Her stepmother struggled with the two stepchildren and one of her own. Marion described her stepmother as a mean and cruel woman. The stories my wife told of how she was treated were quite disturbing. Looking back, I can understand the stepmother's frustration and anger at her own predicament. I don't know if she can be excused for her actions, but I do have some understanding. At thirteen, Marion couldn't take it anymore and was taken in by her paternal grandparents. Four years later her grandmother had a slight heart attack, and one of her five uncles told her, at the age of seventeen, that she was too much for her grandparents and would have to move out. Two weeks later she found a small apartment in Massachusetts, moved in, and slept on the floor with a coat over her until she could afford a bed.

My wife had been severely scarred emotionally. She didn't deal well with change and felt unworthy from childhood on. Fear of loss was a deeply troubling issue that caused her to be very possessive and insecure, with insecurity leading to matters of trust. Laughter came hard and infrequent; something bad was always going to happen, and when would the other shoe fall? Throughout her bouts of depression, she refused to seek medical help, no matter how hard I tried to convince her. Forty years of sometimes frequent behavioral difficulties were hard to navigate. That said, we had many wonderful times and memories together, and although I choose not to recount some in this narrative, it's in no way meant to diminish their significance. There were some lofty highs that we both cherished.

Marion was honest. She would not and did not ever lie. She was a perfectionist, keeping a beautiful home, and was a loving, attentive mother to our daughters. She was generous in giving but denied herself. Those fortunate few who gained her trust earned her friendship and loyalty forever. Marion's life experiences were hard, yet although she struggled with them throughout life, she overcame many. I had, early and often, been shown the errors of my thinking and other ways to handle particular problems. It took me years to realize fully that I possessed none of the life tools that my wife had acquired after having gone through such hardships. These lessons, these tools, and so much more, she taught me. She was a critical and necessary part of my growth and maturity. I can't imagine the person I might have become without her influence.

Marion often made the statement to friends, "I don't think Randy has ever said *no* to me." It's not an absolutely true statement, but pretty close. Coming from a secure home and raised by loving parents with a normal upbringing with none of the anxiety and fear that Marion suffered, I felt that I brought her security and the knowledge that she wasn't alone. I knew what her life had been, so I worked hard to make certain she knew that I loved and cared for her. One of the hardest hurdles to overcome was getting her to believe that I would never leave and would always be there for her and the children. Life for her was full of loss, and nothing was ever permanent.

Early in the marriage we frequently argued over how best to deal with any number of issues because of her profound need to be in control, which had resulted from her inability to trust or depend upon others. She had grown up believing that she could only, truly, depend upon herself. The fight-or-flight response within her was powerful. I always wanted, and tried, to take the gentle approach—you get more flies with honey. Even matters that we agreed upon became problematic because our approaches would be at odds. Mine were not wrong or ineffective, just different from hers, and too often led to arguments. So, over time I simply gave up rather than fight, and maybe rarely saying *no* was a result of my surrender. Our marriage was very rocky at times, but through it all I loved her, and I knew she loved me.

Marion died of lung cancer in January of 2009. I suspected that she was ill for over a year before the diagnosis, but she refused to go to a doctor, or even talk about it. She was less afraid of not knowing what was wrong than she was of learning the truth and dealing with it. Her plan of action, or non-action, was beyond my comprehension. I asked the oncologist for his prognosis shortly after treatment began. He told me six months, and he was right.

Spending countless hours in our darkened bedroom with my semiconscious, sleeping, or medicated wife was an overpowering experience. For me, it was a spiritual awakening. The self-examination that occurred—of my life, of the people I have hurt or disappointed—was profound. As much as I prayed for Marion, I prayed for my own forgiveness, becoming closer to God.

My daughters and I were with her when she passed.

I never thought I would cry, because I hadd been preparing myself for six months, but I was so wrong. The sorrow was harder than I ever imagined. I cried for two months before the pain began to let up. Looking back, the long-impassioned grieving period was healthy and started my rebirth. I began to rediscover who I was. I had been one person at work and another at home, and home was where I became the accepting, submissive, never-say-no and go-along-to-get along personality. It had become the "normal" me, and I didn't even know it.

Beginning my resurrection, I noticed that my daughters were looking at me differently; I had changed. Often, when they came home from college or work, they would share stories about friends whose parents had divorced, with the father remarrying and the family disintegrating. They had become uncertain and wary of their dad, so I understood that the rebirth of Pop would need to be done carefully, and with baby steps.

In retrospect, I suppose buying a Harley Davidson motorcycle, joining a club consisting of all police officers, then going on a road trip to learn you need a second, bigger Harley, was a leap too far for my girls. I had ridden bikes since I was sixteen, and rode them for the state police, so this was nothing new, just different behavior. I sat them down with reassurances that I wasn't going to run off to Vegas with a new wife, looking for a new life. I was still their same father and wasn't going anywhere. The transition would take some time, but that didn't mean I couldn't have a little fun—or payback.

The motorcycle gang went to Laconia, New Hampshire for Bike Week. We all dressed the part with our helmets, chains, and vests adorned with the club's colors, but we stayed in a three-million-dollar home across from Weirs Beach. We roughed it.

Anyway, I had told my girls that I was going, and although they expressed enthusiasm, I knew that it wasn't sincere.

On the third afternoon, two of the guys wanted to go to a tattoo parlor near Weirs Beach to check out their art, so we all went for the ride. I can't remember the name of the place, so for the sake of this story, we went to Sally's Tattoo Parlor. Four of our "gang" went inside, while the rest of us waited outside. I sat down on the front porch steps to wait and pulled out my cell phone to check the news.

Being from my generation, barely post-World War II, I had been accustomed to seeing tattoos on sailors, servicemen, and a lot of "shady" characters. Tattoos didn't belong on my daughters and I had told them so. But sitting on the stoop of a tattoo parlor in 2011, my views had "moderated"—somewhat. Admittedly, had one of my girls got herself a small discreet tattoo I would have accepted it, but I wasn't going to tell them so.

Acutely aware that my daughters' phones were no more than a centimeter or two beyond their reach, and with my cell firmly in the palm of my hand, I figured it was time for a text message.

> Hey, Guys, I just wanted to check in to tell you that I'm OK, and having a good time, but I wanted to ask you a question. I'm with the gang at Sally's Tattoo Parlor and I want to know what you think about a Dragon tattoo? There's a full color one that starts at the neck and winds down the arm.

That did it. Within thirty seconds I received two texts and they were both calling at the same time. I didn't answer right away.

I was sixty-three, lonely, and knew I didn't want to spend the rest of my life hugging a couple of motorcycles. Another decision, that I had cast in stone, was that I wouldn't settle for just anyone. Awakening, so to speak, from a forty-year slumber, I was determined to find the right person, or spend the rest of my life alone. That said, where does a sixty-three-year-old go to find a girlfriend? I was never into bars, even as a single young man. I was a novice with a computer but was assured by friends that I *needed* to go on internet dating sites like eHarmony and Match. All I can say to my concerned and helpful friends is that if any one of them had actually tried internet dating they would never have recommended it.

Each new aspect of this journey could be a writing bonanza all its own. The dating experiences generated by those sites were discouraging, a waste of money, and just plain awful—every single one of them! So I'm not wasting my time or an ink cartridge writing about my "rendezvous"—too scary.

The Harleys were large bikes, eight hundred pounds each, and I had some trouble handling the weight, so I went to the gym for some muscles. Supplementing the workouts, I purchased, not a five-pound dumbbell, and not a ten-pound dumbbell, but a twenty-five-pound dumbbell to do curls at home while sitting on my butt in an easy chair watching TV. Isn't that how one exercises?

An orthopedic doctor, James Wyles, told me that I had strained the lateral epicondylitis and the medial epicondylitis of my left arm. Basically, I had tennis elbow and golf elbow at the same time, and it was going to take weeks to heal. He set me up for physical therapy a few days a week, further suggesting that twenty-five pounds was way too much weight for me to curl, and that I was probably the dumbbell in this case. My words, not his.

My physical therapist's name was Anne. She had me sit in a chair next to the therapy table and rest my arm on top. She was cordial, had brown hair in a cute short style. That's about all I noticed of Anne, because I was focused on me, and what the therapy would consist of, for I had never been to physical therapy before.

It was simple enough. Anne placed a cloth over my arm and began a hands-on muscle/tendon massage. Her technique was nothing like any massage I'd ever had; her fingers were strong, and she went deep into the muscles searching for the damaged tendons. It hurt when she found the spot and held pressure working the tendon from side to side, while explaining this was something I could do at home. Through the pain, I visualized myself sitting on my butt in my easy chair, watching TV, and squeezing my arm instead of curling the twenty-five-pound dumbbell.

Anne was pretty much all business to begin with, but speaking about my injury she was a little more open. I asked a few questions and she answered pleasantly with a smile here and there. When she finished working my arm, she called to a young girl named Katie. "Okay, Katie. He's all yours. Ice and stim him," came the instructions as she left the enclosure. Katie preceded to wrap my arm in a cold compress, and then used electric stimulation to treat the spasms and pain. I was done.

A few days later when I returned for round two, Katie came into the waiting room and brought me inside. I thought she was going to treat me but learned that she was a PT student. Katie set me up at the same chair and table as before, and then Anne came in to begin treatment.

I was more animated and talkative than before, telling her how I had hurt my arm, that I was retired from the state police, that I was married for thirty-eight years before my wife died, blah, blah, blah, and blah. She listened and asked some questions. We had a few chuckles, but she was guarded and revealed nothing of herself. Our session ended upbeat. She once again worked quickly and had Katie finish up, but added a goodbye and said that I was scheduled with another therapist the next time.

At my next appointment, as before, Katie brought me from the waiting room to the treatment area, where Anne was standing. A surprised Anne looked up. "Oh, you again? I thought I was done with you." I knew that my expression of surprise was bigger than hers, and I didn't know how to answer, but then she smiled and gestured for me to follow.

This session was the most enjoyable yet. We talked, bantering back and forth, and enjoyed some silly laughter. She still wasn't revealing anything about herself, which made me curious.

This was the first time that I really looked at Anne. No, it was the first time that I actually *saw* her. She was a beautiful woman. I guessed that she was in her late thirties or early forties, about five feet six inches tall, with a gorgeous figure. Her short dark brown hair framed the smooth features of her face. Her brown eyes with minimal mascara and eyeliner sparkled against her light skin, red lipstick, and telltale freckles. I guessed she might be Irish. Her smile is what held me the most. I couldn't stop taking in her brightness—she glowed.

At this point in my life, my interactions with any female regarding dating or a possible relationship was underdeveloped and awkward at best. Being near her now, I felt like a silly junior high school kid with his tongue tied. Nevertheless, I managed to put together a few sentences and we had a nice conversation. As before, we bantered and laughed, while I hoped that she was starting to like me. She seemed to have a wonderful sense of humor, that is, until I got enough courage to ask if she was married.

She contemplated the question, then added sternly, "Yeah, three times. I knew you were up to something." The remark stopped me cold. I held my words, not speaking for about thirty seconds, which I would term as a very long pregnant pause, before getting the nerve enough to go again. "So," I ventured, "does that mean you're involved?"

Anne called for Katie to finish up and left the room.

The next week Anne worked on my arm for my last treatment session. It was good. She was friendly, we laughed and joked once more. I stayed away from any marriage questions, wanting to be a perfect, polite, gentleman throughout. When the session was almost over, I sincerely thanked Anne for our time together and told her how much I had enjoyed our conversations. I thought that was going to be the end until she asked, "So, what if I decided to go out?"

Flabbergasted, I asked for her phone number and said that I would call her. "No, no no, you give me yours and we'll see," she admonished.

It was more than I could have hoped for while writing down my number and saying goodbye.

I waited almost a week and didn't hear a peep. Determined to take matters into my own hands, I sat down at the computer and brought up a notepad screen to write her a message.

Hi, Anne.

OK . . . OK . . . one of two things is going to happen . . . I'm either going to hurt myself again so I can come in . . . or . . . I'll have to come in for butt therapy because my rear end is killing me from spending hours sitting and waiting for the phone to ring.

We are not going to elope . . . it's dinner, and it's easy!
I hold a chair so you can sit down, you stuff a napkin down your blouse and pick up your fork. You stab the fork into some food, put it in your mouth and chew. Then I make you laugh. There . . . isn't that easy?? Call me . . . anytime on my cell (except Thursday before 4 p.m.), or any evening after 7:30 on my home phone.

Now . . . just in case you burned my numbers in a fit of "why the hell did I ever tell that guy that I might change my mind?" Here they are again, and don't burn these, because I still have friends in high places and one of them is the State Fire Marshall.

Annie, you will have a nice evening, and if after that you're never hungry again . . . I won't bother you. Promise.

Randy

Message completed, I sealed it in an envelope, wrote ANNE on the front and headed to her office, planning to leave it with the receptionist. The parking lot was full, but I found a spot right in front. I got out of the car and met Dr. Wyles at the front door of the office. He remembered me and asked how my arm was doing. I told him that it was getting better and thanked him. Producing the envelope, I asked if he would mind giving it to Anne. I said it was a recipe that I had promised to give her. He said he'd be glad to and went inside. I waited almost another week and she never called. Apparently, I wasn't very good at this sort of thing.

I was a good cook but often tired of the job. I also liked going to a local diner late in the afternoon for dinner and visiting with a couple of regulars. Feeling the need for comfort food, I went to the diner earlier than usual, ordering meatloaf and mashed potatoes. When I'd finished eating and small talk at the counter, I said goodbye and pushed out through the door just as my cell phone rang.

"Hello," I answered, stopping on the stairs so that I could hear.

"Hello back," said the female caller. I hesitated, trying to figure out who it was. There were no women in my life, and it was neither of my daughters, so I guessed.

"Anne, is that you?" I asked, pausing to listen to several seconds of silence.

"Yeah, it's me." Again silence.

"Oh, I'm glad you called." Excitedly, I added, "I was afraid you wouldn't. Did you get my note?"

Another long pause, then she said. "Yeah I did, eventually!"

Now it was my turn to pause. "Eventually?" I inquired.

"Yeah, eventually—my boss's name is ANN."

"Oh. My. God. Your boss got my note?"

"Yup, my boss and the whole office too."

"Dr. Wyles?"

"I imagine all the doctors saw it, I'm sure it made the rounds before I got your recipe."

I can't recall the rest of our conversation. In the end, she was adamant that dinner was out, but I could take her to lunch. No, I couldn't pick her up at her house. She would meet me at her office and we'd go from there.

I suggested a hilltop restaurant for lunch with a view that was agreeable to Anne. Aside from her pushing my hand away when I tried to take hold of hers to walk up the steep staircase, it was great fun. She was great fun. The food, not so much, my corn cob salad was lousy, but I didn't complain. Anne ate all of hers, and had just swallowed the last mouthful when I asked if she'd like anything else. Whilst I was thinking dessert, she blurted out. "How about a cheeseburger with onions and mushrooms?" This lady wasn't shy. We laughed, split a cheeseburger, and talked a good while after.

Cautiously, she began going out with me, and after a time she gave me her address so I could pick her up at home. After several months, I was well on my way to falling in love with her. Anne was fifty, but didn't look a day over forty. She'd had a boyfriend in her twenties, one in her thirties, then one in her forties. She had never been married, had no children, and had no baggage. I asked if I could be her boyfriend in her fifties.

Anne and I dated for about nine months. It was special, sweet, and I was happy. Unfortunately, there are always some bumps in the road of any relationship. We hit a bump and parted. I was devastated. I went on a couple of road trips with the motorcycle club, writing to her about the places we went, but she didn't reply.

In early December 2011, I was cleaning a drawer in a side table. Inside was an old unused ashtray holding a necklace and broken chain that Anne had placed there. I remembered she had told me that one of her sisters had made it and had given it to her as a present. I was able to restring the beads into the original sequence, but I couldn't fix the chain, so I took it to a jeweler. I mailed her the necklace with a short note telling her I had found it in the house and thought she would like to have it.

One of the motorcycle trips had been to Key West, Florida. I trailered my bike to Boca Raton, parked the trailer at my daughter's, and then rode the Harley to Tampa, where I met up with the gang.

Once off toward Key West, we stopped our first night in Fort Myers Beach. Crossing the tall bridge into Fort Myers Beach gives a beautiful view of the back bay. I remembered Phil's brother-in-law, Hugh Briody, had a place there. I had gotten to know Hugh well through playing golf with him and Phil. Anne was gone, and I was loving the looks of Fort Myers Beach, so I decided that when I got home I'd check out condos for sale in the area. Check them out I did, found a one-bedroom that I liked, and placed a deposit contingent upon my coming to look at it.

A few days after Christmas, I flew down to check it out. Having second thoughts about a one-bedroom condo, I asked the realtor to find some two-bedrooms to see before committing to the single. My daughter drove over from Boca to help with the decision. The second two-bedroom condo we looked at was the one I wanted, so I made an offer.

My daughter and I had a nice dinner together before she went back to Boca across Alligator Alley, and I went to my motel. It was about 6 p.m. when I got to the hotel, but before I could get into a parking space my cell rang. It was the realtor saying that my offer had been accepted. I was on cloud nine. Nothing could have made me any happier. The conversation lasted no more than twenty seconds. I finished parking and shut the car off when my phone rang again.

I knew the number. It was Anne. She had called to thank me for the necklace, and to say hello. I asked her to give me five minutes to finish parking and get up to my room to call her back. It took me less than two minutes. Realizing that I wasn't at home she had asked where I was, so I told her the story of how I'd found the condo, the purchase, and everything else that popped into my mind over the next two hours.

I ended by asking if I could call and wish her a Happy New Year when I got home. That was a yes, and I was clearly so wrong in thinking that nothing could have made me happier than buying the condo, because my happiness at the thought of Anne being back in my life far exceeded that. By April she and I were dating steadily once again.

Annie has every one of the good and wonderful traits that Marion had. Every positive that Marion owned was a part of Anne, but more importantly, she was all the things that Marion could never be. I know Marion tried with everything she had, but could never get past all the heartbreak, hurt, and most of all, the losses that tortured her soul.

Spiritually, I've grown so much with Anne. We both strongly believe in God. Marion and I were meant to have been together, for I'm convinced the multiple meetings were not coincidental. We were destined to meet, just as I know that Anne and I were predestined to find each other.

Anne also taught me how to say *no*, and that it isn't a dirty word. I learned the importance of, and how to set, boundaries with both friends and family to make life and getting along easier. Boundaries aren't an impediment to good relationships, they're essential. She helped and encouraged me to validate myself. At long last, I understood how and why I had lived with two personalities, one persona during work and in public, another at home. No longer was I the submissive, all-accepting man that I had once been.

Lastly, laughter and love fill the home that Anne and I built. She is silly, funny, and a joy to be with. As for love, I believe the unconditional affection known as love, which we all seek, consists of many different degrees. I loved Marion and will forever. But I must confess to a deeper feeling for Anne than I've ever felt before, because it has been so easy and free and I've never been happier. Marion, Anne, and I all needed each other at critical times in our lives. We battled; we cried; we loved; we laughed; and, most importantly, we learned from each other as God intended. Now, Anne has given me back my life.

Red Ruby, Oh Red Ruby

Strange, odd, and interestingly peculiar characters can be found everywhere, but it was my experience that many towns in Russell's area had more than their fair share. Red Ruby was one such person we often dealt with. He lived with his elderly mother on their seventy-five-acre family farm in Chester.

The first time I met Red was after his mother called the barracks requesting a trooper be sent to the farm because Red was acting up. In truth, Red was acting up *again*, as everyone in the barracks knew from previous visits to "settle Red down."

The small farm was located on a rural dirt road. It was a pretty drive to the Ruby farm, with stone-walled pastures alongside the road and fields of multicolored cows that lazily lifted their heads to glance indifferently at passing cars. Nearing the farm, large maple trees stood shoulder to shoulder, having grown up through the ancient walls and, like sentinels, they kept watch over the century-old farm. Several of the trees had old maple syrup taps stuck deep into their trunks, and from another hung a badly rusted bucket. I imagined the bygone taps as old wounds. I wasn't a farmer, but knew it wasn't maple sugaring season—the taps and bucket should have been removed long ago.

Passing the last maple, I saw the property, which from a distance reminded me of a typical old New England farm. The barn had grey weathered vertical boards with a faded red door. The metal roof appeared relatively new. The house was a small two-story Victorian in the same faded red as the barn door, with a straight porch across the front. At first sight, the spread was appealing, and I warmed to the scene before me. I had come to love exploring the remote back roads to discover old farms tucked into some obscure hidden hollow, many beautifully frozen in time.

Unfortunately, the Ruby farm was nothing of the sort. Pulling into the barnyard, all the years of neglect became evident. It saddened me because I so loved the old farmsteads. The barn's missing boards, broken windowpanes, and piles of broken and rusted machine parts littering the yard gave evidence. The house had cracked siding and the wooden steps from the back door to the barnyard were missing a tread. The front porch, which looked like such an inviting place to sit rocking away warm evenings, was dilapidated. The white paint was peeling, and rot was the only thing supporting two of the four porch columns. I worried that the porch might topple onto an aged Chrysler sedan parked on the far side. Several scrawny chickens pecking along the side of the house were being eyed by a huge farm cat that looked part tabby, and only God knew what else. It had obviously been feeding itself well on a diet of mice, and maybe an occasional chicken. The grass hadn't seen a lawnmower this year, and I guessed the machine was at the bottom end of a mower handle reaching up through the tall weeds.

When I got out of the cruiser, an elderly woman came through the back doorway and navigated the broken steps. She was in her eighties, or maybe older; it was hard to tell. At five feet five inches, she wore old black rubber slip-on boots. I guessed she kept them by the rear door, stepping in and out of them as need be throughout the day. There wasn't a railing for her to hold onto, so she clutched the skirt portion of her worn blue-green print dress for balance. Nonetheless, she nearly fell at the missing tread. Her hair was a stringy salt and pepper grey that was partially held up with a man's red handkerchief. Her skin was elderly pale, and she fought to catch her breath while struggling with her bulk to reach me. Her wide eyes seemed fearful and she started talking before I could ask what the problem was or even say hello.

"Hold on. Are you Mrs. Ruby?" I asked calmly.

"Yes, he's out there, he's out there, over in t'barn."

I knew she was talking about Red, and I also knew that the previous visits by troopers had never been violent, so I wanted her to simmer down and relax.

"Red is in the barn?" I asked. Mrs. Ruby nodded and took a deep breath as her tension eased.

"Okay, Mrs. Ruby, what's the problem?"

Excited and animated, she began. "He won't do nuttin'. He's lazy 'n' no good. I tell 'm he's gotta get t' cows and milk 'm 'fore two o'clock, but he jus' takes his time 'n' does as he damn well pleases. He don't mind me no more. Ya gotta talk to Red. He's mad now. He's mad a' me and I'm not gonna make 'm no supper if 'n he don't stop it."

"Okay, Mrs. Ruby, what's your first name? What do they call you?"

"I'm Ida."

"All right, Ida. Why don't you go back inside and I'll find Red, is that okay?" Once again she nodded, then grabbed hold of both sides of her dress to climb back into the kitchen.

Leaving Mrs. Ruby, I went to the barn and pulled the right side of the double door open. I was surprised that it worked so smoothly. Looking inside, there were five cow stanchions on the right with troughs for hay against the wall. The concrete floor behind the stanchions had a channel to catch the cow plop and urine. The rest of the barn floor was dirt, mostly covered with fresh hay. I loved the smell of active barns—I'd been in many and never found the smell offensive. Loose hay was piled high in large bins that filled the rest of the barn floor. It was curious that the hay wasn't in bales.

Red wasn't in the barn, so I went out the back door, where more junk and scrap metal was piled against the back of the building. An old model Farmall tractor rested against a stand of overgrown bushes. The tractor looked in working condition, and appeared to have been recently used, but the rusted hay bailer with flat, rotted tires explained the lack of hay bales in the barn. The loose hay had been manually moved, hauled, and tossed into the bins. Haying is hard work *with* a baler. It is beyond backbreaking when done by hand with a pitchfork.

I looked all around and couldn't see where Red might be, then spotted an old Ford stake body truck parked a couple hundred feet in front of the Farmall, also against the bushes. I caught a glimpse of a person in the driver's seat peeking at me, then ducking out of sight. Was it Red, was he trying to hide? Approaching the vehicle, I saw that it was quite old. I couldn't guess its age, but the color was now a rusty red, with rust having replaced the paint years ago. Side and rear wooden stakes were held upright by side slots in the truck's bed frame; the bed was made of wood with a number of oak floorboards missing, and others rotted. If the engine and three-speed floor shift worked, I figured the truck was probably what Red used to haul hay from the field to his barn. The cab had a leather bench seat and a large rectangular rear window into the rear bed. The window had lost its glass long ago.

I walked up to the driver's door. The window was gone—not rolled down but gone. As I studied the fellow behind the wheel, he looked back at me with one of the saddest faces I had ever seen. His face was farm work dirty, not filthy as if he never washed, and I could see dried tear tracks down both cheeks. He had been crying. "Are you Red?" I asked gently, and he nodded.

Red Ruby, I later learned, was fifty-four years old and had spent his entire life on the farm with his mother and father. His father had died fifteen years earlier. Red was less advanced mentally, socially, and, I would add, emotionally than most people his age. Obviously, with no expertise on the subject, I can't label his mental state or condition. I simply thought of him as slow, but I sensed a gentleness in the man.

Red, or his mother, kept what little hair he had on the sides and back of his head cropped short, making him appear bald. He had a large head, large ears, a prominent nose, and a small roundish mouth that just didn't belong to his face, but it did partially hide the only two teeth of his I ever saw. Brown eyebrows followed the downward slope of his green eyes, giving him a perpetual look of sadness or deep sorrow that even a rare smile couldn't hide. He had smooth skin with a healthy tan from working the farm in the sun. I don't think he ever wore a hat, but for our introduction today, he wore bib coveralls with a grey sweatshirt and black rubber boots.

"What's the matter, Red? Your mother told me you were mad."

He cast aside my question to ask, "What's your name, trooperrr." He spoke slow and deliberately. The word trooper he pronounced with two elongated syllables. There was no anger, or surliness. He was curious, with a childlike nature.

"My name is Randy." I answered.

"Is that your nick . . . name?" continued Red, slowly. He was long past my initial question and going off in his own direction.

"Yes, Randall is my real name and Randy is my nickname."

He repeated my name, Randall, long and slowly. This was the way he spoke. Red wasn't dumb by any stretch. Thoughts came slowly as he brought them forth in speech. One needed to be a patient listener when dealing with Red, and this, surely, would be part of the difficulties between him and his mother, because Ida was not a patient woman. For sure, I didn't know the causes—maybe it came with her age, or maybe from the years of dealing with Red alone without her husband. But in any case, from that day on Red called me Randall, using elongated syllables as was the habit with so much of his speech.

Red got out of the truck and stood beside me. He was my height, somewhat stocky, but every bit of him was muscle. His wrists were as thick as my bicep, and his hands were massive and callused from years of farming and milking.

I reminded him of the first question I had asked of why he was mad and why his mother had called the police. It took him a few seconds to come back from wherever his mind had been, and he said that he couldn't take it much more. The conversation was all in slow motion, but I pushed. He told me that his mother was always yelling at him to get things done. He was too slow; he never worked hard; he never did things right; he never helped with anything at all; and he was stupid. When I asked, he said there had never been anyone else to help him with the chores, adding that it had been okay when his dad was alive, but not now. Probing as to why he had gotten so mad, I learned that he had a driver's license and drives the old Chrysler, but never alone. His mother wanted Red to take her to the local store, not far from the farm, to get a few things. Red asked her if he could get some licorice and she had told him no, so I asked why he couldn't just buy some himself when they got to the store.

Red stared hard at the ground, and shamefully said, "Ma wouldn't give me any money."

I was astonished and tried to hide the look on my face. "Don't you get any money from your mother for your work?" Face still aimed toward the dirt, he shook his head and said nothing. Then, looking at me with tear-filled eyes, he said that he was sorry for getting mad at her; that she had made me come, and that he didn't mean to do anything wrong. I damn near cried myself.

This was beyond my skills. The Academy never covered anything like this. These people needed professional help. I told Red I wasn't mad and that it was all right. It was my job to help, and I was going to go up to the house and speak with his mother. I didn't know what else to do with Red, so I reached into my pocket, pulled out a five-dollar bill and told him to buy some licorice the next time he took his mother to the store. He lit up, sort of, with a woeful smile.

Mrs. Ruby was sitting at the kitchen table when I knocked. She still wore her rubber boots when I walked in and sat on the chair she offered. The kitchen was messy and there were dirty dishes in the sink, and though it wasn't filthy, it did need some scrubbing. The table where we sat was covered with crumbs, a couple of empty mugs, a partially eaten sandwich on a plate, and half a glass of milk. The floor needed sweeping and the furniture was just barely holding up.

Angry again, Mrs. Ruby asked, "Well didja find 'im? Where was he hidin' this time?"

"He was sitting in the stake body, Ida. He's okay now. He's sorry that he got mad."

"Yeah, well he's always sorry afta, he's no good for much, trooper. You see 'ow 'e is."

I didn't know how to respond to her, so I changed the subject and asked her about Mr. Ruby. Ida immediately brightened and told me what a wonderful man he was, how hard he had worked to build the farm, and how good he was to her. They had been married just over sixty years when he died of a heart attack. They had another child, a girl, who died of pneumonia at the age of six. She told me how much Mr. Ruby loved their little girl. Ida missed them both and recounted memories of the two of them. I was attentive and listened sympathetically as her face softened with the thoughts, but she hadn't mentioned one word of Red.

Ida talked about this and that for quite a while, and I let her go until she had talked herself out. She had settled down once more and was in a better state of mind. I brought her back to the subject of Red's behavior, wondering how that might go. Surprisingly well, I would have to say. She still wasn't ready to cut Red any slack, reminding of me how useless he was, but she was obviously no longer mad and said that it was time to make his supper. I thought that was good enough for one day. I didn't dare ask her why she wouldn't give Red any money for his work. It really wasn't any of my business, and I feared making their relationship worse if she knew Red told me about money, licorice, and the store. Ida walked with me out to the stake bed Ford to get Red and bring him back to the house. All was at peace.

Ida and Red lived in a time when elder services, welfare, and help for people like them wasn't as available as it is today, if at all. I cared for them both, Mrs. Ruby because of her losses, the loneliness she must have felt, and the burden of looking after Red. Red's childlike innocence was often very endearing. He was strong as an ox, slow, yet capable of keeping up with the work of the farm, but outside their acres he'd be alone, lost, and wouldn't make it. One couldn't help but feel compassion. Over the next few weeks, I made it a mission to stop and check in on them. Things seemed to be okay. Ida would get a little grouchy and bitch about her son, but nothing too bad. Red always gave me the same unhappy smiles, and it was the same old talk, but I always left him happy with a few dollar bills for licorice.

Patrols were busy the next working trip and I couldn't get to the farm. Almost a week later, on my middle day, I received a radio call that sent me to the Ruby farm. Mrs. Ruby had called the barracks, as so many times before, to say Red was acting up.

It wasn't an emergency, so I didn't speed to get there, but it was a routine Red Ruby call requiring that I go directly.

Pulling into the barnyard, Ida came out her back door all flustered, holding her skirt as usual, sputtering that Red was mad again and out back somewhere. It was the same behavior for Red, so I went through the barn as usual, then out back looking for the stake body truck, which was nowhere to be seen. Looking into the fields and back up toward the maple trees along the stone wall, there was still no sign of Red or the truck. I gazed straight into the field, then looked down the slight hill over to the right and saw Red's truck facing toward me uphill. It was partially obscured by an old wooden trailer in front and appeared to be backed against an oak tree. I started off toward the truck trying to see Red in the front seat, but he wasn't there. I opened the passenger's door, first looking at the steering wheel, then at the sole of a rubber boot sticking into the cab through the rear window of the truck. The next step told me everything that I didn't really want to know. Red's body was on the floor of the truck bed. His right foot was still in the boot through the truck's rear window. From where I stood, I couldn't see the other leg or foot, but his right arm was torn from the socket and lying beside him. His head was almost completely severed from his neck. Red was a gruesome sight, and there would be no need for an ambulance.

What poor Red had done to himself was grotesque, yet effective. I wondered if it was purposely hideous, as a reflection of how he saw himself. I didn't know, but I couldn't shake the image of Red sobbing uncontrollably with tears streaming down his face planning his end, and how he would do it.

Climbing up next to his body I saw the rope noose still around what little remained of his neck. I followed the other end, finding where Red had tied the rope to the oak, then where he ran it up over the truck bed and through the rear window into the cab. Apparently, he had then got into the driver's seat, tied the noose around his neck, started the truck, and in first gear floored the accelerator. His whole body was ripped up, out, and through the window. Red had had enough!

I found Ida back at the house and told her what had happened to Red, and I wasn't surprised at her lack of emotion. Delivering death notices to families, telling them that a loved one had died or been killed was never a pleasant assignment. Sometimes the news brought hysterics, with people being uncontrollable and inconsolable, and it wasn't a pretty picture. Other times the news was received as altogether untroubling. I would place Ida in the latter category.

On the drive back to the barracks I thought long about Red and his suicide, just wondering how deeply troubled he must have been through all his years. I never remembered Ida uttering one word that would make me believe that she ever had a care for him. It was so sad for them both.

My thoughts drifted from Red back a couple of weeks, when Trooper Patty O'Neill went to Huntington for a report that David Davis was trying to kill himself. David was in his midthirties, another troubled soul familiar to us, and the source of many calls.

I worked Route 91 that day, so I wasn't there, but I got the story firsthand from Patty when I came in. Parking my cruiser in the garage, I went into the guard room where Pat stood, instead of sitting, because he was literally covered with blood. It was in his hair, on his face, arms, and huge stains besmeared his uniform. Staring in disbelief I thought, what the hell?

Pat had sped into Huntington, just before the center of town near the Davis home, to find David lying unconscious on the ground surrounded by several people. He was covered in blood

136

with his fingers wrapped around a handsaw. Knowing that an ambulance was on the way, O'Neill quickly checked to make sure that Davis was still breathing. Then, noticing deep ragged wounds on his neck, he ran to get the first aid kit. Pat said that he was going apply pressure bandages to the wounds until the ambulance arrived.

Pat had almost made it to the cruiser when David regained consciousness and picked up right where he had left off—trying to saw his head off. Bystanders screamed, backing away as David stood up sawing his neck with a wild look in his eyes. Patty tackled him and David fought like an untamed beast, but not one bystander lifted a frigging finger to help. O'Neill wrestled with the wild man for a couple of minutes. David passed out just as the ambulance arrived.

They made it to the hospital with their patient still unconscious. Fortunately, David hadn't damaged his spine, nor did he cut into his carotid artery, so he was allowed to go home several days later.

Unfortunately, the family, apparently as nutty as David, continued to believe there was nothing wrong with him, until he took a shotgun and blew his brains out in his bedroom a week later.

I guess David had had enough, just like Red.

A Transfer

Over the past few months, I had been assigned a number of guest patrols at Northampton. I'd come to love the area and all the new experiences, except for my late-night takeoff and crash landing at the dike. Figuring the mishap was a one-time event, and a flight that I would never attempt again, I submitted a letter for transfer.

I liked working at Russell, but it was the only place I had been. The noncommissioned officers were great leaders and fine examples to emulate. My brother troopers became lasting friends; we could count on each other without question, and one couldn't ask for more. Nonetheless, each of Troop B's substations had a different character, or one might even say they had different personalities. Some of Russell's senior troops had worked at different stations, but most eventually returned to the comfort and slower pace of Russell. It was possible I would end up doing the same thing, but for the time being, I wanted to see what was out there.

Transfer requests were sometimes ignored by headquarters, simply because of a dislike for the officer making the request. Egos, grudges, and clashing personalities exist in every profession, and the state police are no different. Apparently, I was in good standing where it mattered, and headquarters approved the transfer within a month.

Wintertime was upon us. It was only my second winter season, but this time I was ready. After the near-disastrous search for the lost hunter in Blandford, I had totally prepared myself for anything the arctic could throw at me. Authorized equipment or not, I intended to be warm.

The clock above the desk read 2:45 p.m., and I had about fifteen minutes to relax before heading out on patrol. Lighting a Winston and sipping a coffee, I leaned back against the wall on an aged wooden chair, not built for leaning, and the legs strained and the stiles groaned. My only concern was the storm outside.

It had been snowing hard for the last twenty-four hours, causing dozens of accidents, some serious, but most minor. Winds had been especially strong earlier and had built impressive snow drifts, but it was weaker now. The sky was a light grey as I watched the snow billow gently against the houses across the street, then fall slowly to the ground—a good sign the storm was coming to an end.

There were always a few guys who complained and hated to work in snowstorms, but most didn't mind. Some people may find this odd to say, but for me it was exciting, busy, and one never knew what to expect. But for the time being I was content to finish my smoke and watch the desk officer go nuts answering the phone.

Trooper Mike Rogalewski was on desk duty. Mike had been an extra man, so the station commander put him on the desk while he caught up on some paperwork. It was obvious to any casual observer that Mike's patience had run out. Desk duty at a troop headquarters substation is busy any day, but during a snowstorm it borders on insane.

Mike had been with the State Police two years longer than I had. He had a long, slim face, a long nose to match, and blue eyes. His ears were small for his head, and troops weren't shy about telling him how funny they looked. Mike kept his brown hair short on the sides and back, but the rest was long, without a wave or curl anywhere. It was the straightest hair I'd ever seen. He could wet it with water, comb it in any direction, and it stayed put all day. I'll admit that some of his hairdos were a little strange, but nonetheless he was liked and respected by his fellow troopers. Mike was an excellent police officer, always displaying a natural confidence and smoothness. I would have bet that he could handle virtually anything. But the white knuckles gripping the telephone receiver gave him away. Mike was about to blow.

"This isn't a radio station, lady. If you want a weather report call WHMP or look out your window. I can't tie up emergency lines to give you a weather report," sputtered Mike, slamming the receiver into the cradle.

Uniformed officers manned the desks and answered the phones. Prerecorded message systems would have relieved so much stress, but we lacked the equipment necessary to set up dedicated lines to provide routine information to the public. We knew it existed, but in those years the technology hadn't been adopted by the State Police in Western Mass.

Joe Baran walked into the room and leaned against a file cabinet to my left as Mike spun toward us, red-faced and exasperated. Joe, too, held the rank of trooper, and had been around a few years longer than Mike and me.

At five feet nine inches tall, Joe was a bit overweight. He appeared much heavier than he actually was, but he'd still never catch anyone in a foot chase. As one might expect, Joe had round features including large round blue eyes, a round nose, wide mouth, and large lips. His wide, short neck quickly disappeared inside the collar of his shirt.

Wearing his usual broad smile, Baran cupped his mouth and whispered loudly into my ear:

"I think someone is letting their Polish temper show."

I laughed, nodding in agreement as Mike shot back.

"Yeah, well, I've seen your Polish temper, Baran, and it ain't no different."

Laughing, Joe said something back at Mike in Polish, prompting a middle finger response. Both troopers were of Polish descent and spoke the language fluently, often yelling at each other in Polish or in English with a heavy Polish accent. It was hilarious when they got on a roll. On a serious side, the Northampton area had a huge Polish population, making the troopers' ability to converse in Polish invaluable. Joe and I kept at our conversation for several minutes, while Mike continued to answer the phone, call after call, nonstop.

When there was a momentary pause in the calls, I glanced at Mike, noticing that he had folded his arms across his chest and was staring straight ahead. The phone resumed its incessant cry once more, and Mike made no move toward it.

Four, five, six, seven times it sounded. What the hell is he doing just sitting there like a bump, I thought. With a last swig of my coffee, I pushed my chair away from the wall and started to get up just as Mike answered, in his thickest Polish accent.

"Ah-loh. Polish Bak-ery, Mike speaking."

"Hello? State Police?" asked the excited caller.

"No-gots stat po-lice," replied Mike. CLICK.

I slapped a hand over my mouth to keep from spraying coffee everywhere. Tears began rolling down my cheeks, mixing with the coffee oozing through my fingers and running down the front of my shirt.

The phone was ringing again, and Mike answered.

"Ah-loh. Polish Bakery, Mike speaking."

"Hello? Is this the state police?" The same man was on the phone sounding a little desperate.

"You wait," Mike said into the phone as he held it away from his ear and yelled to Joe.

"Hey, Joe, you gots stat po-lice?"

"No gots stat po-lice—got rye bread," replied Joe.

"Am sorry. We n'gots stat police—only gots rye bread." CLICK.

That did it. Joe and Mike laughed uncontrollably. Joe's face was a contorted mix of pain and pleasure. Clutching his belly with both hands, he pleaded to the Almighty, "No, no more, please stop, no more."

Still again, the phone began to ring. I could hear it, but knew the other two couldn't. It was probably just as well, because neither of them could talk anyway. Wiping my cheeks with the back of my hand, and my stomach still fluttering with laughter, I took a couple of deep breaths to gain control, then with one final breath, I answered.

"State Police, Northampton, Trooper Stevens."

The unmistakable voice of a telephone operator was on the line.

"I have your call now, sir, go ahead."

"Oh, operator, oh, thank God! You got through. Hello? Hello, officer? Do you have any snow up there?"

Magnolia

The winter of 1969 to 1970 in Northampton seemed to have no shortage of snowstorms. My impression, not supported by actual facts, was that we continually patrolled in snow, sleet, wind, and freezing rain. Once more, not supported by any facts whatsoever, I believed the worst weather most often made its appearance on the night shifts.

When thinking back to my first winter at Russell, and specifically to February 22–28, 1969, I'm intrigued, for that was the week of the infamous hundred-hour New England snowstorm, and I don't remember it. I don't recall being out in any large snowstorms that winter, except while searching for the lost deer hunter.

That hundred-hour period marked the occurrence of the longest snowstorm in recorded history across New England. Boston got 26 inches, Pinkham Notch in New Hampshire received 130 inches throughout February, and Mount Washington got 164 inches. The entire monumental event must have leaped right over the Town of Russell, or maybe my memory had begun to fail, for I have no other explanation.

Reminiscing on a particular patrol, and one of my favorite anecdotes, I was assigned to cover the entire Northampton area, except for Route 91, because we were short personnel, leaving me to cover twenty-one towns. Thankfully, about a third had organized departments, which meant the other fourteen were mine. I prayed for a quiet midnight-to-8:00 a.m. shift.

At 2:00 a.m., traveling south on Route 116, it was hard to see the road in front of the cruiser with the snow and sleet driven hard by the wind. Wipers on high and defrosters blowing full speed could barely keep the windshield clear. Off to my left, and barely visible except for the brilliant dorm lights, sat the University of Massachusetts' southwest dormitory towers. No doubt the students were up late studying, or more likely partying.

The weather was making it a long shift. About the only good thing having a large territory to cover meant that I could stay on the main roads unless sent elsewhere. Priorities mattered as well, so as much as possible, I kept to the center of my patrol area, never too far away from any one place. Hopes for a quiet night were dashed when the radio awoke.

"Station L to cruiser 478," said the dispatcher.

Station L was the radio code for Northampton and cruiser 478 was me.

"L to 478," came the call again.

"478 is on L," I answered.

"L to 478, report of a hit-and-run accident on Route 9 in Goshen, with unknown personal injury."

I gave a simple "received" and headed out.

A hit-and-run accident with unknown personal injury wasn't as bad a call as it might sound. Most often, bad accidents with significant personal injuries were described as such, with many calls reporting it. I'd investigated many hit-and-runs, usually involving a lot of leg work, but we actually solved quite a few. Motor vehicle accidents were frequent and a routine part of any patrol; fatals and other serious events were not routine, and, thankfully, not as frequent. I hoped the hit-and-run wouldn't be too hard; actually, it was better than driving around all night dealing with stranded motorists who had run off the road or out of gas. One would be surprised how often people decide they need a loaf of bread during a storm, then end up as a tree ornament because their car didn't have snow tires. Almost every time I come across a driver who had a mishap for a lack of snow tires, I remember a similar story of a Connecticut State Trooper.

The Connecticut State Police were assigned cruisers of their own for patrol and limited personal use. The cars were unmarked, and the roof lights could be put on or taken off as need be. The CSP instituted a policy mandating troopers put chains on their cruisers during storms. It was a good policy. Police everywhere have favorable working relationships with gas stations, garages, tow companies, and the like. The CSP, being no different, would head to the nearest garage to get the chains mounted during heavy snows. The troopers were quick to adhere to the policy, because both Connecticut and Massachusetts took a really dim view of cruiser accidents. Disciplinary action was fast and severe if the officer was faulted.

Contrary to the belief of some, troopers are human, and being lazy comes just as easy to a trooper as it does to a plumber. No offense meant to plumbers. Regardless, this particular trooper was one of the lazy ones, deciding he needn't bother having his chains mounted. That is, until he skidded off an icy road into a deep ditch landing the cruiser upside down.

Although this officer may have been lazy, he certainly wasn't dumb, nor one to panic. Before calling his station to report the accident, he got his chains from the trunk, climbed onto the cruiser's undercarriage, and began mounting the chains. A woman driving by the scene just after it happened raced to the next phone booth (before all the phone booths disappeared) to report the crash. She described, in explicit detail, the scene of the trooper's accident to the sergeant on the desk. Concerned for the trooper's condition, he interrupted the woman to ask if the officer was injured.

"Oh, no," replied the woman. "When I saw the officer standing on the top of his patrol car, I stopped and asked if he was all right. He told me he would be fine, just as soon as he got his chains on."

The drive to Goshen on Route 9 was mostly uphill, about sixteen miles from where I got the call, and I hoped no one was injured because it was going take a while to get there. Activating the overhead blue lights, I increased my speed as fast as I dared to go. One of the first lessons troops learned during break-in was the necessity of actually *getting* to any scene before you could help. Wrecking along the way meant no help to anyone, and it was something I always remembered, especially at very high speeds.

Entering Goshen some thirty minutes later, the snow had lessened along the two-lane winding road, making it easier to see, but it was still sleeting heavily. A set of headlights pierced my windshield through the sleet, and in the road ahead someone waved a red light. Fortunately, there was little traffic. Anything coming downhill from the other direction would have trouble stopping.

Drawing near, I could make out a large snow-covered form lying in the middle of the road. Stepping from the cruiser, it took me several seconds to realize that I was looking at a horse, a very large horse. Scratch that, a huge horse. Even with its coating of sleet and snow I could tell the animal was dark brown from its long thick coat of winter hair. A portion of the poor animal's belly had been gorged, spilling intestines far and wide. Thankfully, it was dead. Blood covered and spotted the snow ten feet on either side of the road, and its bulk, more or less, blocked both lanes, leaving little room for a car to be guided around the carcass.

I'd seen many collisions with deer, and even though deer are much smaller than horses they can cause a lot of damage, often requiring the car to be hauled away. Here there was no other vehicle at the scene, and the fact that whatever hit the animal had driven away only confirmed that it was big. First things first, the road had to be opened, then I would talk to witnesses, if any, and find whatever evidence might be lying about.

John Emery introduced himself, telling me the horse was his, and that he and his family had owned the small farm alongside the road all their lives.

"What 'ya gonna do about Magnolia?" asked Mr. Emery, grabbing his snow-covered cap and shaking it off.

"I'm Trooper Stevens, Mr. Emery. I take it that Magnolia is yours?"

"Yup, I've had 'er eight years. I keep 'er over there in the pasture. Don't know how she got herself out."

"Well, first we have to get her out of the road. I can call the Department of Public Works."

Route 9 was a state highway in front of the Emery's property. Even so, I knew the DPW would not be happy with a 3 a.m. call requesting a bucket loader for Magnolia, but I could see no other way to deal with the carcass.

"Trooper, I've got a small dozer in t'barn," offered Emery. "I'd jus' as soon take care of 'er myself."

That suited me just fine. It would have taken the DPW a couple of hours to get there, and I had no desire to spend the rest of the night directing traffic around a dead horse.

Mr. Emery's son, Scott, handled traffic while we waited for the dozer. I wanted to find anything that might tell me what happened to Magnolia. Using my flashlight and the cruiser headlights I searched the ground as my boots crunched broken glass, which surely belonged to whatever had hit the horse. The eastbound lane on the downhill side of Magnolia had the most litter. Presumably, the vehicle that killed Magnolia was going eastbound downhill, but there was always a possibility the driver swerved lanes to avoid the horse. Magnolia would never tell me her side of the story.

In hindsight, I regretted taking a shortcut through Northampton toward Goshen instead of following Route 9 all the way. Had I stayed on Route 9, the odds were good that I'd have seen the hit-and-run vehicle.

Dismissing my what-if thoughts, I noticed a piece of chrome sticking out from beneath Magnolia. Taking hold, I wiggled it out from under the animal and brushed off the snow. It was a large piece of grill from a car, possibly a General Motors product. Continuing my walk along the edge of the eastbound lane I sought anything that might add a piece to the puzzle. If the point of impact was, in fact, headed east down the hill, then more debris would be found in front of Magnolia, which is where I picked a hubcap off the ground. Luck was with me, for in another few minutes it would have been covered with snow and I would have missed it. Feeling quite sure the hit-and-run vehicle was most likely a Buick or an Oldsmobile, I tried imagining how the car must have looked after the collision, and how anyone could have possibly driven it away. It had to be a wreck.

I was placing the scraps of metal and hubcap in my cruiser when I heard Emery's bulldozer approach. It looked like a midsize Caterpillar or Case. Many farm owners would have a bulldozer or backhoe for a myriad of tasks. There were always boulders, stumps, and piles of dirt to be moved, as well as towing broken or heavy equipment, and burying dead horses.

I joined Mr. Emery and his son in the middle of the road and raised my hand to stop a small pickup truck approaching the horse. I hadn't been paying much attention, but I believe it was only the third vehicle to drive by. Emery stopped the dozer several feet from Magnolia. In his hand he held a length of chain that he wrapped around her rear legs. Then he jumped back onto the machine and slowly dragged Magnolia off the road. Once off the roadway, he made two quick turns, and with its blade lowered he pushed Magnolia into a corner of the yard.

"I'll bury her tomorrow," Mr. Emery said to his son as I approached. "I don't think t' frost is too deep. It'll be hard diggin' for a foot or so, but after that it will be okay."

I didn't say so, but whatever they wanted to do with Magnolia was fine with me, because, as a city boy, I had no idea what anyone did with a dead horse.

"I picked up a couple more pieces of car out there in the road, Mr. Emery. I'm pretty sure I know what we're lookin' for. Now all we have to do is find it. Did anyone in the house hear the accident?"

"We didn't hear a thing," offered Scott.

Then Emery added, "I woke up and had t' pee. I remembered when I was gettin' back t' bed that I forgot t' put more wood in the stove after supper. In t' kitchen I looked outside t' see how much snow we got when I saw Magnolia in t' road. I musta got up right after it happened—couldn't been more than a few minutes. I don't think she suffered none. I think she died right when she fell."

I told the Emerys about the radio call that I made to the barracks while I was moving the cruiser from the road to their yard. With information provided to the dispatcher he would broadcast a BOLO (Be On the Lookout) message over the radio to the area police departments. He would briefly relate the incident and give a description of a heavily damaged Oldsmobile or Buick possibly heading east on Route 9. It would be followed up with a teletype message containing more details. There wasn't much else I could do for the Emerys. I'd taken a picture of Magnolia, the scene, and taken all my measurements. Saying goodbye to the father and son, I told them I'd be in touch when

I knew anything. I was hoping for some luck on this, because there were never many witnesses to things in the middle of the night.

It was 3:50 a.m. when I finished a much-needed Dunkin Donuts coffee. Leaving the parking lot with four hours left on my shift, I decided to check some of the side roads off Route 9 to find the culprit—that car couldn't have gotten very far. After exploring two roads I got a radio call. I had paid slight attention to the radio chatter from the six Troop B substations, but it had been steady all night. Russell had a personal injury accident, three accidents in Pittsfield, and a crazy husband took a wild shot at his wife in Shelburne Falls. Wondering what might be next for me, I grabbed the mike and answered.

"478 is on L."

"L to 478, Amherst PD believes they have the party involved in your hit-and-run at their station. They're requesting you stop there."

"Received, en route," was my reply.

From the Chief on down, the officers on the Amherst Police Department were the most crazy wonderful bunch of cops you'd ever want to meet, unless, of course, you happen to be a bad guy.

The Chief, John Hurt, was for some unknown reason allowed to also work as a court officer when the Hampshire County Superior Court was in session. His good friend, and APD's midnight desk officer, Fred Sanford, also worked with the Chief at courthouse. Hurt was in his late sixties and for some reason reminded me Winston Churchill, only bigger. He had a full head of white hair and a red nose that stood out magnificently against his pasty white complexion. If he put on a red stocking hat and grew a beard, he'd make a good Santa as well. His most distinguishing feature was his voice—always overly loud, deep, and gravelly. No one ever mistook who was speaking when the Chief had anything to say. Fred Sanford was almost the same age as the Chief, yet his build was slim. His eyes were brown, nearly matching the color of his thinning short cut hair. A long nose and medium complexion finished the picture. Physically, they were almost complete opposites, but together they were quite a pair.

An interesting tale involving the Chief and Fred is the story of a prisoner transport they made to Walpole State Prison, since renamed Cedar Junction. On this particular day a man had been convicted on multiple charges of bestiality, which at the time was a felony in Massachusetts. The offender was a laborer working at a local farm who apparently fell in love with the farm's sheep, goats, and quite possibly some other livestock—but they weren't talking or complaining. In any case, the two court officers began their prisoner transport before lunchtime. Fred was doing the driving and the Chief was in the backseat with the animal lover.

They hadn't gone far before the prisoner complained that he hadn't been given lunch and was hungry. The officers weren't going to stop for him, or for themselves, and told him to just suck it up; he'd get fed when he got to the prison. Persistent, though, he complained all the way to Walpole.

Arriving at the prison, they pulled onto a long approach road leading to the entrance. Having just turned onto the drive they came upon a farm wagon being drawn by a horse and driven by a prisoner moving slowly along the side of the road. Prisoners often worked on the grounds doing all sorts of chores, so the wagon was nothing unusual. The Chief, sitting behind Fred, spotted the wagon up ahead and told Fred to pull alongside. As they did, the Chief opened the rear door, jumped out, and grabbed a handful of hay from the wagon. Then jumping back in, he threw the hay into the prisoner's lap.

"What's this?" asked the angry prisoner.

"It's lunch," replied the Chief. "If it's good enough for your girlfriends, it's good enough for you."

The APD was always a frequent stop during patrol. The troops at Northampton enjoyed the best of relations with Amherst. That's not to say relations with the other departments were bad, it's just that Amherst was special. Troopers could walk into the PD, ask for the world and most likely they'd get it. The reverse was true as well.

I arrived at the PD a little after 4:30. The police department was located in the basement of the Town Hall, just off the common in the center of town. To the south of the common was Amherst College and to the north was the UMass campus. The common was quite beautiful as I drove up to the station. Only one item in the picture marred the beautiful freshly covered snow scene, and that was a nearly demolished black Buick. It was sitting at the curb directly in front of the police department. Parking behind the Buick, I grabbed my clipboard and a few accident reports without ever taking my eyes off the car. It was totaled. To describe the vehicle as it sat there was a challenge. To imagine that the car had been driven eighteen miles to get to where it was parked was impossible.

To begin, the roof was caved in, almost touching the top of the steering wheel. From a side view the vehicle looked half its normal height. The windshield was gone, both front doors were ajar, and I don't know what held them shut. The hood ornament was sheared off, probably inside Magnolia somewhere. The hood itself had been buckled backwards and then flattened, more than likely resting atop the engine's carburetor. Nothing of the front grill remained, nor of the left headlight. The bumper dangled an inch or two above the ground, and had surely dragged along the highways on the trek to Amherst. Steam hissed from the space previously occupied by the grill, and radiator fluid had melted a large puddle of snow underneath the car. The left fender buckled six inches from its original shape, and the tire was severely sliced. Only God would know why it wasn't flat, and the hubcap in my cruiser matched the three that remained on the car. The final clue was a handful of brown horsehair I lifted from the bumper. Yup, I'd say, without doubt, I had the murder weapon.

I walked into the station and was greeted by Fred Sanford from the desk.

"What's happenin', Fred?"

"Nothin' Troop, how you doin'?"

"I'm okay but I'll be glad when it's time to go home," I said.

"Can't say I blame ya," replied Fred with a smile. Then, nodding toward a side room he said, "He's in there."

"Okay, thanks." Then I turned and opened the door to the interrogation room. Officer Gordie James sat at the desk in front of me. He had just poured two cups of coffee and handed one to his guest in the corner. "You want one, Randy?" asked Gordy. I nodded. "Yes, cream and sugar, please."

Seated in a chair, huddled and shivering in the corner of the room was a small figure of a man holding his coffee with both hands. His face was beet red and his lips were purple, except for the white of an old scar that began just below his septum and disappeared into his upper lip. His eyebrows and grey hair were covered with melting ice, and his clothes were soaked from the waist up. Seeing this pathetic looking man, I could envision him driving through the sleet and snow with only his face for a windshield. It was in the next moment, when Gordy handed me my coffee, that I noticed the collar around his neck.

Gordy's introduction was formal. "Trooper Randy Stevens, this is Father John Ayres of Saint Brigid's Catholic Church here in Amherst." I knew, right then and there, that Jesus had taken the wheel of that car to get it to Amherst.

The predicament was a hard one for me. I'd just started my second year on the job, and I was still missing a whole lot of experience. Another, more seasoned, officer would have filled out the paperwork to cover the accident; known that the insurance company would pay for the damages; would file no charges against the priest, and would accept the fact that he reported the incident to the APD. However, the inexperienced young tended to see things as black and white, because it was easier that way. They also didn't know any better. Things were right or wrong, and laws were written to follow—simple. I wanted to see, and use, the gray as it could be applied to this accident. I just didn't know how I would justify it on paper to my superiors. I decided to go one step at a time and began with a conversation. "Nice to meet you, Father," I said, more nervous than he was, as I readied my pen to a pink accident report.

Our conversation went easily. I instantly liked the man. He was gentle and soft-spoken with a little lisp, obviously from the old scar. He had a genuinely warm smile, as one might expect from a man of the cloth. The fact that I was raised Catholic had nothing to do with my fondness for him, because I'd met several priests that I didn't like at all.

With the necessary information complete on all the forms, I began feeling anxious again. Father Ayres knew every officer in the station, which made me uncomfortable in view of the decision I had to make.

"So, Father," I began. "You left the scene of the accident and it was two hours before you reported it. The farmhouse was right there and the road was almost completely blocked. What I mean is, I don't want to cite you with hit-and-run, but you've got to give me something to account for filing the accident with no charges."

There, I had said it. Now the priest was going to have to give me a reason I could use.

Father Ayres sat for a moment or two before I saw the hint of a smile as he started to speak.

"Trooper," he began. "I don't know what to tell you, I really don't. I was in shock and scared after hitting the horse. My mind was a blur. I couldn't focus. I remember getting out of the car, I was cold, I was shivering and shaking. There was blood everywhere and the horse was still kicking when I walked up to it. I felt so sorry. When it stopped moving, I knew it had died, so I, instinctively, did what priests do—I prayed. After a few minutes I got into the car and drove off, hoping that I could make it to the Amherst Police. I had gone about halfway when my mind started to replay the awful event. It was during those thoughts, when I realized that I had just given the Last Rites of the Church to a horse."

Father Ayres was staring down at the table with a stone serious look on his face as Gordy and I started to laugh at the priest's admission. He perked up with our laughter, realizing the amusement of what he had just said, and broke down giggling himself. Gordy got us a second cup of coffee as Father recounted the whole episode to Fred and another officer who had come into the station. Amherst called for a tow truck to remove the car from the front of the PD, and I drove Father Ayres home to the church rectory.

I submitted the hit-and-run report the next day, and I documented everything exactly as it had happened with no charges filed against Father Ayres. I had learned a lot that night, discovering there *are* gray areas and possibly things were best handled by bending a rule, or a law, or at times, ignoring them altogether.

In December 1970, Father Ayres performed the wedding ceremony for Marion and me.

Yellow Trucks

Spring was late in 1970, taking its sweet time as it sometimes does. Raw rainy days were the most frequent menu item Mother Nature served for winter's recovery. A few forsythias started to blossom, but halted awaiting warmer days, along with the tulips and crocuses still in hiding.

The mood at the barracks was light, everyone was in good spirits. Winter had been a long slog with too many storms and hundreds of accidents throughout Troop B. Change was coming and the troops were ready.

The cast of character personalities wearing state police uniforms was as varied as a jar of jellybeans. Every station had an officer, or two, who could only be described as truly unique. One officer I would describe as unique, or a little different, was Bruce Swift. Bruce was senior to me by several years. He was a worker, making more arrests and solving more cases than anyone else in the barracks, but he could be a little rough around the edges. Swift was of medium height and build, had black hair, dark brown eyes, and a rough complexion. Smiles didn't come often— one rarely saw a sense of humor from him, and he was described by many as distant and unapproachable. In my opinion, it was his outward appearance that caused most of his public relations issues. More to the point, people, even troopers, tended to be careful, cautious, and I'd go so far as to say fearful around him.

I was with Bruce almost every day, except for an occasional change of assignments, for as line mates we worked the same days and shifts. I got along with him just fine, and he had saved my butt more than once from being seriously hurt. I'm not saying that he had never been ill-mannered or discourteous to the public, but I hadn't seen it. He got his share of letters complaining about his actions, prompting higher-ups to scrutinize his behavior and provide counseling, which in those days was a highly professional ass-chewing with threats of a transfer. I learned fairly early to set the tone with anyone that I had encounters with, be it a speeder or a felon. I believe that Bruce, because of his intense expressions, was perceived as aggressive before he even opened his mouth. Timid individuals would not usually argue with or challenge him, but in the end they would discover that Bruce had treated them fairly. Those choosing a belligerent or combative stance received more than they had bargained for, with things going badly for them after that point.

Bruce was an enigma, even for his brother troopers. I suspected he harbored a deep insecurity, but about what, I didn't know.

Many of the troops who had worked with him were standoffish, simply because they were unable to figure him out, and quite frankly, few could. I never felt threatened or intimidated by Bruce, only intrigued, and treated him like everyone else. Maybe that was the basis of our good relationship.

One day the troop mechanics wanted my cruiser for a few hours to do a brake job. The sergeant had me double up with Bruce for the rest of the afternoon, so after delivering my cruiser we went to Route 91, where we wrote a number of good quality Vs (violations). Bruce was his normal stern self and treated everyone respectfully. Finishing with a motorist and sending him on his way, we hadn't gone a mile before pulling over behind a new Mercedes in the breakdown lane with a flat tire.

Bruce got out first and strode up to the driver's door, while I waited outside by the right front fender. I noticed the car had MD (medical doctor) plates.

From where I stood, I heard Bruce politely tell the operator that we would call him a tow truck, or if he had AAA, we'd call them to come out and change the tire. I couldn't hear what the operator was saying, but could plainly see that he was animated and holding his car keys out the window toward Bruce. Bruce took a half step backward holding both hands up, palms forward, suggesting a *no* to whatever the motorist had in mind. The operator opened his door and started to get out, but Bruce took a step forward so he couldn't open the door any wider.

Motorists frequently want to get out of their cars to walk around or "discuss" things with an officer while traffic is passing within a few feet at sixty-five miles per hour. They don't realize how utterly dangerous it is, so we don't allow it, unless it's absolutely necessary or unavoidable. You can bet your life's savings that if we allowed a motorist onto the highway and he or she was struck, injured, or killed, we'd be hit with lawsuits.

Bruce calmly asked the operator to stay in the car for his own safety, but the Mercedes man was having no part of it, and plainly demanded that we change his tire. Hearing that, I slid onto the front seat and radioed for a tow truck to either change the man's tire or tow him off the interstate. It would be his choice.

I picked up bits and pieces of the conversation. He was a doctor. What was he paying taxes for if we wouldn't change his flat? What's your badge number? What's your name? How dare we tell him that he couldn't get out of his car, blah, blah. Bruce was stoic, taking the doctor's abuse without batting an eye, as the man slammed the car door and rolled up his window. We stood by as the tow truck driver changed the flat before we drove off. Bruce was unflustered and carried on exactly as he had before the exchange with the doctor. I don't change tires, was the only comment that Bruce made, and I detected no anger.

It must have been the day for bad tires, or nails, because heading back to the station we came upon another car with a flat. This one was on a VW Beetle. Pulling up to the rear of the Beetle I noticed two young ladies standing outside the car, safely beyond the guard rails. They'd had their arms wrapped around each other as we approached, then unwrapped themselves and held hands while walking to my side of the cruiser. I guessed the women were gay, which was fine with me. I didn't care or have a problem with them, but I wondered about Bruce's attitude. I waited for his signal for me to call a wrecker.

I had never personally seen or heard stories from, or about, officers mistreating anyone because of color or sexual orientation. I wasn't so naïve as to believe that it didn't exist in places or in some individuals, but it wasn't prevalent in the universe of police that I worked in. Had it been so, I would have known the extent. Secrets were never well kept.

Well, I must admit that what Bruce did next astonished me, upheld my belief in him, and cemented his status as an enigma. He asked the women if they had a spare tire and a jack. When they answered yes, he asked for the keys to the trunk and proceeded to change their tire. Go figure. I would have never imagined. I helped.

Trooper Al Delisle was another character, quite the opposite of Bruce. Al had jet black hair which he kept at medium length, barely short enough to meet MSP requirements. He had a fair complexion with brown eyes that seemed to have a perpetual gleam of playfulness. The guy was also in great shape, strong, and one wouldn't want to be on his bad side. Al's demeanor was naturally friendly and personable. Everybody liked him for his smile and fun-loving sense of humor. And he was a prankster.

Delisle and five other Northampton troopers were assigned to the 55 Team. During the oil crisis of the early 1970s the Federal Government lowered the speed on the country's interstate highways from sixty-five to fifty-five miles per hour. As part of the implementation of the new speed limit, the Feds issued grants to the states for enforcement of the new rule. Massachusetts set up "55 teams," whose primary duty was to run radar on the interstates. Some guys loved the assignment, but it wasn't for me. I had no interest in running radar traps all day long, everyday. I had had enough trouble being on the occasional radar detail because of my issues with red and green colors. A radar operator would routinely call out something like, "The green Chevy in the passing lane at 86." Now, that would seem simple enough, but waiting at the pickup spot ready to wave over the offender, I'd watch the three lanes of traffic bearing down on me, with three Chevys in the passing lane, and I often had no idea which one was green.

The 1970s gave birth to one of the decade's biggest fads, the Citizens Band radio. Though CB radio actually started in the 1940s, and although they were most popular with truck drivers, the oil crisis made them popular with the general motoring public. It was a tool for finding out which stations had gas available, and how long the waits in line were.

Hollywood soon got on board with movies like *Convoy*, then *Smokey and the Bandit*, along with TV shows like the *Dukes of Hazard*. Everyone had a handle, or name, they adopted to identify themselves when talking on the CB. Kind of like chat rooms today. There was Road Runner, Hot Dog, Dice Man, and thousands more. Not to be outdone by the male population there was Kitten, Big Dolly, Long legs, Georgia on Your Mind, and Fast Sally. Interestingly, a lot of the handles chosen by the ladies had obvious sexual connotations.

By this time, Massachusetts had begun providing troopers with their own cruisers, but unlike in Connecticut, personal use was not allowed. We were, however, allowed to install CB radios in the cars at our own expense, and most of us did. Truckers used channel 19 to chat back and forth, and most of the public listened in. Users would report accidents and other hazards on the highway, along with providing the location of every "Smokey" working radar or simply parked on the road, so troopers listened, too.

Even though the 55 Team guys liked their assignment, it didn't mean they wouldn't succumb to boredom on occasion. Al Delisle was no exception, and a comedic genius some days, who actually created chaos at a number of truck stops along interstate 91. He was fair though, because he divvied up his antics equally between truck stops, and didn't do it very often out of consideration for business.

Keep in mind that the price of gas and diesel fuel had skyrocketed, and not all gas stops had fuel, often running out without notice. Truckers and the general public were always monitoring the availability, falling right into Al's scheme.

Parked in a rest area not far from a targeted truck stop, Trooper Delisle keyed his CB mic on channel 19 and began to broadcast with the deep southern drawl of an out-of-state driver passing through Massachusetts.

"Breaker 19, breaker 19, Tennessee Jimmy hea' come back, y'all."

Motorists didn't often engage with the truckers when they called out, but it only took a few seconds before a trucker answered.

"Hey, Tennessee, you got Side Car here, come on."

"Yeah, Side Car, did y'all go on by that exit 2-4, that Maverick Diner stop?" asked "Trooper" Tennessee Jimmy.

"No, man, how's the food? I gotta stop somewhere, I'm goin' up t' Brattleboro to make a drop."

"Tennessee back at y'all, I jus' ate. Th' foods good, but they be givin' away ten free gallons o' diesel to truckers for the next hour and they jus' started. An' they be givin' five-dollar meal coupons to regular cars that come t' eat. Bes' make some time, Side Car, so y'all don' miss out."

Every trucker and motorist within range heard the broadcast, which was instantly repeated by others, starting the rush to cash in. Troopers in the area knew that the trucker, Tennessee Jimmy, was Al. We'd all be sitting, or driving along, listening to the radio chatter spreading news of the free diesel fuel and dinner coupons as we headed for the diner to have a look at the chaos. I'm pretty sure that some of y'all reading this will think it was awful or cruel to pull a stunt like this, so to those offended I'm sorry, but it *was* hysterically funny. And remember we are, after all, human.

I can't speak for today, but during my career the officers of the state police held a great respect for truck drivers, often cutting them a lot of slack for their hard work and long hours. Many, many truckers would stop when they saw a trooper alone on the road in a situation to offer their help. They were appreciated.

Trooper Delisle appreciated the truckers as much as the rest of us, but that didn't mean he wouldn't mess with them. Sitting high on an entrance ramp to the interstate, Al would watch the traffic passing below to pick out just what he was looking for. It wasn't long before a brightly painted tractor trailer with the name E-Z Trucking Co. passed Al's perch. Trailing behind the tractor trailer was a pale-yellow pickup sporting a CB antenna, following along in no particular hurry.

Al let a couple of cars and another truck pass his location before he swept down the ramp to follow Mr. E-Z Trucking and the yellow pickup.

Al then proceeded to introduce himself in the most effeminate, melodious, and lisping voice imaginable.

"Breaker 19, breaker 19, this is Rodney Round-bottom looking for all you big strong truck drivers . . ."

CB radio chatter instantly stopped at Rodney's introduction. Then came, "What or who was that?" from an unknown.

"It's just me, Rodney. Who's this? What's *your* handle?"

From someone else, "Ignore it, he's just some asshole!"

"No, I'm not an asshole. I'm Rodney Round-bottom. I know a lot of you truck drivers. Come on, tell me, what's your handle. I bet it's a cute one."

A new voice, "Oh, God. Where is he, what's he driving? Somebody should run that guy over."

Ignoring the new voice, Al turned Rodney's attention to E-Z Trucking.

Friendly and invitingly, Rodney spoke, "Hey there, Mr. E-Z in the pretty truck. Where ya going?" No reply. Silence.

Rodney tried again. "Your rig, oh, pardon the pun, is really big. Can't we talk and be friends? Wouldn't you like to teach me how to shift your gears?"

Al kept swinging in and out of the passing lane to keep an eye on E-Z Trucking and the yellow pickup, then spoke again.

"Ya know, Mr. E-Z, didn't I meet you in the northbound rest area a couple of weeks ago? I'm sure that was you. If I'm right you were 'Eeee—Zeee'. I never forget a truck."

Exploding onto channel 19 came Mr. E-Z, yelling. "Look you creep get off the radio, YOU SICKO. If I find you, I'll be the one running you over."

"Oh stop, silly, you couldn't run anything over if you tried. Probably got your license at Sears and Roebuck," stabbed Rodney.

Mr. E-Z was furious now, "Where are ya, WHERE ARE YA, YOU ASSHOLE, I'LL RIP YOUR HEAD OFF."

Rodney answered softly and ever so calm, "I'm in the yellow pickup right behind you, Darlin'."

To which, the guy in the yellow pickup, who'd been listening all along, screamed into his mic, "IT AIN'T ME, NOOO, SIR, IT AIN'T ME, I'M NOT RODNEY!"

A few weeks later spring had finally come to the Connecticut River Valley and it was beautiful. I had a rural patrol in the western sector and was looking forward to heading into the hills to see it all. I planned on visiting a few farmers whom I hadn't seen since late fall to see how they were doing and catch up on the goings-on. The main road through the western sector was Route 9, which took me past the spot where Mr. Emery had buried his horse. I laughed again thinking about the snow- and ice-covered Father Ayres administering the Last Rites to Magnolia. My frame of mind couldn't have been better as I looked forward to a peaceful day exploring and reconnecting with friendly acquaintances. Positive thoughts, the day was going to be great.

"Station L to cruiser 478," shouted the radio, robbing me of all the pleasant thoughts.

"478 is on L."

"478, proceed to the Edwards residence on River Road in West Cummington. Meet a cruiser from SP Pittsfield re an A&B with a DW."

"Received," I answered. "Do you have a better 6 (location) on the Edwards house?"

"Stand by one . . . it's on the north side of River Road just before the Windsor State Forest."

"Received, en route."

That was a pretty quick end to all the plans I had for the day. Assault and battery with a dangerous weapon was a serious felony.

Twenty minutes later I arrived at the Edwards' home. A woman came out of the house as I got out of the car and identified herself as Mrs. Edwards. She told me that the other trooper was down the road and that I should go there. Thanking her, I continued along River Road, eventually passing a "Welcome to the Windsor State Forest" sign and pulled up behind cruiser 425 from the Pittsfield Barracks. Trooper Butch Thomas got out of his cruiser and greeted me with smiles and a handshake. I'd gotten to know, and like, Butch while working with him in the past.

In front of his cruiser was a blue 1967 Chevrolet Camaro. The area surrounding the vehicle was marked off with crime scene tape. The windshield, headlights, passenger door, and rear windows were smashed; inside I could see droplets of blood spattered on the front and backseats. The Pittsfield trooper led me to the front of the Camaro, picked a battered baseball bat off the ground, and tossed it inside the car.

Butch told me that the photo and print guys had been to the scene, taken pictures of the car, footprints, tire tracks, the bat, and dusted for prints. The victims were taken to the Berkshire Medical Center in Pittsfield, where Butch was going to meet up with troopers from the DA's office after he secured the Camaro and bat. Butch asked for my help searching the area for the bad guys.

According to Butch, this was the probable abduction of a guy and a girl from Hinsdale, which was a part of Pittsfield's area. The two victims had met with the men in a parking lot concerning some type of business deal. There were four perpetrators, or perps. Two arrived at the meeting in a beat-up yellow Ford pickup truck, and the other two were on Harley motorcycles.

One of the perps got into the backseat of the Camaro with the male victim while the girl drove, supposedly, to a camp somewhere near the Windsor State Forest or in West Cummington. The second perp followed in the yellow truck while the two bikers brought up the rear.

When they got to the Windsor State Forest something went wrong. A fight broke out in the backseat between the two males.

The girl stopped the car and the other three perps joined in. The male victim was beaten unconscious with the bat. They broke the girl's arm with the bat, then beat her with their fists before turning the bat on the Camaro and leaving. The girl made her way to the Edwards home, and Mrs. Edwards called the Pittsfield barracks. Trooper Thomas, an ambulance, and the technicians were dispatched and worked the crime scene before I arrived.

My confusion was answered when I learned that Pittsfield had requested an officer from Northampton's area to help Trooper Thomas with a search of the surrounding towns to find the perps. The radio message that I got never made that clear. Some of the towns were in Northampton's area and some in Pittsfield's, and since the crime actually took place in Windsor, the investigation was Butch's. That was fine with me. I would help search.

We finished picking up after the tow truck removed the Camaro and were almost ready to go when Butch got a call with information on the bad guys. It was somewhat sketchy, but for the time being it was the best they could get from the girl. The male victim was in surgery. The four bad guys were thought to be part of a local gang and their names were unknown. The girl claimed she didn't know them, but thought two names might be Jack and Chuck, no last names. Jack was in the back seat fighting with her friend, but she wouldn't or couldn't tell anymore. The detailed descriptions provided by the young lady were vague and not much help, which was not unusual under the circumstances. She was hiding something and was probably very afraid.

So Butch and I headed out looking for two badass biker guys with leather colors and beards, most likely in the company of the two other, randomly described, bad guys driving a beat-up yellow Ford pickup.

I spent the next couple of hours combing the back roads of West Cummington looking for anything that might be considered a camp, cabin, or some other hideaway with motorcycles and/or a yellow truck parked or hidden on the property. I gave the search a good shot but had no luck. Time to call it a day and return to the barracks.

It felt good to be off the dirt roads and on pavement once again. Cruising eastbound along Route 9 beside the Westfield River was a calming end to a stressful day and search. Up ahead on the left between the highway and the river was the Captain's Den. It was a local watering hole we had been to a few times for fights, but no more so than other distant joints. Passing the Den, I saw a beat-up yellow Ford pickup parked at the front of the building with two cars on either side. Off to the left were parked three Harleys. My heart began to pound.

I drove past and stopped a couple hundred yards past the Den and keyed the radio mic.

"478 to station L." Nothing.

I tried again, "478 to station L." Shit, I thought, I'm in a dead spot.

I thought there would be little chance of contacting Butch, cruiser to cruiser, but I gave it a try hoping that station L might hear me trying to call him—they didn't. There were too many dead radio spots throughout the whole of Troop B, and this one was certainly not fortuitous.

Lord, what do you do? I could have driven off toward the barracks and safety, without anyone ever knowing that I saw a yellow truck and motorcycles—no one except me. I couldn't do it, so I turned around and went back.

I drove into the Den's lot and parked parallel to Route 9 so that looking out my side window I could see the whole front of the building. The Den had an annex on the left side of the establishment with pool tables. The annex/pool room had two swinging barn-style doors at the front that were wide open. The main portion of the structure, to the right, held the bar that was open to the pool tables, letting patrons walk back and forth between the two sections. From where I was parked, I couldn't see the people sitting at the bar. But the three Harleys were parked in front of the pool hall, and the riders inside leaning on their pool cues had just spotted me. Their game of pool stopped to check out the state police cruiser parked just beyond their bikes. Two of the three bikers had scruffy beards. The other was somewhat clean-shaven, but they all had leather vests with the bike club colors, their chains, skull patches, and no doubt, brass knuckles and probably a knife or two, at least. I focused on the one biker who most caught my attention. He was about five feet nine or ten inches tall, his head was huge and mostly square, with hardly a neck that I could see. It looked like his square head just sat on his shoulders. He was wide and big with a huge belly that looked hard as stone. His arms, covered with tattoos, didn't hang straight down at his side. They couldn't. They hung out at an angle as if waiting to grab something, or someone. I hoped it wasn't going to be me.

I took the night stick that I kept stuck between the seat cushions, slid it into my belt ring, unlatched the door handle and stepped out of the cruiser. By now, people at the bar had seen me too. I felt myself shaking and prayed that no one else could see it. Putting on a firm, yet non-confrontational face, I stared at "Square Head" and walked into the pool room as every eye in the place watched. Half turning toward the bar, with an eye still on the bikers, I addressed the afternoon barflies with as much confident as I could muster, "Who owns the yellow pickup truck out front?"

Answered by only a dozen pair of curious eyes, I asked again, louder. "Who owns the yellow pickup truck?" Then, near the far end of the bar, a thin trembling hand was raised high, and an eighty-year-old gentleman weakly admitted, "It's mine, trooper, is there a problem?"

To which, I damn near fainted with relief.

I asked "Square Head" and the other two bikers where they were from and to show me some IDs. They were from Worcester and said they were taking Route 9 on their way into New York. We talked about their Harleys and our state police bikes. They asked if I had ridden them. The fact that I had owned bikes, of one sort or another, since I was sixteen years old, and that I routinely road the SP bikes on patrol seemed to interest them. I suggested, depending on their destination, that they consider taking Route 7 down into Connecticut. If they hadn't been that way before, I told them it was a great ride. These guys were not trouble and weren't looking for it. Sometimes stepping back, giving people a chance and benefit of the doubt, can bring some surprisingly good results.

It Comes in Threes

Police work is occasionally mundane, but it's actually a roller-coaster of emotions. I daresay that over my career I have experienced every emotion. Some were easy to embrace and hold onto, yet I would have gladly avoided others, given a choice.

Although I was involved in numerous criminal investigations, from homicides on down, I have chosen to tell the stories that I remember most fondly, along with some others that I will never forget. And, since I love silly humor, it's no wonder to me that the emotions of happiness, surprise, joy, awkwardness, amusement, sympathy, and excitement account for the majority of my remembrances. On the other side, however, were emotions that I felt too often: anger, fear, horror, pain, disgust, and sadness. They're still with me today, occasionally troubling, but altogether too significant for me to exclude the telling of a few.

As always, the evening shift was my first day back at work, and the desk officer, my current line sergeant, was John Bass. Bass had been extremely hard for me to figure out, never mind get to like, and the fact that he made it difficult didn't help. The sergeant was one of the old-school officers who was never able to make the transition to post-Miranda changes in law enforcement. He was stern, showed little tolerance, especially for the newer troopers, and exhibited no sense of humor that I ever witnessed.

Bass was a former Marine who kept his Marine Corps haircut, now aged to a salt-and-pepper gray. Although he never drank, he had a drinker's nose, a ruddy complexion, and green eyes. At five feet ten inches, his build was stocky, strong, and he walked heavily wherever he roamed. In the barracks he was known as Thunder Boots. The man's face was oval with a slightly square jaw. He looked good in a campaign hat, I'll give him that.

Sergeant Bass was not a favorite of the men. The one habit that made him the most unpopular was when he would round up a team of troopers and take them onto the interstate for radar details. He loved running the radar and calling out speeders to the troops waiting up ahead. There were two problems with being on Bass's detail. One problem was the radar machine itself, because of an operational glitch. When a vehicle entered the radar beam, it caused the needle on the dial to jump to the car's speed. However, inertia caused the needle to shoot past the actual speed of the car, for just an instant, before settling back to the real speed. The "inertia bump" could add ten or more miles per hour, and the faster the car was going, the greater the bump. The second, and most irritating, problem was that Bass radioed the speed with the added bump to the pick-up crew. As one might expect, very nearly every motorist swore they weren't going as fast as the officers said—and wanted to argue. The troopers operated these machines on a daily basis, and they all knew the bump reading was bogus. Bass gave them no choice but to issue the citation, because he kept track of every car's speed and collected the tickets at the end of the detail. The troopers hated him for it, especially because he refused to listen to reason. A few higher-ranking officers had even spoken to him, but it proved useless. It was the sergeant's opinion that both he and the machine were infallible, which added unreasonable ignorance to his list of attributes.

I began my tour with the 1-3-5 area patrol, which was okay with me, because UMass was in the eastern sector and I didn't feel like dealing with the drunken college kids on that side of the river. Early on, I stayed in the lower valley instead of roaming the hill towns, deciding that after dinner I'd go up through Chesterfield to Worthington, then off toward Ashfield. It was a nice warm evening for a rural patrol.

I took my dinner at a favorite Northampton diner, then made the circuit as planned. Returning to the valley via Route 116 into Deerfield, I got a radio call for a bad accident on Chestnut Plain Road in Whately. The report was for serious personal injury, so with lights and siren I sped off Route 116 onto Route 5 south towards Whately. A right turn off Route 5, onto and up Christian Lane, and then a left put me onto Chestnut Plain toward Westbrook Road. I knew the road well, so passing Westbrook I slowed for the hill that curved across a small bridge right at the bottom of the hill.

As I approached the bridge, I saw a VW bus that, at a glance, looked to be parked on the west side of the span. Several residents stood randomly about, and there were two pickup trucks stopped on the far side. Their red lights flashed as two volunteer firemen tended to a bloody someone lying on the ground. Stopping the cruiser, I saw that the VW Bus had broken through the wooden bridge rail and was teetering on the edge of the road deck, ready to topple into the brook. It leaned impossibly over the side. I couldn't imagine how it was balanced. I walked toward the fireman to check the guy on the ground and get an update. They introduced themselves as Bob and Dan. Bob, the older of the two, spoke first, saying they thought the guy was already dead, neither fireman could get a pulse, his eyes were fixed, dilated, and he wasn't breathing. It should be noted that the firemen, police, and the ambulance people were trained in first aid, but they were not EMTs with today's equipment or training. Bob and Dan were both excited, talking rapid-fire, but in control and providing crucial information.

Small towns in those days didn't have full-time fire departments or ambulances, with neighboring towns sometimes actually sharing an ambulance. Fireman Bob said that a firetruck would be on the way shortly and the ambulance had been called. This was not unusual. Part-time police, fire, and ambulance responders would most often receive a call at home, or on a pager, then drive to their station to pick up the emergency vehicle and go. They were great people, but that was the extent and nature of rural emergency services back then. With ambulances routinely slow to arrive, or occasionally unable to respond at all, troopers transported many a victim with life-threatening injuries to hospitals in the backseat of a cruiser.

Fireman Dan interrupted Bob's update to tell me that we had to go help his brother Jimmy in the back of the van.

"Was he in the accident?" I asked a little confused.

"No, he came with me, there's other people hurt and we can't get them out. This guy here was the driver. You can't see from here, but the bridge rail went into the truck and that's the only thing holding it up."

Bob stayed with the driver on the ground to cover him with a blanket as Dan and I went to the bus. One look at the gruesome interior told it all.

The Volkswagen came down the hill at a pretty good clip, and for an unknown reason veered to the right side of the road and struck the end of the three-inch by ten-inch wooden bridge rail. The rail pierced the front of the bus like a javelin, dead center, just below the VW emblem, splitting the dashboard in two. The driver's side dashboard and steering wheel struck the driver with tremendous blunt force, ramming and squashing him against the driver's door and pinning him there. The passenger side dashboard hit, and trapped, a female passenger against her door. She was hurt, hysterical, in pain, and crying to get out, but the only way was a twelve-foot drop out her door to the brook below. The wooden railing passed between the two front seats, eviscerating the passenger seated behind the driver, and ripping into the side of the other backseat rider. Fireman Dan's brother Jimmy was inside leaning over the rail between the front seats trying to calm the girl, and every time he moved the bus became more unstable. The compartment was a bloodbath.

We needed to get the injured out soon, and, again, the only way out for the female was through her door. The two in the backseat needed to be removed through the rear hatchway, but the old oak bridge railing, after skewering the rear passengers, continued into the back compartment. To pull the massive railing out would be impossible—it would have to be cut, but it was the only thing holding the bus from falling into the brook.

With the ambulance, fire truck, and its volunteers still among the missing, we had to make do. So we first asked if any one of the bystanders had a chain saw. Helpless, expressionless, faces stared back until one man, almost reluctantly, said he would get his saw. Next, I recruited the hesitant spectators and put them to work. I didn't ask, I told them, with urgency, to grab hold of the teetering bus so it wouldn't fall while Jimmy and I were inside.

With all my heart, I am thankful and appreciative of all the bystanders I have encountered over the years, who unselfishly rolled up their sleeves and got a little dirty in order to help those seriously injured. Having said that, my opinion of the others, who just stood around watching, unwilling to lift a finger, would not be kind.

A few minutes later the "saw man" returned with a crosscut handsaw from his toolbox. Good God! It was going to be a challenge cutting the rock hard, ancient, oak rail with a handsaw.

Gingerly, I climbed inside with Jimmy and positioned myself to begin sawing. One man in the back was unconscious, the other was unconscious forever. The girl in the front became more hysterical, screaming uncontrollably as she looked around at the carnage. Neither Jim nor I could calm her, so he held onto the rail as I sawed. We needed to cut it as far forward as possible to clear the front and rear seat compartments. Jim and I sawed like mad men and were three quarters of the way through when the fire truck and ambulance showed up. Jim jumped out to see if they had a chainsaw, and to our relief they did. I didn't want any more weight in the bus, so Jim came back inside and finished the cut in about ten seconds.

I'm still unsure why it took so long for a tow truck to get to the scene, but the driver went to work right away hooking a chain to the bus to prevent it from going over the side. Once secure, Jimmy and I passed the two male passengers out the back door, then attempted to calm the female while the wrecker pulled the bus back from the brink. Once safely on the road, the ambulance attendants removed the girl onto a stretcher, placed her next to the surviving male in the ambulance, and headed to the hospital. Unknown to me, a second ambulance from Northampton had arrived and had already taken the dead to the hospital. The savvy Northampton ambulance driver told fireman Dan, even knowing the men were obviously dead, they were going to take the bodies to the hospital and have them pronounced dead there. If they hadn't done that, I would have had to call the Medical Examiner to get his permission, or wait for him to come to the scene before removing the corpses, and I had enough to do.

The female and male who left the scene alive recovered. Neither of them knew what made the driver crash into the bridge. My guess was that he was just going too fast. Anyway, that's how I wrote it up, taking with me the gut-wrenching emotions of horror, disgust, anger, and sadness that would stay with me for a long time.

The next morning, I was scheduled to work a day shift in the station area, but Sergeant Bass, for reasons known only to him, wanted me on Route 91. So, with no rationale explaining the change, I went into the bright sunshine to ride the interstate.

Traffic had been very heavy, but the day was uneventful. I helped a couple of disabled motorists but didn't write any citations. After yesterday, I didn't feel much like interacting with anyone, let alone a motorist. I was nearing the southern end of the stretch of my patrol, where the road opened up from two lanes into three, just before the Riverdale Road exit. A half mile into the three-lane section I pulled into the breakdown lane and stopped, for no particular reason that I remember, except maybe to collect my thoughts, I guess. The highway curved slightly to the left at this juncture, so I parked a little cockeyed, giving myself a better view of the approaching cars.

Five or six minutes had passed when a motorcyclist rode his bike from the middle lane over into the breakdown lane and stopped about two hundred feet behind me. Thinking that he might have had a mechanical problem, I watched to see if he got off the bike. He obviously didn't have a problem and wasn't dismounting, because he kept looking over his left shoulder at the oncoming traffic, so I figured he was waiting for an opening to reenter the travel lane and continue his journey. He wasn't, and didn't wait for an opening, either. Instead, he made a U-turn right in front of, and into, three lanes of oncoming traffic. I watched, aghast, as an 18-foot box truck struck the motorcycle broadside. The bike and rider were dragged sixty or seventy feet before the truck, with brakes and blue smoking tires locked, ran over the motorcycle and its rider. Cars skidded and careened in every direction to avoid joining the collisions. All I could hear was the screaming of tires on pavement as I watched, and heard, the car behind the truck hit and bounce over the biker's mangled body.

I was on the radio in an instant begging for all the help I could get before someone else got run over, most likely me, since I was the one standing in the middle of the tangled mess dodging cars and trying to stop traffic. When a thing of this nature happens, all else, like yesterday, is forgotten to deal with the now.

Traffic was a shambles, people had gotten out of their cars to help or more likely to gawk. Either way, I wanted them to get back into their cars and stay there. I needed reinforcements before clearing a path through the shambles to begin cleaning things up. Three blankets in two lanes hid the poor motorcyclist from the spectators.

The accident wasn't as hard to cover, or investigate, as many others had been. The cyclist was the only victim. No one else was injured—in shock, yes, but injured, no—and I was grateful for that. Personal, insurance, and vehicle information from the truck driver and the young lady who also drove over the biker, along with their brief statements to be put into the report, and my own detailed statement about what I had witnessed were all that was necessary. Family and friends swore the twenty-seven-year-old biker was untroubled and happy, and we never learned the reason he turned into the oncoming traffic.

Help quickly cleared the scene and traffic flowed once again. The day shift was complete, and I headed north to the barracks for supper, once more reliving the emotions of horror, sadness, anger, and disgust from the day before. Today, I added fear.

I couldn't wait for the three-day tour to end. I wasn't only weary, but emotionally drained as well. Sleep didn't come for a long time after supper. My alarm went off at 11:15 p.m., and the shower didn't help my spirits or the tiredness I carried downstairs to be greeted by the ever "jovial" Sergeant Bass before my midnight shift.

"So, Trooper, you had quite a day, I see," Bass said.

I didn't know if that was a question or a statement but ignored it anyway. I wasn't up for any conversation with my duty sergeant. All I wanted was out the door to finish my last shift before starting time off.

My line mate, Trooper Woody Banes, walked past the office door on his way to the garage level to start his own midnight shift.

"Hey, Woody, wait up," I yelled following him out the door.

I stopped myself at the doorway, then turned toward Sergeant Bass. "Are we all good, Sarge? You need me anymore?"

A wave of dismissal was all I got as I caught Woody in the kitchen.

"Hey, what's up?" he asked.

"Nothin', I can't deal with him tonight. Let's go."

I waved a "see ya later" at Woody as he pulled out of the driveway, then I gave my cruiser a quick wash and cleaned the film coating from the inside of my windshield. I had never known the origin of this mysterious windshield film until reading that it came from the plastic inside our vehicles. Plastic heated by the sun creates a gas containing plastic molecules that settle on the glass, which aside from appearing dirty produces glare from oncoming headlamps.

I went south to Dunkin Donuts to pick up a much-needed coffee. And, for those curious, yes, I love Dunkin Donuts and the coffee. Usually, I get a cup from the barracks kitchen while spending a few minutes going over the station logs, but in tonight's hasty exit, I forgot.

Driving through Williamsburg then over to Southampton, I found that I was more exhausted than I realized. It was going to be a long night, and staying awake would be a struggle, so I parked in a used car dealership's lot to be quiet and rest. Twenty minutes later a radio call ended my peace, sending me to check for a bad accident on Route 5 in Hatfield a mile north of the barracks. Damn, I thought, not another one.

It was 2:15 a.m., and Route 5 in Hatfield was sparsely populated, so I wasn't surprised that there were no other reports called into the station with more details. Without any traffic, I made it in ten minutes. The scene was without all the usual stopped cars, the flashers, and stray flashlight beams shining everywhere. The cruiser's high beams and spotlight illuminated a Camaro that had driven straight into the thirty-inch trunk of a maple tree. There were four residents standing on the sidewalk, two with flashlights. They had been awakened by the crash.

Walking to the car, one gentlemen with a flashlight stopped me to say that one of the boys was Bobby Burns from Hatfield. Dear Jesus, I thought with my heart throbbing, I knew Bobby and his whole family. With a fearful dread, I looked inside. There was nothing left to the front of the car. The engine, still steaming and hissing, rested where the dashboard and front seat had once been. There were two crushed bodies partially buried under contents from the front end and engine compartment. The boys' lower extremities were tangled in what was left of the backseat. From what I could see of the young man, who I thought to be the passenger, he looked like Bobby. A feeling of utter sorrow and hopelessness took hold of me as I wondered if the driver was his brother Freddie. I went to the driver's side. The boy's smashed face and red hair were hard to look at, but it wasn't Freddie, whose hair was long and black. Back I went to the other side, but I still couldn't tell for sure if it was Bobby. Struggling, I was able to roll the boy's lower torso toward me just enough to get his wallet. It wasn't Bobby. The victims were two twenty-year-old boys from Greenfield. The relief I felt knowing it wasn't Freddie or Bobby was short-lived, for the badly mutilated bodies of two young men, not much younger than me, lay dead.

There was nothing that could be done with the boys except to cover their bodies. We would have to wait until the tow truck and volunteer firemen arrived with tools to pry or cut them out.

I walked the skid marks from the rear of the Camaro over a hundred feet back down the road. I would get exact measurements for the report later, but the marks told me they were going at an extremely high speed.

Woody showed up at the scene to help, but there was naught to be done. I gave him the boys' IDs to bring back to Sergeant Bass, because the families would need to be notified. I also asked him to tell the sergeant that I would appreciate not being the one to do the notifications.

I got back to the barracks around 5:30, got a coffee, and sat at one of the round dining tables with my back to the wall. Too tired to think of what new emotions I might have just undergone, to add to the list, I simply decided that I had suffered them all. Where had all the joy gone?

Goose Chase

Marion and I drove to my parents' home in Auburn to stay the night and hook up with a couple of civilian buddies and their girlfriends. It was a welcome change. Reminiscing about old times over drinks and dinner brought some much-needed laughter. I had told Marion about the three accidents, skipping all the gory details, and didn't mention any of it at dinner. In a sense, I grieved for those who died, kind of a private thing, and it was not something that I wished to share in casual conversation. Marion had understood, and never brought it up. Since becoming a trooper, I had become subtly aware of feeling that my friends looked upon me differently than before. Unable to describe exactly how they saw me, or what they thought, is something I couldn't put my finger on, and I couldn't say that it was necessarily bad, but it was real. I didn't believe that I was suddenly unfamiliar, and I consciously strived not to be any different around them, but my everyday world *had* changed. All the emotions both good and bad had become recurring affairs, tests, and trials for one's normality. Maybe, in hindsight, I had changed. Marion was good that way and understood, probably because she had only known me as a cop, but she got it. Nonetheless, we had a good time, it was a well-deserved getaway, even if only for a day.

Reporting back for duty I was surprised to learn there had been several transfers within the troop. Most interesting was the transfer of Sergeant John Bass from the Northampton sub-station into the Northampton Headquarters. In reality he had only moved to the office directly across the hall from our sub-station but was no longer my line sergeant. He would carry out the duties of a headquarters desk officer, answering phones, overseeing and directing troop-wide events, or as a patrol supervisor inspecting substations and troops on the road.

The Northampton barracks is a large two-and-a-half story brown brick structure with five rear access garage stalls beneath the building. Sleeping quarters for the troops were on the second and third floors. The first floor held the kitchen and dining hall, dispatch office, an office for the substation duty desk and troopers, with another for the headquarters duty desk and staff. Located down the hall were offices for the Troop Commander, his Executive Officer, civilian clerks, and finally the cell block. The substation and headquarters were distinct and independent entities, and to say they worked in close quarters is an understatement.

As was my habit, I got to work early, grabbed the logs, cleaned my car, made a coffee, and sat in the dining room to relax before patrol. I had just finished reading the log entries concerning the Hatfield double fatal, and reading where Sergeant Bass had assigned the north patrol out of Shelburne Falls to deliver the death messages, when someone slid a chair to my table and sat down. It was John Bass.

"You had quite a few days for yourself last trip, didn't ya," said Bass. It was another partial statement and question, but this time I answered, setting the logs on the table.

"Yes, sir, I did."

Bass took a sip of coffee, hesitating before continuing. "I didn't get a chance to talk with you the other day before you left.

I wanted to say that you did a really good job handling every-thing that came at you."

I was a little stunned. I had never heard the sergeant praise anyone for their work or performance, on anything.

I wasn't usually at a loss for words, but here I was.

I began haltingly. "Thanks, Sarge, I appreciate you saying that, and I appreciate you assigning the death notifications to someone else. I'm not sure I'd have handled it well."

"You didn't have to ask, Randy. I'd already decided to give it to someone else."

Now, I was really at a loss for words after he called me by my first name.

"Well, again, thanks. I guess I should get on the road," was all I could manage.

"Nah, sit down, have another coffee. I took a transfer today, so I'm the duty officer. Relax for a bit."

For the next forty minutes, give or take, Sergeant Bass never stopped talking. He talked about his time on the job, the guys he had worked with, and spoke with a longing about how things used to be. He was glad for the transfer and thought it would be a better fit for an old dog like him. He asked me what I thought of the job, Troop B, living in the barracks, the challenges I'd had so far, and on and on. He actually smiled and laughed when I told him about stuffing my belt with lead to make the weight requirement. John Bass was something other than the picture my mind had created of the man. To answer why he opened himself to me would only be a guess. He knew that he was disliked by the men; he may have been a lot of things, but stupid wasn't one of them. He was ridiculed and made fun of, and he knew it, for I had been in a room when he let hurtful remarks di-rected at him slide by. I began to get the sense of someone feeling and believing that he was out of place, and didn't know which way to go, or to whom he could turn. The thought made me consider that he hid a deep insecurity with bluff and bluster.

Being teased as a young boy for being skinny was something that bothered me for years. Although I was strong and athletic, I always judged my body as inferior to others'. So, having experienced torment, I didn't belittle others and felt uncomfortable when it would happen to someone else in my presence. To my knowledge, I never showed any outward disdain toward Sergeant Bass. Maybe he realized I didn't judge him as harshly as others did.

Thinking back on that day in the kitchen many years ago, I find that age and life experience give one a very different perspective. I'm able to appreciate now that underneath his bark and rough exterior, and behind the thick wall he placed between himself and others, there was a good man. I had seen, many times, that he was a dog unable to bite if it meant hurting someone. It's like the story of the sixteen-year-old boy thinking how stupid his father was, who then at twenty-one couldn't believe how much his dad had learned in five years. I was the sixteen-year-old at the dining table with my sergeant, who understood that five deaths in three days were, indeed, traumatic events for a young officer. Drawing on twenty years of experience, he understood what I was feeling, and in his way, offered me support and some comfort.

Over the next weeks, busy with his new duties, the troops and I saw less of Sergeant Bass, unless passing him in the hallway or at meals. On the positive side, he went out of his way to talk with the troops, showing a friendliness I hadn't seen before. He began to dine with troopers instead of joining a table with senior officers, and he was well received. The man was sincerely trying to change, and genuinely appeared happier. I occasionally noticed that if he was stressed, or on a mission of sorts, he'd become tense and show some of the old irritability, but then again, who wouldn't under those circumstances?

Woody Banes was still one of my line mates and our rooms were side by each at the end of the second-floor hallway. We had both finished our day patrols, had dinner, and were in our rooms resting before the midnight shift. A little after 6:00 p.m. Woody walked into my room, interrupting my reading.

"Hey, Rand, you wanna go t' the 300 Club?"

Now, when the state police lived in the barracks, beginning with one's arrival on the first workday up until dismissal at the end of the third day, troopers were absolutely forbidden to leave the substation or its grounds. That's right, grown men with badges, guns, and powers of arrest could not leave the compound between shifts to go anywhere, but that's not to suggest that some didn't sneak out, and that's precisely what Woody had in mind.

"No, I'm tired, Woody. Not tonight, I feel like I could sleep right now. You go."

"Ah, c'mon, it'll be fun. Couple of beers and we'll be back by ten. Plenty of time before patrol."

"Thanks, Woody, but I'm staying home."

"Okay, I'm goin'. Don't lock the window," said the runaway trooper.

"Why would I, is somebody gonna break in?"

The escape route was common knowledge. Conveniently located at the end of the hall right outside our doors was a large double-hung window leading onto the fire escape. So, Woody climbed to the ground, then walked out past the service garage, now empty of mechanics, past the basketball hoop that no one ever used, and slipped among the pine trees just north of the barracks. From there it was a short walk to the 300 Club.

I had dozed off while reading when I heard the unmistakable goose step cadence of combat boots pounding down the hall toward my room. I knew instantly it was Thunder Boots, Sergeant Bass, and I wondered what he could want with me. Rolling off the side of my bunk I sat up, expecting company, but he passed my closed door and pounded loudly on Woody's.

"Banes," he called. Then another loud knock. "Banes, you asleep?" I heard him open the door to Woody's empty room.

I opened my door and stepped into the hall, "Hi Sarge, what's up?" I asked.

"Randy, where's Banes? I need to see him."

"I don't know, Sarge. He was in there a few minutes ago. I was just talking to him."

"Okay, thanks, I'll find him."

Bass retreated along the hall the way he came, and I listened as he bounded all the way down to the first floor. God, I thought, doesn't he realize how loudly he walks?

I gave it a minute before running to the wall intercom to buzz the substation desk officer, Jim Peterson.

"Jim, It's Randy. Is Bass there?"

"No, he went downstairs, why?"

"He was just up here lookin' for Woody, and he's at the 300 Club. You gotta call up there and tell him to get his ass back here, *now*."

I went back to my room and sat on the edge of my bed, rocking nervously back and forth, thinking I'd have been sound asleep by now if Woody had only stayed put. A long four or five minutes passed before I heard the hall intercom buzz. Running in socks, I slid to the phone and picked it up.

"Jim?" I asked.

"Yeah, it's me. I got Woody, he's heading back. But Bass was just here a few minutes ago asking me if I'd seen him. I told him I thought Woody said he was going to get something from his cruiser then go to bed."

With that bit of news, I crept back to my room as Sergeant Bass marched back up the stairs. Along the hallway he pounded once more, until I stopped him outside my room.

"Sarge, Woody, was just here. You missed him. I told him you were lookin' for him. He said he was downstairs and didn't see you. I think he went out towards the radio building."

Exasperated, and a little out of breath, Bass cried, "Son of a bitch!" Then turned on his heel and stormed off.

I went back to my nervous bunk-rocking, which seemed like the only thing to do. Finally, I heard him on the fire escape, open the window, then enter his room and close the door. Thank you, Lord, we were all safe.

I fell back on my pillow breathing a sigh of relief, as once more Sergeant Bass thundered past my door to Woody's room.

With a forceful shove of the door the angry sergeant stomped inside.

"Banes, where the *hell* have you been?"

With a scared, chickenshit grin, Woody answered, scarcely, looking him in the eye, "I was at the 300 Club."

I couldn't believe my ears—the jerk had just sunk us all.

I could hear the sergeant's angry whispers, but except for a word or two I couldn't make out what he was saying. I could imagine but would wager a bet it had nothing to do with why he was looking for Woody in the first place. Woody and I stayed pretty quiet on our mid-patrols and snuck out of the barracks the next morning to start our days off.

Back at work on the next trip I suited up and went downstairs for the usual cup of coffee. I walked past Sergeant Bass in the hall and gave him my normal greeting, unsure how he felt about the wild goose chase we had sent him on.

"Hi, Sarge, how ya doin'?"

"Good, you goin' for coffee?"

"Yessir," I answered, as Bass turned and followed me to the kitchen. We filled our cups and sat at a table.

John Bass was back to his better self, and our conversation friendly and normal.

Woody walked through the dining room and Bass looked up and gave him a genial, "Hi, Woody."

Lord, I thought, another first name?

Woody kept walking, responding with his own friendly, "Hey, Sarge." But when the sarge wasn't able to see, Woody turned toward me with a questioning expression of surprise while shrugging his shoulders, then bolted to the garage.

People are strange. I had seen Woody wade into a brawl without a thought, and I could always trust him to have my back, but in the matter of Sergeant John Bass, Woody was a chickenshit. It took him weeks to stop hiding from the man. In the end, as best we knew, the sergeant had never reported Woody's AWOL.

Caught a Big One

The craziest trooper I had the pleasure of working with at Northampton, and I say that with affection, was Eddie Krajick. He was on a line opposite mine, so we didn't normally work any shifts together, but we nonetheless lived, worked, played, and hung out in the same building. There were times when I wondered if Eddie ever slept between shifts. His room was at the opposite end of the building from Woody and me, and he never seemed to be "home." He was always joking around, playing cards, shooting the bull with whomever, or pestering active patrols while they tried to write reports.

Putting together this memoir, I have come to realize that I prefer applying similar criteria when writing anecdotes, a longer story, or something focusing on a particular individual. No one gets along with everyone they end up working with; it's a fact in the workplace and in life itself. Human beings range from saintly to abhorrent and everything in between. I haven't come across any truly saintly troopers and, gratefully, no abhorrent ones either, but there were a few that I didn't like for their egos, personalities, or other conduct. Those same men were not particularly well liked in general, and although there are stories that could be told, I have no interest in doing so. Those narratives were long ago discarded into the why-bother-to-remember trash bin. In truth, I've consciously forgotten most of those people, and their troubled behaviors, in order to show the human side of the guys I knew to be fun, caring, and hard-working police officers.

I know it's sounding like a broken record, but Eddie Krajcik *was* another good guy. He was smart, worked hard to solve the cases he was assigned, and was considerate and empathetic to anyone in need. He was five feet ten inches tall, of average build, and he was balding with close-cropped sandy hair. His blue eyes were too close together, causing a few double takes, to go with a long straight nose.

His outlandishness and outspokenness drove his supervisors and strangers nuts. He'd throw out an opinion or thought on whatever topic of conversation was being discussed, whether or not he was a participant. I suspect this is something we all occasionally do. Lots of things pop into my head that I would like to inject into conversations, but an inner voice tells me to keep my mouth shut. Not so with Eddie. He would toss it out there regardless. Kind of like sitting around a peaceful campfire with friends, chucking a firecracker into the flames, then running away to watch what happens. In any event, he wasn't out of his mind, deranged, insane, or mad, but he was a little off, in a harmless sort of way. Hence his nickname, "Crazy Eddie."

Eddie and I had often talked about going fishing sometime when we could get a day off together, but months passed and we never did. One day, before going back out to patrol, he came up to my room to say that he had taken a couple of vacation days and was wondering if I wanted to go fishing. I did and told him so, but since Marion and I were now living together, I wanted to check with her to see if she had made any plans. I was learning it was best to check *first*, before trotting off to fish.

Eddie picked me up at 5:00 a.m. We tossed my fishing gear, bag, and beer into his trunk. I thought that I was supposed to bring the beer, and he thought that he was to bring the beer. So, needless to say, we had plenty of Budweiser as we began the thirty-minute ride to Gate 8 at the Quabbin Reservoir.

The Reservoir was built between 1930 and 1939 and is roughly seventy miles west of Greater Boston. It provides water to Boston and forty other communities. The story of the Quabbin is interesting. In the early 1920s, eastern Massachusetts found they needed drinking water. The Metropolitan District Water Supply Commission focused on the Swift River Valley for the project. Initially, the plan was to relocate 2,700 residents from the towns of Enfield, Dana, Prescott, and Greenwich, which had been settled as far back as the 1700s. The legislature passed the Swift River Act in 1927, paying $108 per acre, and giving the residents until 1938 to move elsewhere. A few months later they began the flooding, which took several years to complete.

Stories of the four communities and residents are truly bittersweet. Sweet because the towns were taken for the betterment of millions in eastern Massachusetts, and bitter when one reads the stories of those who gave up their own histories, homes, livelihoods, and futures.

The Quabbin today is the largest manmade water source in the region, covering thirty-nine square miles of beautiful scenery and holding 412 billion gallons of water filled with fish for Eddie and me to catch.

In Belchertown, we turned off Route 202 at the Gate 8 fishing entrance and stopped at the bait shack before picking up our boat. Ed grabbed the brand-new bait bucket he'd bought a day or so before, and we went inside to buy some live shiners and any other incidentals we might need. I wanted to get a dozen night crawlers, but Eddie said shiners would be all we'd need. Doing a little fishing as a kid, I often had luck using an "Al's Goldfish Lure." The lure had a treble hook, making it wicked good at holding anything that grabbed onto it, so I bought one, just because, and tossed it into my tackle box.

Our next stop was at the water to arrange for the boat rental, where I asked Eddie if he remembered to bring Billy's fishing license. I guess I'm a little ashamed of this point, because neither Eddie nor I had fishing licenses. We needed state licenses to fish and rent a boat. It's no excuse, but we put together this outing in a rush and we simply didn't get them. Knowing that no one was going to arrest two troopers for fishing without the proper paperwork, we didn't worry. As for the boat rental, Eddie hit up Trooper Billy Wagner, an avid fisherman, to borrow his license for the boat, and that worked just fine. For anyone concerned, a few days later we both got our own fishing licenses for future outings—but on this day, we were outlaws.

The Ranger, worker, boat custodian, or whatever his title may have been, was a very friendly and accommodating gentleman in his sixties, welcoming us to the Quabbin.

"Hi, there, how you doin'?" Eddie asked the Ranger.

"I'm good, son. What can I do for you?"

"I called yesterday to reserve a boat. I'm Billy Wagner," Ed told the gent.

"Oh, sure, I pulled boat number 10 over to the side so you could load up. Not many people here today. Shouldn't be too crowded on the water."

I wondered about the fishing, knowing that some days they were biting and other days not so much. "How's the fishing been? They getting any with shiners?"

"You bet, seen some largemouth bass, and some nice rainbow trout taken with shiners. They're good most anytime. Lures have been doin' good too. You boys fished here before?"

"Yeah," said Ed. "I've been here a few times. Are they biting up this end near your boat docks?"

"It's okay here, but I like to go up the finger four miles or so. There's some big boulders and low granite outcroppings coming off the shoreline. That's a real good spot for the bass."

The western portion of the reservoir is a finger-shaped body of water running north/south about eight miles from Belchertown into the town of Pelham. So the Ranger suggested that we boat north four or five miles and fish there, which sounded like a good plan, because we certainly didn't have another one.

Our boat was an aluminum runabout about twelve feet long with a five-horsepower motor. It had three wide seats—one at the motor, one at the bow, and a middle seat we could sit on to row if we broke down. There were two oars under the seat, which I hoped we wouldn't need.

Eddie said that I could be captain of the ship, running the motor and steering. He wanted to be the first mate and ride up front.

"Okay," I agreed, "but if we break down, it's the first mate who rows."

The air was still, and the water was like glass with a light mist just above the surface. Bits of pale yellow sunlight began working through the mist, promising a beautiful morning. The local weather report was for little wind and a partly cloudy afternoon.

The Ranger gave us a shove away from shore and the engine started on the second easy pull. We turned slowly northward toward our fishing grounds. I was almost sorry watching the bow of our boat slice through the mirror-like water, leaving a bubble-filled wake behind us. Ed suggested that we pick our spots and fish for a while along the way. If we found a good place, we could stay there and not have to go so far north.

We had gone about a half mile when Eddie pointed to a spot where a large tree hung over into the water.

"Randy, go over there. Let's see how we do." Then with the familiar sound of a beer can gushing open, he offered one to me.

"No, Ed, it's waaay too early. I need some food first. Later, though."

I knew right then why he wanted me to drive. He planned on having a few.

We fished on both sides of the downed tree without success. I wished that I hadn't listened to Eddie and had bought some night crawlers. Catching pumpkinseeds, or perch, off the bottom is still a lot of fun. Hooking something is always better than catching nothing. Anyway, I had a ham sandwich and my first beer. Eddie finished his third—and didn't want a sandwich.

My partner picked out a few more prospective fishing holes for us to try over the next mile and more beers. Our luck wasn't any better, so we continued north, stopping once again at a favored spot for the rest of our lunch and, of course, more beer. Eddie had a good buzz on, because he giggled when he tangled his line, and laughed when he showed me how to fix the mess by cutting off a hundred feet and tossing it into the bottom of the boat. Before he finished tying on a new hook, I started the motor for another trek northward to fish the Ranger's outcroppings. I was tipsy after a couple more Buds, but Ed was a step or three ahead of me.

It was slow going in a twelve-foot boat powered by a small motor, so it took much longer than I imagined, but we found the Ranger's spot and tossed our lines into the lake. I had given up on the live bait and fished with my new Al's Goldfish Lure. My headstrong friend stuck with shiners.

We fished and fished without a nibble, which probably had more to do with us as fisherman. Or, it could have been punishment for fishing without licenses. In either case, we hadn't caught a thing. It was getting late. I was tipsy. Ed was blitzed. And we had a long ride back. "Come on, Ed, it's time to go, we suck."

"Wait, wait a minute. I got an idea. We can't go in without a fish. I'm gonna get us some."

I had no idea what was swirling around in that brain of his until he pulled a paper bag out of his tackle box, filled with M-80s.

An M-80 was a large class of firecrackers. They were made for the military to simulate explosives and artillery fire. They're made from a cardboard tube an inch and a half long containing three grams of gunpowder with a fuse coming out of its side. In 1966 they were banned by the Consumer Product Safety Commission and made illegal by the ATF in the 1970s. They were unique because the fuse would stay lit, allowing the M-80 to detonate under water, and they were quite powerful. I don't know where he got them, but I had an idea what he was going to do.

"Okay," announced Eddie, "we're gonna depth-charge us some fish."

"Oh, no, Eddie, come on, we gotta go," I slurred.

"This'll only take a minute, we gotta do this. Gimme a cigarette, so I can light this thing."

"Eddie, don't." I warned. "They float, you can't have them blowin' up on top of the water."

"You're right, I forgot," he said, standing, almost falling out of the boat as he looked under the bow seat, and, just his luck, came out with four or five small rocks.

"These will make it," he said, "hand me that fishin' line, and light me a cigarette," which I did. Handing it over, he stuck it in his mouth, and squeezed it awkwardly between his lips as smoke filled his nose and burned his eyes, which sent him hacking. Eddie didn't smoke. Tears streaming down from his too-close-together eyes gave me a silly fit of the giggles before I settled down.

The drunken First Mate took a knife from his tackle box and cut several lengths of the nylon fishing line. Taking a piece of line, he tied one end around the M-80 and attached the other end to one of the rocks. His next move was to light the fuse and drop his depth charge over the side. Several seconds later there was a muffled kaboom from deep beneath the surface. Eddie was ecstatic and hurried to look over the side and watch stunned fish float to the surface. Seeing the fish-less water around the boat, he undauntedly grabbed another rock and M-80 and dropped his next charge over the other side of the boat. Again, he hadn't blown up any fish, but he was getting a charge himself hearing the underwater explosions and watching thousands of bubbles rush to the surface. It's amazing how one so inebriated can find such unabashed humor in something so stupid. Had I been as drunk as Eddie, I might have enjoyed his antics, but I was sober enough to realize that we had to get going.

"Okay, Eddie, come on, we gotta get outta here before dark," I warned.

Agreeing to "just one more," I watched him tie a rock to the last M-80. Ed leaned to the boat rail and lit the M-80 just as the rock slipped off the nylon line and plopped into the water. Eddie didn't notice.

"EDDIE, EDDIE," I screamed, "THE ROCK, *LOOK*".

"Oh, SHIT," cried Eddie, reaching over the side and shoving the M-80 into the water. We both breathed a sigh of relief, but unbeknownst to us—because M-80s don't sink on their own, which we *did* know but were too drunk to consider—the explosive hugged the bottom of the boat. Where it blew up.

Sitting on the back seat next to the motor with my feet firmly planted just behind Ed's new shiner bucket, I heard first a loud WHOMP from under the boat, then watched in awe as the shiner bucket shot into the air in front of my face and crashed back to the floor. The lidded bucket was smashed from the bottom. Totally squished may be a more appropriate description, and the shiners were swimming around the bottom of the boat. Ed was aware of nothing, and it was worse.

The shiners were able to swim around in the boat, because the M-80 had blown a perfectly round shape into the boat's bottom, half the size of a basketball, splitting a floor seam and letting water into the boat. Eddie had just blown a hole in our twelve-foot rented boat.

"WE'RE SINKING, EDDIE," I screamed.

He laughed, "Yeah, right."

"NO LOOK," I yelled, holding up what was left of his bucket. "THERE'S A HOLE IN THE BOAT, WE GOTTA BAIL IT OUT."

He finally snapped out of it, and wanting to see for himself, he moved to the middle seat, which, unfortunately, was where I had placed my fishing pole, and he sat right on my Al's Goldfish Lure, with its three barbed hooks. OUCH!

"OWOEEE, Jesus! What's that," howled Eddie.

"Never mind, bail the friggin' boat or we're gonna end up at the bottom of this lake," I pleaded emphatically.

In that second of pain he forgot about our predicament and pushed the tip of my rod aside, driving the lure hooks deeper into his backside.

"YEOW EEEE, NO, STOPSHITGODDAMN IT HURTS," he cried, not knowing which way to move.

In his current state, Ed had no idea what he had done to cause so much agony. I didn't know either, and frankly, I didn't care. We were going to sink if we didn't do something.

"C'mon, Crazy, help me here, gimme the hand towel, take the bucket and bail." I wanted to stuff the towel into the open floor seam to slow the flow of water. It wouldn't stop it, but I thought it would be enough for us to stay afloat if we bailed.

"I can't, Randy. I can't move, it hurts too much. What'd I do?" Eddie asked with water-filled eyes. At that point I realized I was on my own.

Scanning the shoreline, I spotted a small sandy bank about 200 feet away, big enough to beach the runabout. One tug coughed the motor to life, and I aimed the bow right for the spot.

"Where ya goin'," asked my surprised friend.

"To shore, hang on!" Then I plowed the boat at almost full throttle into the sand, stopping us dead and rolling Ed off his seat with another scream of pain. I was starting to feel a little sorry for him, but not too much.

Safe for the moment on dry land it was time to see what was troubling my First Mate. None too kindly, I ordered him to stand up so I could see what was going on. Gingerly he stood. I could tell it was pure torture, but saw my beautiful new lure dangling between, and through, the legs of his jeans. He was hooked in a location that I really didn't want to think about.

"Crazy, you got my lure stuck in your ass. We gotta get outta the boat."

Realizing what had happened, along with the pain, he began to sober up—slightly. At least to the point that he followed my suggestion to grab the fishing pole and carry it ashore with him. I must have been drunker than I thought because, honestly, in Ed's condition it was a stupid idea. So, instead of picking up the operational, reel, end of the pole, he picked it up by the flexible tip, dragging the reel behind him until it caught on the side rail of the boat and elicited another blood-curdling scream. All I had to do, to save more pain and suffering, would have been to take the scissors from my tackle box, cut the line, and leave the pole in the boat, but NO, that was what a sober person would have done. Instead, I grabbed my pole and opened the bail to release some line, and walked Eddie ashore like a huge fish I'd just caught. My composure was slipping away at the ridiculousness of it all, and I began to laugh.

"C'mon, Rand, you gotta get this thing off me, it hurts like a bastard."

I went back to the boat and got my tackle box full of the tools I'd be needing for surgery. I deftly cut the fishing line about a foot below the lure and tossed my pole out of the way. Whatever I ended up doing was going to hurt, and the only anesthetic was more beer, but I chucked the thought, figuring he'd just have to suck it up.

The little beach had several inches of soft white sand, so I made Eddie turn around and I got on my knees behind him. The bright gold lure was hanging at eye level, and there was a silver-dollar-sized ring of blood on his pants. "Spread your legs and bend over a little," I ordered, but as soon as he spread 'em, it dawned on me that I was operating without a plan and his blue jeans would have to come off.

"Okay, Crazy, I gotta cut your pants to get this thing out."

The firm reply, "WHATEVER," was the first sign that he was getting angry. He had better not be mad at me, I thought, I didn't blow up the boat, and he better not have broken my new lure.

Scissors in hand, I poked a hole through his pants and cut around the ring of blood, using it for a guide.

"Unbuckle your belt and drop your drawers," I ordered once more, sounding firmly in control, though I wasn't. Another indignant "WHATEVER" remark struck me silly, and my stomach was beginning to quiver with laughter. Not waiting for his pants to fall, I pulled them down to his feet and turned my attention back to the job at hand, which entailed cutting around another blood-stained ring on his jockey shorts. My laughter became more debilitating with every snip of the scissors.

Ed, still bent over with hands on both knees, turned his head sideways to inform me, with righteous indignation, "You are an asshole!" Yanking his underwear down, I realized I couldn't argue the point, for in front of my face, the sight of my goldfish lure stuck in his butt adorned with the little cutout pieces from his jeans and underwear dangling and swaying between his two hairy balls, was just too much to handle. I fell over onto the sand laughing hysterically. I couldn't have stopped with a gun to my head.

Eddie was beside himself pissed off, yelling at me, and calling me every name he could think of. It didn't matter what he did or said, for I was beyond getting hold of myself. But, to finish the surgery, I reached blurry-eyed into my surgical instruments box, grabbed a pair of pliers, and yanked out the lure. "YOUCH!!"

A minute or so later I was able to sit up and wipe away the sand stuck to my wet cheeks. The First Mate had pulled his pants up, still calling me names. The good thing was that he appeared way less intoxicated and a tad less irritated. Rummaging through his bag, Eddie found a couple of Band-Aids and held them toward me. Then, glaring in complete seriousness, he suggested that his wound should be covered to prevent infection and keep the dirt out.

I was dumbfounded. "Eddie, I ain't touchin', or wanting to see anything, that's inside your underwear ever again, bandage yourself."

He was moving slowly but did his part to help me cram the hand towel into the ruptured seam, then sat quietly bailing, although he kept shifting from one butt cheek to the other.

We made good time returning to the boat docks, and I worried all the way, wondering if the Ranger would be as friendly when we lied about the hole. I felt shameful at the prospect of lying, but there was no way I was going to tell the truth.

Nearing the dock, I watched a young man leave the Ranger shack and move toward our incoming sinking ship. He looked like a high school kid working an after-school part-time job. This could be good, I thought.

"Hi, there," I said, greeting the boy.

"Hello, sir, did you have any luck today?"

"No, no luck, but we did have a little problem. We went up to fish the boulders that your morning Ranger suggested we try out, and a wave from a passing boat lifted our boat. We came down on a rock, it popped a hole in the bottom. We're really sorry."

"Oh, no problem, sir, we have a repairman. He'll pound it back in place and with a couple of rivets it'll be as good as new. Are you Mr. Wagner?"

"No, that's him," I said, pointing at Eddie, who was running away toward the car with a noticeable limp.

"Well, you're all set then. Can I help you carry anything?"

"No, thank you. You've been great. See ya next time."

Ed packed the trunk with the stuff he carried up, then sat behind the driver's seat waiting for me. I added my gear, then jumped in and gave him a look. He returned my stare with a slight grin, so I asked. "What do you say? Wanna do this again next week?"

Marion could tell that we had been drinking when Eddie dropped me off, because he slurred his goodbye. I was fine, so she wasn't mad when she asked if we'd had a good time. "Yeah, it was a good day," I said truthfully. "Didn't catch a thing but it was fun."

Two weeks later a group of troopers at the barracks arranged a deep-sea fishing trip out of Newburyport on Massachusetts' north shore a little south of the New Hampshire line. I wondered if it might be too soon after Quabbin to charge off on another trip, but Marion had no plans for the day and was good with it.

We left Northampton around 3:30 in the morning to be at the dock for a 6:00 a.m. departure. It was a beautiful day on the ocean, we all caught fish, and better yet there were no explosions or surgeries. I got home just after five o'clock, but Marion wasn't there and hadn't left a note. I was unconcerned, but it was unusual, for if she wasn't at work she was always home.

I took a shower, put on some clean clothes, and turned on the TV in the den. I kept looking out the front window hoping to see her drive into our lower level garage. At seven o'clock, I was worried, for this was so unlike her. I was back at the TV when I heard the faint rumbling of our garage door. Relieved, I opened the door at the top of our basement stairs and waited for her to come up. I heard the car door close, then what sounded like the trunk slamming shut. Twenty seconds or so passed before I heard her approaching the stairs. She carried several department store bags under her arms, with two more in each hand, and carefully mounted the first step. Looking up with a sheepish grin she mounted the second step while shaking her head and exclaiming, "That was one very, very expensive fishing trip you went on."

Learning the Hard Way

Reminiscing about the Quabbin fishing adventure brought to mind an interesting lesson in geography and local history I received courtesy of my troop commander on a flight from Northampton to Framingham. The knowledge he shared with me that day gave me my first grasp of just how little I knew of the world around me, to say nothing of life itself. As the reader will see, it's a simple, straightforward short story, but one that struck me as fascinating. It was time for me to open my mind.

Fast-forwarding to the early 1980s, I had recently been elevated to the rank of corporal and was summoned to a meeting with the troop commander. He wanted to talk about the promotion and discuss my new assignment. Rarely, if ever, did commanders engage in discussions regarding assignments. They just made them. Captain John Hancock (no relation to one of our founding fathers) was a true gentleman who operated differently by showing consideration to those newly promoted under his command.

When the meeting was over, he asked me if I'd like to join him for a ride in the state police helicopter to Framingham. He didn't tell me the reason for his trip and I never asked, but answered with a resounding, "Yes sir, I'd love to go."

We drove to Lafleur Airport in Northampton, boarded the chopper, and headed east. I can't recall whether it was late fall or early spring, but there were no leaves on the trees and a light covering of snow in spots. Nevertheless, the view from 1,500 feet was impressive as we flew directly over the Quabbin Reservoir eastbound toward Worcester.

The pilot, Captain Hancock, and I all wore headphones to communicate because of the chopper's loud drone. Studying the varying landscapes passing below, I was mesmerized by the many miles of stone walls running throughout the woods in nearly every direction. There were no fields, no pastures, no houses, just trees and stone walls. "Wow look at the stone walls," I whispered to myself forgetting that everyone could hear me.

"That's pretty interesting, isn't it?" Captain Hancock commented.

"Yes sir, I've never noticed them before, but who would? There's no roads down there to drive on."

"Throughout the better part of the 1800s this area was being cleared for farms and pastures," Hancock began. "Farmers piled the cleared stones to mark their property lines, pastures, and to designate areas to plant crops, including hay. The walls also kept the livestock from wandering. In the late 1800s Massachusetts was almost 80 percent deforested, and with deforestation came a tremendous loss of the state's wildlife. Populations of wild turkeys, deer, fox, moose, bear, and other species were hunted and decimated through a lack of habitat."

I had heard conversations at the dining table about Captain Hancock and how smart he was, but I'd never taken notice. Articulate, informative, and impressive, at least to me, he continued. "If one were to go down there and measure, you'd find the trees inside those walls are all about the same size; tree ring counts would be nearly the same, indicating eighty to one hundred years old. What we have now, a hundred-plus years later after the small farms disappeared and the settlers moved on, is a state that's reportedly 70 percent forested, and wildlife has returned."

"I've never thought about it," I admitted. "Black bears come into my yard in Hatfield, and I read an article saying that the Williamsburg/Hatfield area has one of the largest black bear populations, per square mile, in the United States."

"That's right," he concluded. "It's a wonderful thing."

Back to the mid-1970s: I was still happy working out of Northampton. Another class had graduated from the Academy that needed to be broken in, and one of the new men was assigned to me, but my feelings were mixed. I liked teaching and sharing what I had learned, but it was hard work. I'd become used to patrolling solo, where the work decisions were for me alone, but training someone meant generating activity and experiences for the new officer. The rub was working your butt off, while a mediocre officer, who would never be assigned a newbie, didn't work half as hard, often getting desk duty and other easy assignments. The only benefit to breaking in a new trooper was the personal satisfaction of doing so. Brian Kent was going to be my "Boot" for the next three months.

I felt like a midget sitting beside Brian in the cruiser. He was six feet four inches tall and all of 250 pounds. I was five feet ten-and-a-half inches and still hovered just over 150 pounds. He didn't seem to care that we looked like an odd couple, but it sure bothered the hell out of me.

Trooper Kent was soft-spoken and his movements unhurried, not in a lazy way, perhaps simply more deliberate, or maybe his size slowed him down. I wasn't sure, but it didn't matter, because he was a quick study and moved plenty fast enough without any questions whenever I told him to do something. The one thing about Brian that gave me a little pause was my suspicion that he had a tendency toward being too kind, too gentle, and too trusting. I'd noticed the same tendency in many of the "big guys." I believed that these officers had become accustomed to people readily submitting to their will, not through force, but due to their size.

Admittedly, I held a heightened sensitivity for my own smaller frame, but strongly believed that size did matter, and the large troopers had an advantage they weren't even aware of. I had seen it too many times to dismiss the likelihood. One evening in particular I was sent to a bar fight in Sunderland. I was the first trooper on the scene. I went inside and spotted the four guys involved, who were pretty much spent but still shoving, yelling, arguing, and spoiling for a fight. This was not going to be easy, I thought. Everyone watched me move toward the troublemakers while drunken patrons continued to egg them on. In the next instant the entire room went silent. Eyes that had watched me now looked to the door I'd just come in. Filling that doorway was six foot five inch, 280-pound Trooper Jim Hunter. It was all over except for "yes sir," "no sir," and "I'm sorry, sir" as we arrested four.

So, trusting my feelings that a big guy might easily become less cautious about his own safety, I wanted to make Brian mindful of the possibility.

A few weeks into break-in we were driving past a bank on Route 9 in Hadley when Brian asked me how I'd decide the need to shoot someone. The question really set me back, because it was a subject that was repeatedly pounded into us at the Academy, and I knew he'd been schooled, too.

I had watched Brian in a few situations, and he showed a calmness with no hint of fear or panic. He impressed me as being sure of himself and having an ability to exercise cool and good judgment. All good things, but I wondered where he was coming from.

"Tell me, Brian, do you have concerns about justified shootings? As I recall, they covered it pretty thoroughly."

"Not really," he answered unconvincingly. "I know it's justified in life-threatening situations, like, when someone's life is in immediate danger."

"Okay," I said. "It's mostly that simple, but I'm not saying it's a small matter. Imagine after we passed the bank back there, that we got a call it was just robbed at gunpoint, and as we pulled in the robber runs across the parking lot with his bag of money and just kept beating feet. I wouldn't shoot at him, because at that point he wasn't threatening anyone's life, but, if he turned and pointed a gun at us or someone else, I would shoot. Understand?"

"Yeah, I see," answered my Boot.

"What I've done many times while riding around on patrol, Brian, is create scenarios, or call them 'what if' situations, and believe me I've come up with some pretty nutty ones. The point is, that by creating these things in my head, I've kinda thought it through. Am I making sense to you? For me, the worst thing is not knowing what to do in a bad situation, so, by living it in my mind, I already have a good idea what to do. Try it yourself."

One of my favorite dispatchers at Northampton was Ray Shea, who had been on board for at least twenty years. He was an avid reader and never showed up for work without a book and a backup read in case it was a quiet night. Dispatchers never looked forward to the graduation of new Academy classes because the volume of radio traffic tripled. They'd be bombarded with license checks, registration listings, and stolen checks on many of the people and cars encountered by the new officers. I readily admit that it could be overwhelming.

I gave Brian the wheel of my cruiser to find his own violators; to patrol wherever he wanted within our sector, and be in total charge of any investigations or accidents we were assigned. I sat back to observe and answer his questions, mostly letting him be, unless he missed something he shouldn't have.

Brian was giving Dispatcher Ray a good workout and I could tell he was getting frustrated. He had already called for a number of M & Ws (missing and wanted checks), and license checks using the phonetic alphabet to spell every name for the dispatcher, and he had another one ready to go. I let Brian go at it, because it was good practice and after a while would become second nature. But he was driving Ray nuts because all the names were simple enough that using the phonetic alphabet was unnecessary. Normally, we only used it when there was a difficult spelling or the chance a dispatcher might misunderstand.

"478 to L," called Brian, with no answer.

"478 to station L," he called again.

Largely frustrated, Ray answered, "L is on, AGAIN, 478, go ahead."

"Can I have a missing and wanted on a Peter J Wade, DOB 9-3-1960, that's P-peter, E-echo, T-tango, E-echo, R-Romeo, middle initial J-Juliet, the last name is Wade, W-whiskey, A-able, D-dog, E-echo."

At the end of his patience, Ray acknowledged loudly over the air. "Okay 478, I could have spelled that one all . . . by . . . myself."

I chuckled, but Brian looked at me nervously after Ray snapped at him for the entire troop to hear. "Don't worry," I said. "He's probably into a good book."

A while later Brian pulled over a car he had clocked at 90 mph, a deserving candidate for a citation. I stood along my side of the cruiser and let Brian handle the motorist without me looking over his shoulder, figuratively speaking only, because I would have needed a stool.

Anyway, the offender gave Brian the car registration and told him he'd forgotten his license at home.

"Shouldn't we get a license data on him?" asked Brian, a little hesitant.

"For sure, go ahead and run him."

"478 to L," radioed Trooper Kent. Silence

He tried again, "478 to L." Silence once more.

Ray was obviously annoyed and being pissy, so after noticing the owner's name on the registration, I grabbed the mic and had Brian give me the guy's papers.

I knew Ray wouldn't ignore my call.

"478 to station L," I spoke loudly into the mic, which brought an immediate response.

"L is on 478."

"478 to L, I need license data on the following white male, DOB 6-24-1957. First name, Stanley, S-Sierra, T-Tango, A-Able, N-November, L-Love, E-Echo, Y-Yankee. Last name Waleszczynski, and that's common spelling."

That brought dead silence, not a radio wave was waving anywhere, until other stations and cruisers piped in.

"Whoa, Ray, can you spell that one all . . . by . . . yourself?"

"He can't even say it, never mind spell it."

"He gotcha on that one, Ray-Ray," laughed the caller.

At a time when the state police no longer lived in the barracks, there's another short tale about a desk officer at the Monson barracks who sometimes felt and acted put out by the excessive radio traffic from his troops. Sergeant Jack Delaney was the second-in-command at Monson and the evening shift supervisor and desk officer. Substations didn't have civilian dispatchers, so the job of manning the radios, phones, and everything else fell to whoever worked the desk.

Sergeant Delaney was red-faced with a deep voice and a permanent scowl. His size, mannerisms, and expressions were intimidating, whereas in truth he was anything but. I had worked with him when I first arrived at Russell, and he did intimidate me until I got to know him. He was another "big" who controlled with size and fearful expressions, yet looking past the facade he was wishy-washy. Decisions didn't come easy for him, which frustrated the hell out of those looking for direction or solid answers. I thought that he was a less than ideal leader, convinced he'd rather not lead at all. But he was harmless, a fact the troopers working for him quickly realized and used to their benefit to take advantage of him—and a loosely run shift.

Sergeant Delaney was another like Dispatcher Ray. He'd routinely settle into his evening shift reviewing area crimes, correcting reports, preparing schedules, scanning the local paper, eating dinner, then settling into the guard room easy chair to watch some TV and hope the night wasn't busy. Unfortunately for Sergeant Delaney, though, ever since patrol of Route 91 south was taken from Russell and reassigned to the Monson barracks, quiet evenings were few and far between. Adding to the hustle-bustle was the evening shift roster of troopers having less than two years on the job. They were enthusiastic and extremely eager.

Night after night the radio calls to the sergeant were endless, and his frustration grew. The more often he had to leave the TV for a stolen vehicle check or license data, the testier he became on the radio. The troops knew they were pissing him off but didn't care. They also knew he would never complain. It was his job to service their calls, so he suffered in silence and did his duty, though without enthusiasm.

The sergeant's exasperation was known to all the Monson troopers, with some of the more senior men actually teasing him about missing his TV programs. Then came a day when the day shift desk trooper discovered a switch on the back of the TV which, when flicked, shut the picture off and replaced it with a screen of white snow. They schemed and shared their plan with the evening shift.

The next afternoon, the day shift desk officer, Dave Garvey, waited for Sergeant Delaney to report for work, then met him in the guard room and engaged him in conversation. Trooper Garvey had previously turned the TV on, then changed the channel, lowered the volume, and finally turned the set off while talking with Delaney. When Delaney went into the office, Garvey flipped on the snow switch at the back of the television and went home.

Garvey had just finished his dinner when the phone rang. It was Delaney.

"Hey, Dave, is there anything wrong with the TV?" asked Delaney.

"I don't know Sarge, why?"

"Well, it ain't workin'. I tried everything I know."

"It was working when I left, Sarge, I don't know what to tell ya."

"Okay, Dave, thanks, see ya tomorrow."

The following afternoon, Dave flipped the switch back to its normal position and he turned the set on just before Delaney got to work.

"God, sakes," uttered the sergeant as he walked into the guard room with the TV blasting.

Hearing him, Trooper Garvey walked into the room.

"Wud you do to this?" asked the annoyed Delaney.

"Nothin', just turned it on. What did *you* do to it? You evening guys musta screwed it up."

"Hey," he sputtered with his irritation showing. "WE didn't do anything."

Before leaving for home, and after the sergeant went into the office, Garvey once again turned off the set and flipped the snow switch.

The next day was a carbon copy of the day before, with Delaney's temper almost at a boiling point.

On the third day, after turning the TV off and the snow switch on, Dave met the sarge coming in, explaining that the TV had given them trouble that morning, and that he had to bang the top of the TV to get it to work.

"Look, Sarge, watch what happens," said Dave. Turning on the television, snow filled the screen as Dave stealthily flipped the snow switch with one hand while in the same instant he pounded the TV top with his other hand. *Poof*, like magic, a picture appeared. Delaney shook his head and went into the office. Dave turned the TV off, flipped the snow switch back on and went home.

On the final day, Trooper Dan Harrington, who had been in station the previous evening writing reports, described Sergeant Delaney's assault on the TV set as nothing short of savage. Worse yet, the sergeant made Harrington climb to the top of the fire escape near the building's rooftop, where the nervous trooper spent fifteen minutes adjusting the TV antenna.

"Operation Snow Screen" was thereafter officially abandoned—not out of any consideration for Sergeant Delaney, but owing to concern for Harrington or anyone else playing TV repairman and falling off the roof.

Trooper Kent had completed his three-month break-in period with me and was assigned a working line opposite mine. I didn't see him too often, but heard good things about his work. I returned to duty one day a month or two later to find a TV news film crew setting up an interview spot in front of the building. I paid them little attention thinking it was probably another routine traffic interview or some such evening news topic. But here I digress, because except for a couple of reporters I had come to respect and trust, I disliked, distrusted, and avoided the majority of the media. I'd been screwed over too many times with their promises of "off the record" or "we'll only print or air it when you give us the okay." Worst of all was giving them a true account of an incident, then reading or listening to a reporter's twisted narrative of the facts I'd provided, with no regard for the truth or the people involved.

I drove into the backyard swallowing the sour taste of the media and went up the back stairs. The barracks was abuzz and the dining hall was filled with people. I excused myself past an Assistant DA, our troop CO, a detective lieutenant from the DA's office, and a bunch of people in plainclothes I didn't recognize. Stepping into the office I went up to Woody, standing in the corner.

"Hey, what's goin' on?" I asked with concern.

"Brian was hurt pretty bad last night right in front of the barracks bringin' in a guy he arrested. He ended up shootin' him."

"*Dead*?" I asked.

"Oh yeah!"

"How's Brian?"

"He's in the hospital, got a bunch of stitches in his neck." Then Woody proceeded to tell me that Brian had arrested a guy for drunk driving. The man was a carpet installer in his fifties who was fine on the arrest, cooperative and friendly, so Brian didn't cuff him. He even put him in the front seat. I cringed. The carpet man had talked to Brian all the way from North Hadley to the front door of the barracks. Then he snapped, or had planned it all along, but in either case he pulled a linoleum knife from his pocket and slashed Brian across the throat.

Brian pulled his weapon and fired.

I assumed the worst at Woody's mention of the guy cutting Brian with a linoleum knife. I had used them—the hooked blade is maybe three-and-a-half inches long, razor sharp, and cuts by pulling rather than slicing. I imagined Brian's throat ripped out. Woody could see that I was shaken. "Brian's gonna be okay, Rand," said Woody. "The guy missed his carotid artery."

I was relieved, but wondered why—why he hadn't hand-cuffed the prisoner and why again, he put him in the front. It's something we don't do, and I'd told him that over and over during break-in. I couldn't help feeling a little responsible, thinking that my lessons weren't emphatic enough. Or was Brian just too trusting?

First thing the next morning I went to visit Brian. He was in a single room filled with sunshine, but he was looking less than sunny with a thick bandage around his neck from his chin to the top of his shoulders. Propping himself up in a bed that looked entirely too small, he gave me a shy grin.

Trying to lighten the mood I asked with a smile, "So, how do you like riding on your own?"

Looking at me and losing the grin he asked, "Am I gonna be okay for shooting that guy?"

Not wanting to go there yet, I dodged the question, "How you feeling?"

"Ah, it hurts bad. They got me wrapped tight, don't want me turning my head yet. I asked the nurse how many stitches they put in. She rolled her eyes saying that I was really lucky, but it took a lot of stitches. I'll be okay, the pain killers help."

"Good," I said. "I was in the kitchen last night and overheard the assistant DA talking to our captain. They're gonna run it through a grand jury. You should be fine. Your drunk driver had some serious priors, so they see no problem. But, I would expect some major reeducation and a serious ass-chewin' when you get outta here. How could you not cuff that guy and put him in the front?"

"I know I know, it was stupid," he said, avoiding looking at me and staring at his big feet at the end of the bed. "I'm sorry," he added.

"You don't have to be sorry to me. You paid the price."

I wasn't going to beat him up or lecture him. He knew he messed up and felt bad enough, so we both sat quietly for a bit until he broke the silence.

"You know, Randy, all night I thought a lot about what happened and how things went. I'm glad that I'm left-handed since he came at me from the right side, but I'm the most thankful for that day in front of the bank in Hadley when you told me about creating scenarios where I might actually have to use my gun. I took your advice and made up my own, so yesterday when he came at me I didn't have to think, I just shot him. He would have killed me if I had hesitated. You saved my life."

I certainly didn't feel like a hero or share Brian's view about saving his life. He saved his own life. But to this day, I credit my coach, Dave, with saving my life twice, so maybe what I taught Brian helped him save his own.

Détente

The 1970s was an interesting decade in my career. I had been assigned many lesser cases to work at the substation level, then a transfer into the District Attorney's Office offered investigations into some of the worst kinds of criminal behavior, then finally came a move to the Narcotics Bureau, where I spent almost four years undercover. I will share a few of my favorite undercover stories later in this narrative, but here I would like to describe two unlikely events that came together in 1975 and resulted in one of the more notable weeks of my career. The first event began way before the later and spawned national headlines. It was United States District Court Judge Arthur Garrity's decision mandating desegregation of Boston schools by means of bussing. The second event was the arrival and docking of two Russian war ships at the Commonwealth Pier on May 12, 1975.

South Boston High became the epicenter for vocal and violent protests, making the schools unsafe and causing South Boston High School to be placed in receivership. The neighborhood was almost like a war zone. Black students didn't want to go to South Boston and South Boston didn't want them—the hatred was palpable. Boston Police rode the busses and provided escorts coming and going. The state police walked the hallways inside the schools and acted as backup.

I'm not knowledgeable enough to comment or express my opinions on the wisdom of the desegregation experiment. Articles that I have read some forty years later describe the effort as a failure. I'll leave that determination to others, but without discussing specific incidents, I *can* recount how it affected the state troopers from Troop B, one hundred miles away.

Approximately forty men were selected from each of the six substations, then divided into two groups of twenty. One group remained back in the troop, while the other division drove to Boston each day for two weeks. At the end of each two-week period the groups switched. It was grueling for those of us driving to Boston. We'd get up in the middle of the night, pick up our passengers, and haul our butts to Atlantic Avenue's Commonwealth Pier.

The pier was built in 1901 as a marine cargo facility to handle large freighters and passenger ships that could also take advantage of the nearby railway and truck transportation. Entrance into, and exits from, the enclosed pier was through three large doorways on Atlantic Avenue. The inside was cavernous, with room enough for all the men and equipment we needed, providing a perfect staging area for the State Police contingent.

Once on site we were divided again. Half were sent into the schools and the rest were stationed inside the pier on standby. There was plenty of call for the standby troops to help with riot control, but it wasn't an everyday occurrence. The Boston PD was, in my opinion, incredible. They dealt with the lion's share of problems and only used the troopers as necessary. So, as far as the men were concerned, the best job was standby duty at the Pier. We could often sit around, play cards, and catnap for a needed rest.

The week began with my group being placed on duty inside the Pier. On the Monday morning drive to Boston I had hoped we wouldn't be needed inside the school, and prayed for no riots, because I was exhausted and needed some idle time. Turning off Atlantic Avenue and driving inside, we saw two large ships tied to the pier, one behind the other. I didn't give them a thought. Once we settled in, Sergeant Red Cady put us in formation to be addressed by our commanding officer, Captain VonFlatern.

"Okay, listen up," said the CO, holding a paper that he was obviously going to read from. "This is a big deal and I don't want any screwups." I thought to myself he was being a little dramatic, because, as a whole, we weren't screwups and usually did a good job.

"As you can see, docked alongside our pier are two Soviet guided-missile destroyers. These are the first Russian warships to visit an American port since World War II." Okay, he had my attention. I was impressed.

He continued, "The warships are part of ceremonies marking the thirtieth anniversary of the Allied victory and they are a symbol of efforts at détente."

Détente is a French word meaning an easing of tensions. The effort began in 1971 between the two superpowers. Then in May 1972 President Nixon made a bold move and visited the Secretary General of the Soviet Communist Party, Leonid Brezhnev, in Moscow.

The captain resumed reading. "The United States has sent two of our warships to Leningrad harbor on a similar gesture of good will. You, gentlemen, are going to guard these ships—the *Boiki* and the *Zhguchi*. They will remain here for five days. A spokesman for the Navy said there were plans to open the ships to the public, but today the Naval Terminal Building and chain link fences are closed and will be patrolled." So much for a lazy work week, I thought.

"That's pretty much it," concluded the captain. "I don't know anything about the plans for public visits. I guess we'll find out later. All right, Sergeant, assign the men their positions. That's all, dismissed."

This was indeed political. United States Vice Admiral Stansfield Turner and his staff, in full dress uniforms, had greeted the Soviet Commander, A. M. Kalinin, and his aides. Similarly, the Soviet Ambassador to the United States, Anatoly Dobrynin, reviewed a detachment of Russian sailors taking part in the ceremonies. Admiral Turner had also paid courtesy calls on Massachusetts Governor Michael Dukakis and Mayor Kevin White of Boston. Now I could understand why our CO had a case of the jitters.

Sergeant Cady spaced our detachment at intervals along the wharf beside the ships. They were impressive, but then again, I'd never been up close to any warship, so what did I know. The vessels were gray with red stars on their bows, colorful signal flags draped from the highest reaches of the ships, and uniformed sailors walked the decks.

Later in the morning the chained gates at the street end of the wharf were opened to allow a collection of news media inside. Carrying their pads, pens, cameras, and whatnot, they were escorted up the gangplank and directed onto the fantail of the leading ship. Tables filled with drinks and hors d'oeuvres awaited the horde of reporters clamoring for the best seats, while others smothered anyone who could speak a little English or provide an interesting picture. I know I'm hypercritical, but what I witnessed from the media was a lack of etiquette and nearly frenzied activity. I wondered what the Russians thought.

In the meantime, we troopers dutifully guarded the Russians and their warships to forestall anything that might trigger World War III or bring down the wrath of our troop commander, whom I noticed had been joined by two lieutenant colonels from headquarters. They would not have been there unless this whole thing wasn't significant.

On Tuesday we all arrived at the crack of dawn and assumed our positions on the wharf. It wasn't long before sailors were wandering about the deck of the lead ship, with some of them even walking down onto the wharf. Clearly the sailors were curious, for they looked us up and down, occasionally pointing and appearing to stare at our uniforms. Dress uniforms of the state police, with breeches, riding boots, blouses, and garrison hats were, and still are, sharp looking. I believe they wondered about our station, our function, or simply who we were.

Trooper Mike Rogalewski, line mate and Polish-speaking frustrated desk officer, was in the same rotational group as I was. We'd been placed side by each about twenty feet apart on the wharf, and that would be our assigned position until someone changed it.

Down the line I watched a Russian sailor talking, or more precisely, using hand signals in an attempt to communicate with one of our troopers. Then I watched the trooper unpin one of his collar ornaments and hand it to the sailor, who handed him something in return. A few minutes later another sailor approached another trooper and did the same thing. I got it—they were trading uniform parts for mementoes. Great, I thought, let the bartering begin. Mike and I made a haul gathering hats, Russian cigarettes, belt buckles, coins, and other assorted trinkets we traded for spare uniform parts he and I had in our duffel bags. We did better than everyone else because Mike and the Russians managed to understand one other with a little Polish and Russian translation. A few sailors would come over and just talk. Mike tried to explain that we weren't federal police, and that we worked as the state police for Massachusetts. They seemed to understand, but Mike said he couldn't know for sure. No matter, we had a great Tuesday watching the comings and goings on the warships. One note of interest, through Mike's observation, was the number of higher-ranking officers from the lead ship who seemed to come and go at will. Some actually walked right out through the gates, returning later with packages. It appeared they had been shopping.

Wednesday was mostly uneventful. The lead vessel was opened for the public to board the ship, walk once around the deck, and then leave the wharf through the Atlantic Avenue gate. It wasn't much of a visit. Sergeant Cady had told Mike and me that the press and some VIPs had complained because they weren't allowed into the ships' lower decks. Apparently, the prize they coveted was to be entertained more formally—instead of outside on the fantail.

Schools were letting out and soon we would be heading west for the day. I was ready to go when a Russian officer walked off the ship directly toward Mike and me. He was my height, stocky, with red hair and a freckled face. Approaching with a smile, he extended his hand to each of us, squeezing with a firm grip. He obviously greeted us in Russian, to which I offered a blank stare, but Mike replied in Polish. They continued their spotty communication with some hand signals, more smiles, and in the end Mike nodded as the officer showed his watch and pointed at the dial. Grinning ear to ear, the officer turned and boarded the ship.

"What the hell was that about?" I asked Mike.

"He asked where he could get stamps."

"Stamps? What kind of stamps?" I asked somewhat confused.

"Stamps," he answered emphatically. "You know, like postage stamps. His kid collects and he wants to get him some. We gotta take him to find some tomorrow morning at nine o'clock. I just gotta figure out where and how."

"Have you lost your *mind*?" I sputtered.

"You gotta help, Randy. I promised him, and he'll be here tomorrow morning."

Being young and unafraid—no, that's not right. Being young and absolutely stupid, I agreed to help.

"Okay, listen," I said, "there's a post office not far from here at all. It's right off North Street near the financial center."

"What about getting there, we can't walk?" asked Mike.

"We take my cruiser. If none of the brass are around, I'll park next to the wharf at nine, we get the Russian, and go out the north door. The big cable doors have been left open every day, so, I don't know, it should work."

I didn't sleep much that night, dreaming about stamp collecting, but I did collect Mike on my way to Boston in the morning.

At 8:50 sharp I gave Mike a nod and slipped away from my post, got in my cruiser, and parked it out of sight near Mike just inside the Pier. At 9:00 a.m. our Russian appeared, accompanied by two other officers. Oh, I thought, this wasn't in the bargain.

Excited, and literally bouncing our way, the Russian shook our hands while nodding and talking to us. Well, he looked at us both, but was talking to Mike. Our new friend gestured toward his fellow officers saying, as best Mike could understand, that we were going to drop them off somewhere. Okay, let's go, I thought as my fear and imagination ran wild. I could see the headlines already. Senior Russian military officers jump ship at the Commonwealth Pier and request political asylum assisted by two as yet unidentified State Police officers. Lord help us, I asked as the Russians climbed into the backseat and we started to drive.

I had to go to the far end of the building before turning around toward the North door. All appeared well. We hadn't seen Sergeant Cady or any brass as we neared the exit. The Russians were jabbering happily without a care in the world when I poked Mike in the thigh and pointed at our escape door—it was shut tight. Through clenched teeth I whispered at Mike, "How does it open?"

"I don't know," he whispered back.

I stopped the cruiser at a point in front of the door and I looked around, then up at the walkway above us. Standing there were Captain VonFlatern and Lieutenant Colonel Griffin. Our CO was glaring at the cruiser stopped below him, but more intently at the Russians in the backseat.

I looked at Mike and whispered, "We're dead meat."

Mike looked out his window and up toward the Commissioned Officers, giving them a hand salute. The lieutenant colonel returned the salute, reached around behind himself, and pushed a large red button that sent the cabled door to the ceiling. My hands shook so badly I could hardly steer.

A couple of miles and a few turns later we arrived at the Hanover Street Post Office, just a short walk from The Old North Church and the Faneuil Hall Marketplace. The one thing that these historical sites have in common is that parking is almost nonexistent. Since walking was out of the question, I parked on the sidewalk at the post office's front door. Mike and I got out and opened the door for our passengers. A security guard came running out of the post office, not knowing what to think or do about two State Police Troopers and three Russians almost blocking the entrance.

Our two additional passengers said, I guess, "See ya later," and walked off. Mike and I then escorted our Russian over to the security guard and told him we wanted to see the postmaster. I explained the Russian was from one of the warships at the pier and wanted to get some collectible stamps for his son. The guard warmed, and realizing that he wasn't being invaded, he said that he could help. Mike joined the two and went inside while I stayed with the cruiser to make sure no one would steal it—one can never tell.

Twenty minutes later they were back. The Russian was the first out the door and gave me a bear hug. Mike and the security guard were all smiles. Our Russian friend had stamps in al-most every pocket and was just plain joyful. Ten minutes later we were parked safely inside the Pier. We were back on post, the Russian was aboard his ship, and apparently no one missed us.

At the end of the day, our Russian came off the ship and over to Mike and me. He was still so happy—I couldn't believe the shopping spree trip had pleased him so much. He and Mike communicated in earnest, and Mike seemed to have trouble understanding. Then he apparently got it and nodded and smiled knowingly. Walking away, the Russian turned and gave us a big wave.

"I think he said that he has something for us," Mike told me.

"What?"

"I'm not sure. I think he said something about tomorrow at noon, but I didn't understand all of it. It's hard talking to these guys, because we only pick up a few words here and there. Guess we'll have to wait and see."

The next morning was Friday, and the last day the warships were to be in port. It had been a good run. The troopers had plenty of collectibles; the Russian had his stamps; Mike and I didn't get in trouble; and the public got to walk topside on the ship. The only grumblings, we heard through our grapevine, were that the press thought they had been shabbily treated, some VIPs shunned, and our brass was miffed because they weren't invited to the first day's gathering on the fantail.

We had taken our normal station along the wharf waiting for the day to end so we could head home, but at 11 a.m. things went sour. Several hundred people had gathered a short dis-tance away from the pier fences to watch the Ringling Brothers and Barnum & Bailey Circus unload at a railroad siding. A number of people then moved down Atlantic Avenue, just out-side the wharf fence, shouting their displeasure about Russia. I didn't know if it was the Russians or the US hosts who made the decision to stop the public from touring the ships, but someone did and the gates to the wharf were closed. At 11:20 Sergeant Cady came with orders for us to join other troopers in forming a line on Atlantic between the crowd and the chain-link entry gates.

Mike and I looked at each other, wondering what we were going to do about our Russian coming at noon.

Mike spoke first. "You stay here. I'll go talk to the sergeant and see if he'll let us wait for the Russian."

"Yeah, okay I guess, go ahead. See what he says."

At 11:30 Mike hadn't returned, and I was getting nervous being the only officer standing on the wharf with everybody else standing guard in the middle of the street. It was 11:35 when Sergeant Cady spoke angrily from behind me, "What are you doing here?"

Startled, I mumble something about Mike going to find him to tell him about the Russian officer, blabber, blabber, and Mike told me to wait blabber, blabber. . . .

"I don't care what Mike told you, get out in the street with the others."

"Yes sir, on my way," was all I dared say, then opened the gate and walked to join Mike in the middle of Atlantic Avenue. Standing off to one side, not thirty feet from Mike and me, were Colonel Griffin, a major whom I didn't know, and our troop commanding officer, overseeing the entire operation.

I estimated there were a couple hundred people who had wandered from the railroad siding to gather behind us and glimpse the ships. Many of them had, initially, come to tour the warships, but with access denied they simply mingled. These people didn't come here to riot. In my opinion, the vast majority were just curious, but I understood the powers-that-be weren't taking any chances on anything going wrong.

We stood at parade rest watching and listening to the murmurings of the crowd when I looked up and saw a commotion on board the Russian ship directly in front of us. I nudged Mike and nodded to the ship, because our Russian was waving his hands at sailors and ordering people about. We watched him move to the top of the gangplank motioning at sailors with both arms swinging as if pushing them onto the gangplank. A moment later sailors lined either side of the gangplank. Mike and I, along with everyone else on Atlantic Avenue, watched. The Russian proceeded down the ship's walkway to the wharf followed by eight sailors in smart-looking attire. Once on the wharf they formed two columns and followed our Russian to the closed chain-link gate onto Atlantic. Our friend shoved the gate wide open and walked toward Mike and me, followed by his men. He had as broad a smile as I had ever seen. Ignoring everything, and everyone else, he walked right up to us. Mike and I were stunned as the Russian grabbed me by the arm, then Mike, saying with a heavy accent, "Come, come, my friends, come," then pulled us from our ranks, placed us between his sailor escorts, and marched us toward the ship.

There wasn't a murmur anywhere, especially from the State Police ranks. No one moved—they just stared as we were led to the gangplank. Following our Russian up the walkway we were saluted by the sailors lined on either side. All I could think was, *OH BOY!* This would either be something great, or Mike and I were going to be in deep shit.

I was numb when we reached the main deck, and almost frozen following the Russian through a hatchway held open by a sailor, and then down through more hatches to the ship's lower decks. I could only imagine what our top brass was thinking as Mike and I entered the bowels of the ship. It was another world. I had never been inside a cabin cruiser, never mind a warship. The trip downward was a blur. I remember only posters on the walls showing Russian workers at different tasks. Farmers, plant workers, men and women, cities and landscapes with large colorful printed text, that, I guessed, were political slogans.

At the end of a hallway, two decks lower, standing stiff and erect were two sailors on either side of double swinging doors. Our host flung the doors aside with a flourish and swept his arm toward a large table on the other side of the room. Seated at the table was a United States naval officer in dress whites, who jumped immediately to his feet upon our arrival. He and the Russian broke into friendly conversation, in Russian, as our host tossed his hat onto the table, motioned for us to be seated, and, giving orders to the sailors, he left the room as looks passed between Mike, the naval officer, and me.

"What the hell did y'all do?" asked the totally dumbfounded officer.

"Took him to get some postage stamps, why?" answered Mike, meekly.

Shaking his head in disbelief he continued, "All I know is that I got a call from Naval Operations in Washington last night telling me to get my ass up here to act as interpreter for this meeting. That's all I was told. You took him to get stamps?"

"Yup," said Mike, "for his son."

"Do y'all know who this guys is?" asked our interpreter, looking at me.

I shook my head and said "Nope."

"He is Admiral A. M. Kalinin, with close ties to the Kremlin, and is here with Ambassador Dobrynin for the anniversary ceremonies. I can't believe this. I'm not even sure my Commander knows what this was all about."

"How 'bout that," was all I had to say.

The waiters entered with trays of fruit, cut and sliced vegetables, cheeses, some bread, crackers, dips, and three bottles of vodka followed by Admiral Kalinin. The interpreter stood, so

Mike and I followed suit as the admiral, shaking his head, motioned for us to sit. The servers opened the vodka and poured each of us about a six-ounce water glass full. The admiral grabbed his glass and, speaking through the Navy guy, offered a toast to Mike and me for friendship, and the kindness and generosity we had accorded him. Mike and I downed about three ounces, which warmed all the way to the pit of my stomach. The admiral drank almost all of his, reached for the bottle, topped us off, and offered another toast to the success of the ship exchange and a hope for better relations.

The meal was delicious—that may be because we hadn't eaten since early morning coffee and donuts, but I think not. The conversation was better. It was so easy talking with this man. Admiral Kalinin was happy, friendly, and inviting. Robust may be the best description. He talked about his wife and son and his home in Moscow. He asked about our families and took the pictures I had shown him from my wallet. He wanted his wife to see the picture of my daughter and my home. The interpreter was having a good time, too, as the laughter came easier with each gulp of vodka. We had spent a little over an hour with our Russian friend when I suggested to Mike that it might be best for us to get back to duty. Besides, I had downed seven or eight ounces of the vodka on an empty stomach and I was beginning to feel it.

Thanking the Navy interpreter and Admiral Kalinin, who bear-hugged us one last time before leading us topside, I found myself staggering and grabbed hold of Mike to keep steady on the narrow stairs. Mike wasn't any steadier, and I realized the staggering had nothing to do with the stairs, for I had all I could do to walk to my post on Atlantic Avenue.

The commissioned officers were nowhere to be seen, but Sergeant Cady was in our faces demanding a full accounting of what we'd done, so I let Mike do the talking. I couldn't, and one of the other troopers had to drive us home.

The next day we were back in good ole Troop B telling every-one the Russian story. We were grateful to learn that we weren't in any trouble, unless one considered how furious our com-manders were over not being included. They would just have to get over it.

Blue Bell

Drunk driving roadblocks, or DUI checkpoints, began in the early 1980s and were created to remove the drunk drivers from our highways. As first used by state police, we would set up a checkpoint, then stop all vehicles entering the site to determine if a motorist was driving under the influence, and place offenders under arrest. Then came lawyers and court challenges, which gave rise to the strict guidelines that all police were required to follow to conduct any DUI roadblock. Specifically, the selection of vehicles stopped could not be arbitrary, safety had to be assured, and inconvenience to the motorist needed to be minimal. Furthermore, the courts ordered the operations be conducted according to a specific plan, having supervisors present, and with advanced notification of the time and place given to the public. There was more, but it need not be detailed here.

I often tell the story of a DUI checkpoint I worked one night at a Route 20 rest area in the town of Westfield. A captain oversaw the detail. At that time I held the rank of staff sergeant, which made me his second-in-command, in charge of another sergeant and seven troopers. All those assigned reported to the Northampton headquarters at 7:00 p.m. It was there that everyone received a copy of the detail plan and then went to the road for a general patrol until 10:30 p.m. Once at the site, the officers helped with setup prior to conducting the actual roadblock from

11:00 p.m. until 2:00 a.m. The location allowed sufficient space for us to direct vehicles off the roadway. It also provided enough room to park our recreational vehicle, which had been modified to process prisoners and house a small office.

Trooper Stanley Polinski was a trooper from the Pittsfield barracks who had been assigned to the night's roadblock. He was a couple of years junior to me, but I had worked with him many times and considered him a friend. Stan was six feet tall with a long thin face, brown eyes, and brown hair with premature gray around his ears. His complexion was medium dark, having the look of someone with a permanent tan. Stan was another one of those with heavy feet. Everywhere he roamed his footsteps stumbled along, and to this day I can't imagine how he made it through close-order drill in the academy. He walked clumsily. Actually, he *was* clumsy.

Polinski was one of the seven troopers assuming a patrol before reporting to the roadblock. Stan was a good worker and liked traffic enforcement. I believe that's the reason he chose to forgo promotional exams. Administrative and supervisory duty didn't interest him.

An hour or so into the pre-roadblock patrol duty, Stan had clocked a New York motorist northbound on Route 91 at 87 mph. Twenty-two miles per hour over the speed limit, in heavy traffic, was a citation fairly deserved. Nevertheless, this gentleman contended that he had been unfairly singled out for obvious police harassment. The discussion went downhill from there.

I don't know, but possibly another reason Stan didn't seek higher rank was that he was a little slower than average and lacked the ability to think quickly on his feet. An exchange of wits with an angry motorist had occasionally been his bane, and this guy was smart and abusive. Stanley wasn't dumb, by any means, but the New Yorker outmatched him, and, unfortunately, when Stan got angry, upset, or nervous, he became tongue-tied, and worse yet he stuttered, badly.

The motorist received his citation, but Stan had given the New Yorker everything he needed by informing the gentleman that "He wa- wa- was b-b-being an a-a-asshole." So, off drove the offended motorist to the next exit, where he proceeded to our headquarters, which was right up the road.

Sergeant John Driscoll was the headquarters duty officer and listened politely to the New Yorker's concerns, but Driscoll had no intention of getting involved when there was another sergeant working the DUI checkpoint. So, assuring the complainant that the state police took these matters seriously, he requested the gentleman wait a few minutes for another officer to take his statement and perform a thorough review of the incident. This guy wanted his pound of flesh, saying he would wait for as long as it took.

Sergeant Jim Patrick showed up about twenty minutes after being called and sat down with the motorist. Patrick was an experienced, capable, and commonsensical officer. He had seen and done it all. Interviewing and reading this guy was second nature to Patrick, and the New Yorker made it easy, for he was as arrogant and abusive to the sergeant as he'd been to the trooper on the road. Patrick let the guy rant, rave, and ramble, agreeing that the trooper should never have said anything suggesting that the man was an asshole. "Of course," assured Patrick. "There will be a record of your complaint and I will be discussing the incident with the officer in a short while. Unfortunately, there's nothing I can do about the written citation, but you can seek recourse in our courts. I appreciate your coming in, sir. Thank you, and have a safe trip."

After interviewing the complainant and facing the man's behavior firsthand, Patrick had no intention of making the complaint official, but true to his word he called Stanley into the barracks for a "talking to." The trooper was given a slap-down for calling the guy an asshole, and though he agreed with Stan's assessment, he told Stan, in no uncertain terms, that he was wrong.

Stanley wanted to explain things further—the guy said this and the guy said that, and why this and why that—but Patrick knew Stan well. He knew the trooper's night was ruined, that he would be nervous, upset and worried, but hopefully smarter the next time. The sarge tried to ease Stanley's mind, but watching the trooper "stumble foot it" out the door with his chin on his chest, he knew it would take him a couple of days to recover.

The troopers began arriving shortly after 10:15, converging on the RV for coffee and a few minutes of relaxation before getting started. Sergeant Patrick had been the first to show up, and remained silent about Stanley's road incident, as he should have been, for it was no one's business anyway. We all sat around quietly except for an absent Stanley, who had probably lost track of time, and Trooper Henry Archer.

Low conversations continued uninterrupted when the RV's flimsy metal door rattled open and Henry Archer bounded into the room, one-handedly holding his coffee and cigarette. Archer joined us with the same smile that he never seemed to be without, and was always ready to entertain with snippets of information, or a need to share his latest joke. Where these tidbits of troop gossip came from, or how they always managed to get to him before anyone else, was always a mystery. I had also come to believe that he couldn't begin a normal conversation without, "Hey, did ya hear?"

Tonight was no different.

"Hey," he began. "Did ya hear about Blue Bell the racehorse?"

Then, waiting for everyone's attention, he took a deep drag from his smoke, swallowed the last of his coffee, and began the story.

"This guy went to the racetrack one day and walked up to the betting window."

"'I, I'd, l- l- like, t- t- t- to, b- b- bet, t- t- two, d- d- dollars, on m- m- m- my, f- f- favorite horse, B- B- Bl- Blue- b- bell,' said the stuttering bettor."

"So," continued Archer. "The guy finds his seat and the race goes off. Blue Bell is screaming around the track, but three-quarters of the way around the horse falls over, landing on its right side. Next week the guy is back and goes to the window again.

"'I, I'd, l- l- l- like, t- t- to, b- b- bet, t- two, d- d- dollars, on m- m- my, f- f- favorite horse, B- B- Bl- Blue B- B- Bell.'

"The horse is in the lead, and once again three-quarters of the way around the track Blue Bell falls on his right side.

"The following week our stutterer shows up early and goes out back to the stables, where he finds Blue Bell's trainer walking the horse around the corral.

"'Excuse, m- m- me sir, I t- t- th- think, I can h- h- help, w- wi- with, B- B- B- Blue B- B- Bell, fa- fa- falling, on, his r- r- right side.'

"So the trainer says, 'We've tried everything and can't seem to fix the problem. We're losing a lot of money, we'd be open to any ideas. What would you do?'

"'I I'd, p- p- place, a p- p- piece, of l- l- lead, in, h- his, l- l- left ear.'

"'Ya know,' said the trainer, 'we were thinking that it might have something to do with Blue Bell's equilibrium. Hmmm, lead in his ear? Maybe, but, how would you put it in?'

"'W- w- wi- with a f- f- fu- fuckin' gun.'"

That did it—Henry's joke struck everyone funny and we laughed hard. Maybe because it was late at night, or maybe because we were all tired, but the hysterics seized everyone, until one by one we settled back to quiet. That is, until Stanley slammed the RV door open, nearly falling up the two steps. Wide-eyed, desperate, and oblivious to anyone else in the room he searched for Sergeant Patrick, because he wasn't finished discussing the New York motorist. Finding the sarge seated peacefully in the corner, Stanley closed in and loudly stammered, "S- S- S- Sa- Sa- S-a Sarge," evoking nearly insane laughter, to the utter bewilderment of Trooper Polinski.

Fall turned into winter and with huge political pressure from Mothers Against Drunk Driving and supportive politicians, roadblocks continued to be scheduled almost every week. The troops were believers in the checkpoints because of the effectiveness of the program for curbing DUIs, as well as overtime from the Federal Highway Administration.

It was very cold one Friday night on Route 9 in Williamsburg, where we set up shop in the large parking lot of a utility company. There was no snow or ice on the ground, making it easier to walk around, but the cold was biting and I had begun to wish that I'd never signed up for the extra detail. Arriving at the parking lot, I went about staging the area according to the written plan, first telling the driver where to position the RV, then grabbing a couple of troops to set our cones and road flares alongside the roadway. From there, I climbed inside the RV to warm myself and wait for the captain to show up. We were a man short, so knowing I would have to fill in, I decided to work the westbound traffic lane. It would be easier for me to supervise and avoid getting involved in an arrest. There were plenty of troopers for that.

Every motorist entering the coned traffic lane was funneled to the road officer, who would stop and greet the motorist and make a quick assessment and then either allow them to continue on or, if the driver was suspected of drinking, direct him or her to the parking lot for a closer look. There was a chase cruiser at either end of the checkpoint for any motorist making a fast

U-turn to avoid the block, or for anyone attempting to speed through without stopping at all. Many had tried it, unsuccessfully. The remaining troops waited in the parking lot to receive, ID, and perform sobriety tests as needed.

In the mid- to late-1970s the television series *Kojak*, staring Telly Savalas, was very popular. I thought that it was a pretty good crime drama, with Savalas playing the cop named Kojak. For those who may remember, his signature feature was a shiny bald head, and he sucked lollipops. I have no idea what one has to do with the other, but I thought I'd throw it in there.

I can't speak for other law enforcement agencies, but I recall that the Kojak look became "in vogue" for our troop during the early 1980s. I'm quite sure that an individual's concern over serious balding was a factor in their decision-making process. If looks were the issue, I didn't know what options were available or even viable at the time, but given a choice between a hairpiece or a shaved head, I'd go with Kojak, or the lollipop.

There were three Kojak-heads under my command that night, Rollie DeWood, Jack Springer, and Frank Kelsey. Frank was the tallest at six feet two inches, strong and muscular, with smooth, porcelain-like skin and deep blue eyes. Rollie and Jack were both five feet ten inches, the same build, fair complexions, and with blue eyes just like Frank. Seeing them seated together in the RV with their hats off, they looked more similar than I had realized. Shiny round bald heads, fair skin, light-colored eyebrows, and deep blue eyes, they could have been brothers, or trolls.

These guys had served under me at different stations over the past years. They were good cops and I consider myself fortunate to have worked with them. We spent the next quarter-hour reminiscing and warming ourselves in the RV, until the captain's arrival and his signal for us to get to work. Grabbing my coat as I went out the door, I was again reminded of the times I nearly froze to death in our old reefer style coat. The new Mighty Mac was one of the best clothing decisions the department had ever made.

I took my position in the middle of the westbound lane and began checking motorists. The traffic was heavier than I had realized, as four cars awaited processing. The night was clear and getting colder by the minute. My warm breath condensed into a huge cloudy mist every time I exhaled. Exhaust pipes from the waiting vehicles bloomed like white clouds and mixed with the sulfur-filled smoke spewing from the flares. I hated the smell, and the foggy mixture gave the site an eerie look and feel as I worked through the line of waiting motorists. After years on the road, it usually took only a fleeting glance into a motorist's eyes, and a sniff of the odors wafting from the driver's open window, to determine whether to take things further or let them go on their way.

Even with the heavy traffic it had been an unusually quiet roadblock. Only two motorists had been escorted to the parking lot for further checks. One was let go immediately, but Trooper Kent decided to play with the other. The trooper's playmate was a guy in his late twenties, most likely a construction worker from the look of his clothes. He had obviously had a beer or two sometime after work and was headed home. Kent could smell the alcohol, so he had the motorist step from the car for a few sobriety tests. The trooper knew after his guy passed the first that he wasn't under the influence, but gave him another anyway, then another. By the fourth test the young man, knowing he had passed them all, was somewhat unsettled by the trooper's firm demeanor, but stood resolutely determined to pass any trial.

"Okay, young man, last test," said Trooper Kent, peeling back the sleeve of his coat to raise his wristwatch in front of his face.

"Ready? Ten seconds, spell your name—BACKWARDS," ordered Kent. Then smiling warmly, he put his arm around a very relieved roadblock acquaintance.

Everyone was ready to call it a night and we were cold and uncomfortable. Another half hour and we'd go home.

Traffic had slowed to almost nothing, but off in the distance I watched a small pickup truck slowly weave its way along the road headed right at me. Taking hold of my portable radio I let the chase cars, and everyone else, know that we probably had a good candidate. Slowly, ever so slowly, the driver aimed his truck between the traffic cones, except for the one he ran over, and then stopped four feet beyond me. I quickly caught up to the driver's door and tapped the window with my flashlight. I could see the small thin driver searching for the window handle while flashing me a happy-go-lucky smile. "One second," he mouthed through the glass holding up a finger. Then finding the handle he wound it down.

"Evenin' osifer," slurred the fifty-something-year-old gentleman. "W wass, goin' on, whoa, you got some accident here. You need some help?"

"No sir, we're good, but thanks, anyway."

"My pleasure," responded the helpful, good-natured drunk.

The alcohol fumes coming out of the window almost made my eyes squint. When I asked the man for his license and registration he sat motionless for a few seconds trying to figure out what I wanted, then when understanding came, he leaned over toward the glove box and toppled to the passenger floor. Leaning through the window, I grabbed him by his belt and hauled him upright again. "Don't worry about it now, sir. What's your name?" "Ames," he slurred, seeming a little less coherent. "My name is Paul Ames."

Paul's face was dark and weathered. His eyes were so bloodshot it was hard to tell their color, and he needed a shave several days ago. There was nothing to him; he was light as a feather when I lifted him from the floor. It was time to get Mr. Ames into the parking lot, so I radioed ahead to let them know I was coming in with one hopelessly drunk gentleman. I considered asking for an assist because I wasn't sure he could walk that far, but seeing everyone busy breaking down the checkpoint setup, I opted to have him drive while I walked along side steering through the driver's window. Paul Ames was docile, friendly, and cooperative. I figured it was better having him drive 250 feet instead of falling down, and I sure wasn't going to carry him.

Mr. Ames and I managed to navigate his truck and park it next to the RV. I helped him out, then walked him a few steps to the front of his vehicle. There he stood looking at me curiously and listened intently as I told him that an officer would soon be asking him to perform some sobriety tests. Paul said that he understood and that it would be all fine with him. That is, until the trooper performing the tests showed up.

Captain Baker, commanding the night's roadblock, was a large man at six feet three inches tall and over three hundred pounds. He was respected and well-liked by all the men. I think one of his best qualities was his sense of humor, so it was no problem when Rollie DeWood asked him if he could borrow his Mighty Mac coat. So, with the captain's coat in hand, Rollie grabbed Jack Springer and the two bald-headed troopers squeezed inside the captain's Mighty Mac, buttoned it up, and this double-Kojak walked around the corner of the RV to give Mr. Ames his sobriety tests.

I was speechless looking past Ames at the two shiny bald heads sticking out of the coat. "Sir, excuse me, sir," called Rollie. Then, ever so politely, he continued as Paul Ames turned around and saw him for the first time, utterly dumbstruck. Rollie said, "I need you to perform the finger-to-nose touch, do you understand?" Then without waiting for a reply he proceeded to reach over with the index finger of his right hand and touch Jack Springer's nose. "Then I want you to do the same with your left finger," as Jack reached across and touched Rollie's nose.

Dazed and totally confused, poor Paul unconsciously raised his finger and completely missed his nose. "That's good, Mr. Ames," said Jack. "Now, watch me balance myself standing on one foot. You need to stand on one foot for a few seconds. See, watch me, Mr. Ames, look at my feet." And Paul, seeing three feet on the ground and one of Jack's in the air, turned white as a ghost.

At that moment the third Kojak-head, Frank Kelsey, saved Paul and took him inside to be booked for operating under the influence of an alcoholic beverage.

At his arraignment on Monday morning, according to our barracks court officer, Paul didn't say one word as his court-appointed attorney entered a not guilty plea on his behalf. To this day, I'd love to know what he told his attorney.

I Knew Nothing

I have included stories from my first few months at Russell, but purposely withheld this short "gap" story because it influenced decisions later in my career and the time wasn't right for the telling. So I'll begin by saying how difficult it was to put into words how I felt about what happened to me in the middle of my break-in training. I could say that I was furtively abducted, kidnapped, or highjacked from Coach Dave, because that's kind of what I thought, but those acts are illegal and our command staff would never do anything illegal—I hoped. So, suffice it to say that during February of 1969 I was simply taken off break-in and away from my coach—which was not a crime.

Dave and I were on a day patrol headed into downtown Westfield. It was a slow and dreary day. The roads were icy and light snow mixed with freezing rain. We hadn't stopped a car, but spent the early morning following some leads and tidying up our open cases.

Just before lunch, Northampton headquarters radioed our cruiser. Headquarters calling a substation patrol was extremely unusual, to say the least. Dave gave me a funny, nervous sort of look, and just in case it was a mistake he waited for them to call again.

"Station L to cruiser 442," came the transmission.

"442 is on L, go ahead."

"442 is Trooper Stevens in that car?"

Dave gave me a curious stare, never taking his eyes off me as he answered.

"That's affirmative station L."

"442 Code 7 directly to BHQ, and have that officer report to the CO. We'll square it with your station commander."

I was shocked, dismayed, and fearful, but no less so than Dave, whose accusatory stare gave me the shivers when he asked, "What the hell did you do?"

"Nothin' Dave, I didn't do anything, honest."

"Don't bullshit me, you did something. Did you get in trouble on your day off?"

Emphatically, "No, I didn't even go out on my day off. I was home with my parents."

Dave kept at me. "Boots don't get called to HQ six weeks on the job unless they're in the shit." I had nothing to say, my head was spinning, and I'd run out of words.

After a few minutes, I saw that Dave had softened a bit. I felt he wanted to believe what I was saying, but the cop in him was leery. We rode most of the way to Northampton in silence and parked at the front of the building. Dave and I got out and walked in the front door where we were met by Lieutenant Garvey. Garvey told Dave that he would take it from there, and if Dave would be good enough to bring my gear into the barracks, he could head back to Russell. I watched my shunned and bewildered coach return to the cruiser for my gear as the lieutenant led me down the hall to whatever fate lay before me.

I walked straight and tall following the lieutenant, then removed my garrison hat and tucked it under my arm before entering the room. The only other time I'd been in the captain's office was the day that new troopers reported for duty and were given a welcoming speech. Empty of troops today, it looked entirely different. Captain Roy Anderson leaned back in an oversized leather chair behind a rich desk placed kitty-corner at the far end of the room. Captain Anderson had a trim athletic build, with a full head of dark blonde hair, and clear blue eyes that looked me up and down as I entered the office. Across the room was a three-cushioned couch holding two men in civilian clothes and a uniformed lieutenant. I had never seen any of them before, and after Lieutenant Garvey left the room I felt totally alone.

Anderson took his eyes from me to direct a comment toward those seated. "Wow, Joe, you were right, I think he's perfect." Smiles crossed the faces of the two men in plainclothes, as the captain rounded his desk, shook my hand and thanked me for coming. "You're welcome, Captain," is what came out of my mouth. Yeah, like I had a choice, was what I was thinking.

Anderson made the introductions. "Randy, this is Lieutenant Henault of our headquarters staff."

"Hello, sir. Nice to meet you," I said, shaking his hand.

"And this is Trooper Joe Deleva and his partner Trooper Bill Williams. They're from narcotics."

I nodded, giving each a handshake.

The captain began by telling me the two troopers worked for the Narcotics Division out of General Headquarters in Boston, but worked cases in the troop with an office upstairs. Basically, he said, they needed an officer for an undercover assignment. He would have to be young looking and unlikely to ever be mistaken for a cop. It didn't take a stroke of genius to figure out that their chosen one was yours truly. Trooper Deleva had seen me at Northampton a week earlier when Dave and I dropped off a cruiser for service. At that time, the captain told me, Joe approached him and asked if they could "borrow" me for a while.

"So, Trooper, I'll let Joe and Bill fill you in on the assignment, but I want to be clear here. You'll be undercover, you'll be alone, and you will tell no one about the assignment or what you're doing. You will report to Joe. You'll use an unmarked car unless using your own would be less dangerous, in which case you'll be paid mileage. You're not done with break-in, you lack experience, and you still have much to learn, so I want this to be your decision. You alone decide whether or not you wanna to do this, understood?"

I offered an extremely relieved "Yes sir," knowing that I wasn't going to be fired, but then wondered what I was getting myself into.

Joe told me their office had been approached by a 16-year-old girl upset about her twenty-one-year-old brother's drug use. In and of itself, Joe continued, they weren't keen on using the guy's younger sister to introduce an undercover officer to buy some marijuana, which was mostly what he used. However, the brother was friends with two dealers well known to Joe and Bill. These friends were active selling pot, hash, LSD, and coke in the UMass dorms and in Northampton. If I could get a couple of buys into these friends through the twenty-one-year-old pot smoker, they'd have me initiate contact with a more seasoned undercover agent and then pull me out. It sounded easy enough to me, so I said that I was in.

They gave me an empty room with a bunk on the third floor of the barracks, and an unmarked cruiser to drive home to pick up some civilian clothes since mine were at Russell. Upon return I learned they had left, at my disposal, a well-used pickup truck that Joe and Bill had "borrowed" from the troop mechanics. These guys seemed to be in the habit of borrowing things as well as people.

The next day I was introduced to the young lady and officially began my adventure. But before continuing the story, I feel the need to address my attire, troop rumors, things I didn't know, and lastly, things that I did know.

My wardrobe consisted of khaki slacks in various colors, long- and short-sleeved dress shirts, pullover and button-down sweaters, penny loafers, dress shoes, and a pair of sneakers. I looked young, naive, well-dressed, fresh out of high school, and still sported an academy hair cut only partially grown out. I was who, and what, Joe and Bill got for an undercover agent, but I'm not so sure I had the exact look they wanted. Frankly, for someone who was supposed to look the part, be knowledgeable of drugs, and hip to the culture, I plainly looked like a dork.

I didn't hear any of the rumors speculating about what might have happened to me, or about my sudden disappearance, until the assignment was over and I showed up, out of the blue, back at Russell. The assignment kept me out odd hours, working mostly every evening and late into the night. A few troopers at Northampton had seen me come and go, but HQ must have put out the word to keep quiet about me. To this day, I haven't figured why my whereabouts was so secretive, but those who knew actually did keep quiet, causing wild speculation among the troops. Someone heard that I'd been arrested upon arrival at headquarters, and they wouldn't let Dave into the barracks except to turn in my gear. From another, my car was still parked at Russell, because I was suspected of drug use and it had been impounded. Two troopers heard that I pulled my service weapon on someone in downtown Worcester. The rumor mill was full on, and I was grateful that I hadn't heard any of the fiction while on the assignment, for I would have been angry and very disturbed knowing the things that were being said. And to think, I thought women were the gossips.

A small sample of things I did't know anything about, was that morphine, opium, cocaine, marijuana, heroin, LSD, ecstasy, and other drugs had been around for a long, long time. The first attempt to stop the spread of opium dens was by one city's ordinance in the late 1800s.

Then, in 1906 a national drug law was crafted as The Pure Food and Drug Act.

In 1914 the Harrison Act was passed to control chemical substances, also making it illegal to use opium and cocaine for nonmedical purposes. The Marijuana Tax Act of 1937 added marijuana to the list.

Cocaine, heroin, and marijuana use rose in our streets from the 1920s through the 1940s. Large-scale smuggling and distribution took off in the 1950s when the Mafia entered the business.

New pills and hallucinogen use exploded in the 1960s during racial tensions and the Vietnam War. Then in 1971 President Nixon declared drug use a National Emergency, and the War on Drugs officially began with the formation of the federal Drug Enforcement Agency (DEA).

My intention here is not to give a history of drugs in America. There are books for that. My point is that at twenty-two years old, being raised in a safe middle-class suburb by decent parents, I was ignorant of it all. I fervently believe that I was blessed for being raised "sheltered" from such things by virtue of where and how I had grown up. As I look back at the young, naïve, unaffected, starry-eyed trooper, the drug culture simply wasn't a part of my world. So, under the heading of "What I Did Know" when I took an undercover narcotic assignment with six weeks on the job, I can write just two words: ABSOLUTELY NOTHING.

I ended up meeting a lot of people during my short stint undercover. The sixteen-year-old girl was sweet and had a genuine concern for her brother's drug use and felt that this was the only way she could stop him. At the first meeting he gave me some pot, because he liked me, then sold me a quarter ounce. A few days later he took me to meet the dealers that Joe and Bill were after, and they sold me hash. A day after that I went back alone and "copped" a few hits of LSD, more hash, and a little coke. Apparently, they liked guys who looked dorky.

It seemed altogether too easy, for when I introduced the new undercover agent as my friend, who actually looked like a druggie, they welcomed him with open arms.

When I reported back for duty at Russell, I was a celebrity of sorts. They had never heard of a boot being taken off break-in for any kind of assignment, let alone something undercover. It was hard to believe that I'd been the only one, but I'll admit I liked others believing it was so.

Several months later, after substantial testimony from my undercover replacement and some from me, indictments were handed down and nearly a dozen were arrested for possession, sale, and conspiracy to violate drug laws. The agent and I testified a number of times in court, resulting in findings of guilty for all involved. But the court system being what it is allowed the defense attorneys to take some of the cases right up to the Massachusetts Supreme Judicial Court. There, the Commonwealth finally won, with my name embedded in Massachusetts case law. (Names of any of the defendants, cases, or appeals adds nothing of interest to this narrative.)

My War on Drugs

My decision to request a transfer into the Narcotics Bureau was undoubtedly influenced by my undercover assignment as a new trooper, which as I mentioned in the previous chapter, had seemed all too easy. I was so naïve, and call me casual and cavalier as well, to have based a transfer request on one successful mission. I was full of myself as I entered the Bureau with a false sense of security. It didn't take long for me to learn that undercover work wasn't particularly easy, and in fact was often very dangerous. Working and hanging out with all the heads—as in coke heads, meth heads, pot heads, addicts, hookers, dealers, and criminal elements in general—made it high-risk and unpredictable.

My hair was long and unkempt with sideburns of the 1970s. A thick full mustache completed the face job, and I ditched the high school grad's clothing for appropriate street garb. It took some time to morph into a new persona and achieve the look I needed to fit into the drug scene. Unfortunately, though, this look was not so good a fit when shopping at the Forbes and Wallace Department Store in downtown Springfield while pushing a baby stroller alongside your stylish and attractive wife. It was the second time in recent weeks we'd been out with the baby when I spotted a dealer I had been pursuing in order to do some business. Each time I was able to do a hasty about-face, spinning the carriage and my surprised wife around before being spotted. Working narcotics in one's hometown area just added another layer of danger and concern, for it was highly possible that I'd be recognized by someone I was working and would never know that I had been found out. I wasn't supposed to be married, or have children, or doing anything associated with that of a normal family man. Just the afternoon before, I was working with a hooker who had been arrested by the Springfield PD. In lieu of prosecution, she agreed to take me on a shopping spree for heroin in the black community of Winchester Square. We spent time in a few bars where I was able to buy, and through her, identify the sellers. Winchester Square was just up the street from Springfield's Main Street shopping district, where Marion and I went on our own shopping sprees for little girl's dresses.

One night a couple of weeks later I was particularly unnerved. I had been in the town of Palmer working contacts trying to hook up with a guy named Gary who was big into coke and LSD. He'd been in and out of jail for numerous crimes including burglary—Gary was a bad guy! A user informant of mine who had arranged several purchases from smaller dealers came through this particular night, having set up a meeting. Conversation with the dealer was easier than I had expected, but Gary was firm on price before coming to terms for coke. Price settled, we all piled into Gary's small two-door clunker for the ride. I was behind him in the backseat, another guy I didn't know sat beside me, and my informant was in front with our pilot.

Our destination was quite a ways out of town. I tried to memorize the way, but we had taken so many turns, and with the conversations flowing, that I'd lost track of where we were. He finally drove up a long gravel drive and stopped in front of the house. I didn't know if it was his or not, but I'd find out later from my connection or from his license plate number, if I didn't forget that too, before getting a chance to write it down. I've never claimed to possess great memory skills, clearly evidenced by my high school grades.

The house was as dark as the night, not a light anywhere. Gary left his headlights on and told us to stay in the car while he unlocked the front door. A few seconds later a blinding spotlight lit the parking area and lights went on inside the house. Gary reappeared through the glare of the spotlight, opened the car door, and reached inside to turn off the engine. He kept the driver's door open, which was my invitation to get out of the car.

The State Police Firearms Section had issued me an American Arms .32 caliber automatic to carry undercover. It was small and easily concealed yet packed a fairly good punch if used at close range. My issue with the automatic had to do with the gun's safety lever, which after jostling around in one's pocket all day, would inadvertently move from the safe to the firing position. Several times I'd removed the gun from my pocket to find the safety was off. With a chambered round it could have easily discharged in my pocket, so with that knowledge, I never loaded a round into the firing chamber. In order to shoot, one needed to first pull the slide to the rear and inject a round from the magazine into the chamber. In an emergency, it was an extra time-consuming step, but it was better than shooting myself.

My contact, in the front passenger seat, jumped out of the car right away, and the guy next to me in back shoved the front seatback forward and pulled himself out the passenger door. When he got out I was then able to move the driver's seat-back forward and climb out, but as I did the .32 automatic slipped out of my back pocket and landed on the running board with the unmistakable sound of metal striking metal. My heart thundered as the gun landed at my feet in front of Gary, whose look was an unsettling mixture of fear and anger.

I don't know from where the thought came, or the calm and coolness to speak without my voice quavering, but realizing my gun didn't have a round in the chamber, I bent down, picked it up, ejected the magazine, and handed it to Gary. He had an un-loaded gun, and I had the magazine. What I had counted on was that the savvy ex-con would never figure a cop to hand over his service weapon.

Taking the automatic, his mixed expressions turned to one of smiling surprise.

"I ripped it off two days ago in Springfield, you like it?"

"Yeah," said Gary. "Where'd you get it?"

"Me and my friend broke into a house in back of the Eastfield Mall. We found money and the gun in a bedroom. He needed the money and I took the gun."

"You wanna trade for some dope?"

"Nah, not now, but maybe later, man, I'll give ya first dibs."

"That's cool," said Gary, giving me back my gun as we walked up to the house to complete our dealings. He was obviously ac-customed to villains carrying a "piece," for he didn't seem the least bit concerned returning mine—maybe he was carrying one of his own.

One of the stickiest predicaments of buying narcotics was not "doing" the drugs with the people you were buying from. One al-ways needed to arrange buys under the pretense that you had someplace else to be, or were saving it for later, or had a girlfriend waiting to get high with you, or you trusted the dope was good.

Over many months undercover I had been able to steer clear of using, until one night in a big house on a hill in the town of Ashfield. I'd met a contact who knew people, and where we could buy pounds of marijuana, so I followed him in my car. It was something I wanted to check out and hopefully arrange a buy, provided I could persuade the District Attorney to give us the money. More on that aspect of narcotics work later.

We arrived around 7:00 p.m. It was dark and the house was full of people enjoying a full-blown party featuring marijuana brownies. The boy and girlfriend pot dealers had baked and set out several pans of samples—I guess for hors d'oeuvres? They said the baked goods contained the product I wanted, and they'd be willing to talk at another time to see if we could make a deal. Meanwhile, the girlfriend gave me a huge brownie on a napkin, which I held, and held, and held without eating. After twenty minutes I broke the brownie in two and slipped one half into my coat pocket for evidence. The other half I carried around the room until I suspected the girl was becoming suspicious, so I ate it. I have to admit it was delicious.

A while later I said goodbye and promised to return. I jumped into my car to go to Northampton and drop off the evidence before going home to Springfield. I had just gotten onto Route 91 when the pot hit me. I was stoned and totally paranoid. I couldn't go home in my condition. Marion would kill me. And I was afraid to stop at the barracks, but logging and securing the evidence in our office was required.

I drove, or maybe floated into the barracks back yard, then tiptoed upstairs all the way to our office on the second floor. After storing and logging the brownie, I sat and tried to figure out what I was going to do next. That's when my pot-conflicted mind decided that having a coffee in the dining room downstairs would be just the thing to set me right. There you have it, paranoid one minute of being caught stoned, and in the next minute not caring at all.

I made it to the kitchen just fine, got my coffee, and sat at one of the big dining tables. I was deep into wondering how long it would take for the stuff to wear off so I could go home when the HQ duty lieutenant walked into the kitchen, poured himself a coffee, and sat down at my table.

"Evening, Lieutenant," was about all I managed, wobbling a little over my cup.

"Hi, Randy, how's it going?" asked Lieutenant Henault.

"Just fine, sir," I added.

Henault was the least talkative person in the barracks. He was mostly stern-faced, and although I'd seen him chuckle or laugh a few times, it was only with his peers. Why in God's name did the man decide on that night he wanted to get to know me? I'll never know, but talk he did, and questions he asked. Where are you living now? How's your wife? Any children? How's the undercover going?

I answered all the questions as best I could because he was sincere, friendly, and engaging. I immediately liked the man, but I was also aware that I was messed up, and I was pretty sure he knew it too. So, with paranoia in control once again, I confessed.

"Lieutenant, I'm sorry. I just came in from trying to make a drug buy in Ashfield and ended up having to eat a brownie laced with pot. I got half of it for evidence, it's upstairs. I thought spending some time here drinking coffee would help, but I'm still messed up." Then for good measure I added another "I'm really sorry."

The chatty person who lives in my brain cells and is known as my subconscious, and *not* focal awareness, would not shut up. Chatty was full of helpful advice. "Oh, you've really done it now. How could you be so stupid to admit to a lieutenant, no less, that you were stoned? Where did you ever get the idea it would be okay to sit your ass in the dining room? What, did you think no one was gonna see you? You're an idiot. What if he makes you stay and won't let you go home?"

It was probably the pot, but gazing into my coffee cup was the reflection of a dejected face staring back at me. It was then that Lieutenant Henault laughed.

"You know, Randy, you're not the first undercover guy to wander in here late at night screwed up on something. There's been two or three that I can recall. Don't worry about it. You did the right thing coming here. Anything that I can do?" asked the lieutenant.

"No, sir, I just think I'll sit here a while if that's okay."

"You bet, stay as long as you like. I'll be in my office if you need me." I hung around for another hour before feeling somewhat better, and my rambling subconscious had finally stopped offering advice, leaving me totally alone to figure out what I was going to tell my wife.

I walked into our apartment at exactly 11 p.m. I had prayed before going in that she had already gone to bed, but she was at the kitchen table giving the baby a bottle.

"Hi, Mar, sorry I'm so late," sounding as cheery as possible.

"It's okay, the baby's been awake anyway," she answered with a long scrutinizing look.

"I was held up at the barracks talking to—"

"What's the matter with you?" came the question laced with a little fire.

"Nothing, why? I had to drop off some evidence and the lieutenant—"

"You're stoned!" She shot at me with a glare that went right through me. "How could you do this? I'm feeding our daughter and you come home STONED?"

Oh, thought I, this is *not* going well. "I'm sorry. I couldn't help it—"

"Couldn't help it? What do you mean you couldn't help it? What did you take?"

"A brownie," I said. "One with pot in it."

"Oh, so now you're gonna tell me you didn't know it had pot in it?"

"Yeah, well, I knew it had pot in it. I got half of it into my pocket for evidence, but everybody was watching me and I couldn't get rid of the rest without them seeing. I had no choice."

"OH? We all have choices," she jabbed.

I was losing the argument and knew it, and that halfwit in my head started up with suggestions again that weren't making any sense, so I decided silence might be best. As I sat quietly sorrowful for a bit, Marion began to soften. I told her that I understood why she felt the way she did with the baby and all. Then asked her calmly if she would let me try to explain.

I told the whole story of the investigation, the possibility of pounds, the brownies, the lieutenant, the coffees, and driving home worried about her reaction to the condition I was in. I didn't, for one second, believe that I was out of the doghouse, but telling her everything took the edge off—for me anyway.

Just before calling it a night, I decided on a "going for broke" attempt to lighten the mood by telling her about running into a friend of ours earlier in the day. We'd been at many state police parties with Trooper Nate Jackson and his girlfriend. They were one of the couples that Marion really liked. We would always talk and laugh at the silliest things late into the night, and often we would be the last ones to leave the party.

"Whoa, I almost forgot, Mar, I ran into Nate this morning, coming out of the DA's office," which brought a slight smile and got her attention. "He looked good, got longer hair. I told him we hadn't been out much because of my sketchy hours and the baby." Then, inexplicably, feeling the sudden urge for bed, I rose from the table and finished by saying, "I told Nate that we'd have to get together soon."

"Soooo, what did he say?" asked Marion expectantly.

"What did who say?" I answered with a bewildered look as the door to the bedroom was slammed shut.

Divine Intervention

As I begin to write the last chapter of this memoir, I find myself somewhat conflicted for choosing to end with a narcotics story. I wondered if it had been a mistake to limit the scope of this account to the early and middle years of my career when there were so many years that I hadn't touched upon. I thought long and hard about including one or more stories from other periods, but ultimately decided that the reasons I outlined in the first chapter made for the right decision.

So, a story from narcotics will provide the ending.

It's hard to put into words what I actually thought about my work and time spent undercover, for it was very different from any position I'd ever held on, or off, the State Police. Some of the tasks were tedious and boring, while others were exciting, yet dangerous. Excitement was often fun, but the danger part, not so much. I worked the streets mostly alone, directed by troopers in the office, but there were occasions when a team of narcs were brought together from other parts of the state to work in one of the cities.

Most of the larger operations came about when a district attorney asked for assistance combatting illegal narcotics in his district. Our Narcotics Bureau was always willing to oblige, especially since the DA would fund the operation with buy money that didn't deplete the bureau's budget. I really enjoyed working with my eastern counterparts. Most of the agents had been active for years and were exceptionally good at their craft. Stories of their adventures into the underworld of narcotics were impressive in scope, and their exploits were on a different level from anything I had experienced. To digress once again, it's important to say that I feel I did an okay job undercover, giving myself a grade of C+, or a B-, whereas, the aforementioned deserve straight A's. So, with the DA's money in hand, we would team up for a few months targeting people and neighborhoods flush with drug activity. To the question of whether these actions were successful, in my opinion alone, I'd have say both yes and no.

When we had spent the DA's cash allotted for *his* war on drugs, he'd convene a grand jury to obtain criminal indictments and arm us with arrest and search warrants to conduct pre-dawn raids. The headlines were impressive.

STATE AND LOCAL POLICE CONDUCT PRE-DAWN RAIDS

> Police arrested 50 and served 11 search warrants in the City of . . .
> District Attorney . . . strikes a serious blow to illegal drug use on our streets . . .

Et cetera.

Hence, under the successful *Yes* column, the raids, arrests, searches, and news headlines absolutely put a damper on drug sales and use in the targeted areas. Mistrust and paranoia ran rampant among the dealers and users as sales and use declined—for a time. Literally, anyone these people didn't know, and some who they knew well, were suspected of being narcs. We saw it play out everywhere on the streets, and once they were in custody facing conviction and jail time, we were effective at turning some prime dealers into informants, giving rise to more arrests.

Under the *No* column in the gauge of success there were a number of issues. First, we were mostly bottom feeding on street users and low-level dealers. Sure, we could slow and hinder drug activity in a particular place, but not for very long because they would go further underground and become even more cautious.

The biggest impediment to more successful drug enforcement at the level we operated, and frankly at every level, was simply a lack of money. The undercover guys were quite good at creating opportunities to "climb the ladder" by using buys to reach sizable dealers. These were the people moving volumes of drugs who needed to be stopped if we were ever to have a more significant impact. That said, our first stop was back to the district attorney to request that he fund our efforts. The answer, more often than not was a *no*. In fairness, the DAs didn't have the kind of money needed to purchase the quantities of narcotics we were after, and we understood; leading to our next suggestion, which was to contact the DEA. It wasn't uncommon for our guys to work with the Feds, for we had good relations with many of the agents and working cases together had been fruitful.

Then came the political considerations, but not on our part. In my judgment, the need for re-election was very often factored into the decisions made by a district attorney financing cases. It was all about money. If a DA funded a drug operation, that operation was over when the cash was gone and the desired headlines made the front page. If the funding ran out, and the operation was still making headway, we would ask permission of the DA to bring in the Feds, which usually brought nothing but funny looks. What went unsaid, but was often heard whispered among some of the staff, was that the DA didn't want the Feds working his district and "ruining" his narcotic investigations.

That was all forty-plus years ago. Are things different now? I have no idea, but it certainly doesn't seem so from news accounts and the number of drug-related crimes and deaths in the country today. I give the "war on drugs" a failing grade. My opinion; enough said.

Pranksters and jokesters were found everywhere I had worked within the Department of Public Safety. The guys in narcotics were no exception, though maybe they were a little more "whacked"—but in a good way.

I had moved from undercover to the Narcotic Bureau's Diversion Investigative Unit (DIU). There were three of us in the western part of the state, Ron Uminski, Vinnie Blanchard, and me, who were tasked with combatting the diversion of legal drugs through pharmacies and physicians. It was boring duty, but necessary because there was a surprising number of doctors and pharmacies bending the rules. Traipsing from pharmacy to pharmacy, day after day, we would physically run through thousands of paper prescriptions searching for scripts that had been illegally obtained from doctors. Addicts would "doctor shop" by making appointments with multiple physicians and claim to be suffering from certain maladies to get a prescription. They would even steal prescription pads left lying about a physician's office, which gave them the option of forging a script for themselves or selling the blank scripts to others. In either case, the ploy was highly successful as a means to obtain prescription drug scripts that could be filled at multiple pharmacies. Unfortunately for the doctors, the prescription addicts who were caught had no qualms giving up the names of the shady doctors who were willing to write prescriptions for Schedule II narcotics. Thankfully today, technology and the electronic transmission of scripts has changed the way physicians and pharmacies receive, store, and account for the drugs they dispense.

I've offered a glimpse into some of the tame, monotonous, and unexciting nature of the work in DIU hoping one might understand our occasional desire to "go off the reservation" in search of excitement, which we always found working with Detectives Robby and Bay of the Springfield PD Narcotics section. I'm certain we spent more time working with those two detectives than we did hounding pharmacists. It was fun and great work, so long as our Bureau Commander didn't find out how much time we "wandered."

Robby and Bay were several years older than we were, and I also didn't know two more savvy detectives. They loved their work and the five of us got along great. They would call Vinny at home whenever they had a good bust going down so we could hook up. After jointly running some of our cases, we began the back and forth sharing of intelligence for search warrant affidavits. All we were interested in was getting the bad guys—we cared nothing for getting our names in the paper. They trusted the three of us completely and the feelings were mutual. Trust wasn't always the case when multiple departments joined together. Jealousies, rivalries, and missing drugs sometimes spoiled the relationships. That had never been an issue with Springfield.

Early one morning Vinnie called me to say that we were going to work with Robby and Bay. He said Bobby had gotten permission from a building's owner to put someone into an empty first-floor apartment that was across the street from a three-family brick house where the resident Puerto Ricans had been selling heroin for six months. They had failed to get anywhere close enough to watch a sale go down, or ID who was selling—right off the front porch. I hadn't completely "cleaned up" from being undercover, so they figured I could walk unnoticed into the apartment. The plan was for Ron and Vin to wait in unmarked cars at one end of the short street, while Robby and Bay took a position at the other end. Vinnie decided the next day's pharmacy inspections in Chicopee would have to wait. After all, Bay and Robby needed us. I told him to count me in.

At nine o'clock the next morning Ron and Vinnie picked me up and we headed to the Detective Bureau. Vinnie was half asleep with bloodshot green eyes and his blond hair slightly messed. The rest of him was neatly attired with dark blue slacks, loafers, a light gray button-down collared shirt, and a sporty leather jacket. "What's up with you?" I asked. "Were you drinkin' last night?"

"No, jus' up late watching a good movie. Then I couldn't sleep wondering what I was gonna tell the lieutenant about skipping out on Chicopee."

"I had a few cold ones last night," added Ronnie, with a proud smile, sitting next to Vin. "Glad I didn't watch the movie you did, you look like shit."

Ignoring Ron, Vinnie continued. "I told the lieutenant we owed Springfield a favor, so I said we were gonna help them with something this morning and get to Chicopee in the afternoon."

"Let me guess," said Ron, "he was pissed, but said okay." Vinnie nodded, "You guys know we'll never make it to Chicopee, right?"

Ronnie, Vin, and I walked right into the Springfield Detective Bureau. It was second nature. We'd been there so many times it felt like our second office. The detectives all knew us, and especially appreciated our arrival with coffee and doughnuts. I can't speak to today, but, *yes*, forty-odd years ago cops did love doughnuts.

Bay told us that they had been getting a lot of heat from the residents near the drug house. Drive-up buyers would park curbside, make a purchase, and bugger off, but recently there had been more walk-up customers who'd cop, then shoot up behind the building, leaving needles and trash everywhere. It was becoming the city's go-to destination for drive-up smack, and Carlos was the main dealer. That was according to the intel Robbie and Bay had been able to come up with. Additionally, through informants, they learned that Carlos never did a sale himself, but still hadn't been able to learn where he hid the dope. Carlos was nearly a permanent fixture on the porch, but smartly appointed four or five surrogates to handle sales, making it harder for anyone to get "the man" himself.

Springfield PD detectives had done a good job of drug enforcement. It was the third largest city in Massachusetts and they, like the rest of us, ended up running like firemen from one place to the next extinguishing fires, never knowing where the next drug hot spot would appear. So, for the time being, Robbie and Bay's hot spot was run by a man named Carlos, yet I hadn't realized how badly they wanted him until Bay spoke to me on the way out the door.

"We gotta get this guy, Rand. The captain told me and Rob this morning that the chief was really pissed and didn't want any more calls from the North End about this house. God better give us some help on this one, we don't need the chief up our butts."

We set up a little before noontime. I waltzed up the street like I belonged there, and no one took any notice of me walking to the first-floor apartment's back door and letting myself inside. There were sheer curtains and window shades over the two living room windows, making it perfect to observe without being seen. The apartment was dark, musty smelling, and dingy. It was empty of furniture, so there was nothing to sit on, guaranteeing I'd have a sore ass if it was a long day.

I'd stuffed a plain doughnut into my jacket pocket when leaving the PD for something to nibble on, but forgot to bring a drink. I supposed that I could drink from the kitchen faucet, but after one look at the sink, I opted to risk dying of thirst as a safer alternative.

My partners and the Springfield duo were in their places. We had checked our radios and the operation began. It was steady business. Vehicles would pull up, decide to stop and make a purchase, or not. I would radio details of anyone buying to the waiting detectives, who would place them under arrest and then hand them over to uniformed officers for transport and booking at the PD.

At two o'clock I raised Vinnie, Ron, Robby, and Bay on the radio.

"Okay, guys, I see what he's doing. Carlos is there on the porch sitting in a rocking chair next to the front door. He's wearing a wide brim hat with a blue hat band. He's got five guys who take turns selling. I've watched them all make sales. One doesn't look any older than ten. There's two girls hanging out, just doin' nothing that I can see. I watched Carlos come off the porch and into the yard. He goes to my left side of the porch. Under the middle front window there's a loose brick. That's where he hides the dope, in plain sight. Oh, it looks like a sizable stash because he takes a big handful and puts the packets inside his hat band. He gives it to the runners when a buyer shows up."

"Fantastic, we got him," said Robby. "Let's wrap it up. We'll hit 'em in a few minutes."

Ten minutes later, having a front row seat, I watched the two unmarked cars drive over the sidewalk and converged at the porch. All eight of the part-time porch dwellers were instantly on their feet. They were jabbering in high gear and their eyes were full of apprehension. These people could spot an unmarked cruiser a mile away, and being somewhat trapped on the porch they stood frozen, knowing real trouble was coming as the officers got out of their cars.

I will never know for sure, because I never asked Vinnie, but I truly wondered if the real reason he was up late the previous night was because of the good movie, or thinking of an excuse for our lieutenant as he had claimed, or was it his "coming up" with what I saw next. If I had to guess, I would say that it was something he always had at the back of his devious mind. Then again, it didn't really matter.

Ron, Bay, and Robbie had emerged from the cruisers and stood at the foot of the porch looking up at the eight terrified suspects. Vinnie was the last to join them. I could see that he was talking and holding something in his left hand. Too far away to hear, I watched my partner, Ronnie, turn away from Vinnie to look at me in the window across the street. He was holding the palm of his hand against his cheek whispering, giggling, and shaking his head to hide himself from the dealers. He later told me that he was whispering. "Oh, dear Jesus, no, Vinnie, don't do it."

Vinnie held a fork-shaped branch that he flipped around grasping each fork end individually. With the pointed end aiming straight up, I realized, then, that it was a divining rod many people used as a type of divination believed to find groundwater, metals, gemstones, or what have you. In the manner of Vinnie's application—it was *drugs*. He stood there for a moment, as if gathering himself, then with wild gyrations he moved with the rod seeming to yank him violently to the left side of the yard as the frightened dealers watched.

Vinnie, the total performer, released one of the fork ends, hesitated for another moment and bent over pretending to catch his breath. Feigning to struggle, he took hold of the rod once more. Twisting and spinning himself in a circle, he thrust the rod into the air, then to the ground, where it dragged Vinnie toward the building. I could see from the apartment that the mortar had been removed from around the brick hiding the heroin. Vinnie had seen it too, so with his next acrobatic feat the rod took his pointer to the base of the front window, where it ever so slowly rose up the wall and stopped at the hiding place. I watched Carlos and two of his boys run to look over the railing in disbelief as Vinnie removed the brick, reached inside and withdrew a huge handful of heroin.

"Way to go, Vinnie," cheered Robbie and Bay, barely able to compose themselves. Ronnie had stopped trying.

Vinnie gave them a celebratory wave as they cheered. Then, dragged by the rod, he stumbled toward and up the porch stairs waving his rod wildly through the air and knocking Carlos's hat to the floor. Our man, Carlos, actually had a panic attack as Vinnie plucked the bags of heroin from his hat and Bay cuffed him.

For a moment, my thoughts went elsewhere as I walked over to help handcuff the other prisoners. I kept hearing Bay's troubled plea for God's help arresting Carlos, quieting the North End community, and most importantly getting an angry chief off their backs. I guess most would think that Vinnie's "Divining Rod Intervention" was a product of his wild imagination—I like to believe that it was spiritually sent.

We let the girls go. *Someone* had to tell the story. *We* wouldn't!

About the Author

Randall Stevens was born in Cambridge, Massachusetts in 1946. He joined the Massachusetts State Police in 1968 and retired in 2001 after thirty-two years of service. Beginning as a road Trooper, he later worked for district attorneys, investigative bureaus, and undercover in narcotics. He commanded substations, and at the rank of lieutenant served as the Executive Officer of Troop B in Western Massachusetts. He went on to build homes, a mini-mall, and a successful retail business with his first wife, Marion, who died of cancer after forty years of marriage.

He is dedicated to his family and work. An avid skier, he taught his daughters to ski and always involved himself in their upbringing. Randall's hobbies include drawing, watercolor painting, motorcycling, golf, music, old movies, cooking, and writing.

I Hate Campaign Hats, which he began writing fifty years ago, is his first book. His early career notes highlighted the silliest of humor, joy, and sadness that came with the job.

Randall has two daughters and lives with his second wife, Anne, in Western Massachusetts.

Made in the USA
Monee, IL
21 November 2021

82681485R00163